NEW FEAST

NEW FEAST

MODERN MIDDLE EASTERN VEGETARIAN

GREG & LUCY MALOUF

hardie grant books

MELBOURNE · LONDON

Contents

The New Feast 8
How to use this book 12
Menu ideas 14

Breakfast

Summer berry salad with ginger, lime & labneh 18
Blood oranges in spicy caramel sauce with ashta 20
Breakfast couscous with nuts, seeds & blueberries 21
Middle Eastern granola with pomegranate, sour cherries
   & pistachios 23
Glazed apple-raisin fritters 24
Turkish eggs with spinach, chilli & yoghurt cream 26
White zucchini omelette with mint & melting gouda 29
Egyptian breakfast beans with feta, lemon oil & green
   chilli relish 30

Breads

Sesame joujou breads 34
Griddled flatbreads: goat's cheese-za'atar; coconut-date;
   fennel-Turkish chilli; crushed hazelnut-rosemary 36
Turkish milk rolls with yoghurt glaze 40
Semolina bread with aniseed & sesame 43
Saffron fruit loaf 45
Middle Eastern pizzas 46

Butters & preserves

Home-made crème fraîche butter 52
Savoury butters: preserved lemon; almond-saffron;
   Persian sabzi; harissa 55
Sweet butters: apple-walnut; apricot-cardamom;
   pear-ginger 57
Rhubarb, raspberry & cardamom fridge jam 58
Gingered grapefruit curd 60
Candied citrus peel 63

Dips & spreads

Crushed broad beans 66
Parsnip skordalia with garlic, lemon & scarmorza 68
Turkish red pepper paste 69
Preserved lemon guacamole 71
Spicy red hummus 71
Home-made shankleesh 72
Labneh; Turkish-style carrot; artichoke & lemon;
   classic labneh in oil 73

Pickles & relishes

Slow-roasted tomatoes with pomegranate & thyme 79
Baby eggplants stuffed with walnuts & chillies 81
Eggplant relish 82
Sweet peppers & shallots in lemon oil 83
Spicy carrot pickle 84

Soups

Vegetable stock 88
Chilled yoghurt soup with cucumber, currants & walnuts 89
Asparagus avgolemono 91
Fresh corn soup with rice, yoghurt & sizzling mint butter 92
Tomato & bean soup with harissa & honey 95
Mushroom soup with fresh za'atar 97
Lemony lentil soup with saffron-scrambled eggs 98

Stuffed vegetables

Zucchini blossoms with haloumi in olive-brioche crumbs 102
Stuffed zucchini cooked in yoghurt 105
Baked tomatoes with saffron, bulgur & barberries 106
Summer vine leaves with tomatoes, pine nuts & dill 108

Fritters

Wild garlic, leek & currant fritters with honey 113
Hazelnut falafel & tahini-whipped crème fraîche 114
Jerusalem artichoke 'wedges' with green olive aioli 115
Vegetable 'fritto misto' in saffron-yeast batter 116
Pumpkin kibbeh stuffed with feta & spinach 118

Savoury pastries

Teta's pie – dandelion, leek & barrel-aged feta 122
North African eggplant pie with pimento sugar 124
Fatima's fingers with goat's cheese, lemon, tarragon
   & thyme 127
Sweet pumpkin sambusek with oregano 128
Za'atar biscuits 129
Feta cheese straws with Turkish chilli 130

Raw vegetable salads

Celeriac remoulade with tahini & golden raisins 134
Shredded bitter leaves with roasted grapes, almonds
   & avocado 135
Persian soft herb salad with fresh figs & labneh 136
Citrus salad with red radicchio & pomegranate dressing 139
Shankleesh salad with parsley & pomegranate 140
Shaved zucchini with grana, burrata & basil 142
Winter tabbouleh 145

Cooked vegetable salads

Baby leeks in saffron vinaigrette with hazelnut crumbs 148

Turkish bread & roasted vegetable salad 150

Fresh borlotti beans with tomato & pomegranate dressing 152

Green beans with chermoula, shallots & feta 153

Rainbow chard with soused currants & pine nuts 155

Potato salad with peas & Persian spices 157

Braised artichokes, preserved lemon & fingerling potatoes with basil crème fraîche 158

Honey-roasted carrots with dates, dandelions & Moroccan dressing 160

Hot vegetable dishes

Peas with pearl onions & preserved lemon cream 165

Griddled broccolini with almonds & harissa butter 166

Tunisian-style vegetables roasted on embers 167

Charred corncobs with almond-saffron butter 168

Slow-roasted eggplant with saffron-lemon cream 171

Tomato & eggplant baked with tarragon-yoghurt custard 173

Baby carrot tagine with yoghurt & honeyed pine nuts 174

Grains

Cucumber, quinoa & tarragon-yoghurt salad 178

Toasted quinoa with coriander, lime & crunchy pumpkin 180

Golden bulgur wheat with apple, raisins & yoghurt 182

Spicy Turkish kisir 183

Toasted nuts, seeds & grains with smashed cherries, herbs & goat's curd 185

Farro with slow-roasted tomatoes, artichokes, olives & oregano 187

Freekeh pilaf with spiced roast pumpkin & shallots 188

Rice

Persian 'baghali polow' with borlotti beans & dill 192

Long-grain rice with lemon & toasted almonds 193

Lebanese dirty rice 194

Eggplant pilaf with yoghurt & zhoug 197

Zucchini blossom & preserved lemon risotto with ricotta & parmesan 198

Legumes

Baked beans with Turkish spices & crunchy crumbs 202

Spiced Puy lentils with porcini & herbs 203

Lentils with sweet carrots, dates & golden cream 204

Lebanese spiced chickpeas & eggplant with pita 206

Roasted tomato & chickpea curry with coconut & coriander 209

Pasta & couscous

Fregola with zucchini, citrus & basil 212

Goat's cheese dumplings with fresh & dried mint 214

Buttered egg noodles with artichokes, cèpes & saffron 216

Mixed spring greens with golden raisins & couscous 217

Wedding couscous with herbs & flowers 219

Ices

Crème fraîche ice cream 223

Banana ice cream with salted date caramel 225

Stracciatella with orange peel 226

Buttermilk sorbet with bay leaf & lemon 228

Pear sorbet with Prosecco, cardamom & lime 229

Negroni sorbet with blood orange & pomegranate 231

Desserts

Lemon posset with fennel shortbread thins 234

Pavlova 'flowers' with apple jelly, raspberries & vanilla labneh 236

Chocolate muhallabeya with Turkish coffee granita 239

Muscat crème caramel with orange flower cream & candied pistachios 240

Saffron rice pudding with spiced apricots 243

Sweet pastries

Beignets with bay leaf sugar 246

Persian saffron tart with passion fruit curd & mascarpone mousse 247

Spiced currant sfiha with cinnamon-ginger cream 250

Orange baklava cigars 252

Cakes & cookies

Bitter chocolate-hazelnut cake with candied grapefruit 257

Blackberry-sour cream crumble cake 258

Fennel shortbread thins 259

Tarbouche – Lebanese chocolate marshmallow cakes 260

Food notes 262

Index 268
Acknowledgements 272

THE NEW FEAST

It began with a curious moment of synchronicity: at exactly the same time – about a year ago – Lucy and I discovered that we were both, quite independently, changing the way we ate. We were cutting down dramatically on the animal protein in our diets and upping the level of plant-based foods. Not so strange for Lucy, perhaps, who has had vegetarian leanings since her student days, but it was something of a dramatic turnabout for me, a chef and confirmed carnivore.

The reasons for these changes probably won't surprise anyone: we confessed to each other similar anxieties over advancing years and a desire to be as fit and healthy as possible to meet the challenges head-on, as well as niggling long-held issues of conscience about the excesses in our respective diets.

It's that word 'excess' that's always been the rub for me. With two heart transplants under my belt, I'm someone who relishes life, who is unashamedly greedy for all that's on offer – especially when it comes to my tummy. There's no escaping the fact that I love food – live for it, really. It's one of the main reasons I became a chef! But I had reached a point where – 25 kg (55 lb) overweight, facing fresh professional challenges in a new country with a difficult climate – I knew the moment had come to face up to reality. It was time for the feasting to stop! Or at the very least, it had to be a different kind of feast.

So what to do?

For me, it was never going to be about cutting out high-fat, energy-dense snacks and sugary drinks; they've never been part of my diet. In fact, I've always believed that I ate a pretty good diet; the problem was that I was just eating far too much of too many good things! Once I started reading up on the subject, I learnt that most of the current health wisdom suggests that the single most important thing we can do to minimise future health problems is increase the amount of unprocessed, plant-based foods we eat. While other pieces of nutritional advice seem to be endlessly tweaked and revised, this dictum remains a constant. In fact, recent Western government guidelines indicate that even the familiar 'five-a-day' model is woefully inadequate and that we should be eating up to ten servings of vegetables and (to a lesser degree) fruit every day.

The flip side of the 'eat more veg' equation is to 'eat less meat'! More and more studies suggest that levels of meat consumption in the modern Western diet – and saturated fats specifically – are way too high and I'd be the first to confess to loving (and eating way too much of) every part of an animal; offcuts, offal and all. I've never been interested in becoming a vegetarian because I enjoy eating meat and seafood far too much ever to exclude it from my diet. But instead of cutting it out completely, I wondered how hard I would find it to simply cut down the amount of animal protein that I eat? Could I refocus my attention on quality, instead of quantity?

This was something I thought I could manage easily enough because, despite being a dedicated meat eater, I've always been a careful meat eater. It's always been important for me to know an animal's provenance – partly this is to do with quality and flavour, but also because I want to know that the animal has been valued. And in the main I've been fortunate: as a chef I've had access to ethically produced meat and sustainably caught fish delivered by suppliers who really care about their animals.

In fact the 'eat more veg and less meat' approach was something I felt sure I could adopt – a part of me even relished the challenge because I knew that my Lebanese heritage stood me in good stead. It turns out that the Middle Eastern diet is actually pretty good for you and, despite the many long years of restaurant gluttony, I grew up in a family where meat played more of a supporting role at mealtimes. And when meat was used, it tended to be the cheaper, less desirable secondary cuts, instead of expensive prime cuts. When I look back now, I see how much we depended on produce from the garden: Dad's beans were the stuff of family legend, as were his thumb-sized cucumbers and wonderfully tasty tomatoes. I remember the baby cos that Mum used in our fattouche salads, the tiny eggplants that were destined for the pickling jars, the bay and lemon trees, the capsicums and carrots, and the coriander, parsley and mint that ran riot everywhere ... Like many Lebanese, my Dad was crazy about his vegetable garden, and while that's not a passion he passed on to me, I did learn from him the particular pleasure of eating fresh produce that's only travelled a few yards from garden bed to kitchen bench.

But the real point is that vegetables are in my blood. The Middle Eastern diet (with some regional differences) is largely vegetarian: it relies heavily on vegetables and fruit, herbs and spices and complex carbohydrates, such as pulses and grains. There is some dairy and plenty of olive oil. A limited amount of meat, poultry and fish are eaten, but they are really added extras to the daily diet. This is partly because the climate and terrain suits vegetable production somewhat more than large-scale animal farming. Meat has always been expensive, and so is reserved for special occasions. I think this is why Middle Easterners are such masters of vegetable and grain cookery: through the centuries they've learnt endless interesting ways to cook and to present vegetables as the hero of a dish, instead of playing second fiddle to a slab of animal protein.

As it turned out, cutting down on meat and adding more plant-based meals to my diet was so easy and delicious that I wondered why I hadn't always eaten this way. As the new food adventure progressed, I found myself returning to favourite vegetable dishes from my childhood and re-reading all my old travel journals for inspiration. Before long I was busily developing new versions in my kitchen at home. Lucy and I started comparing notes and swapping recipes by telephone and, before long, the idea for a new book was born.

One of the things Lucy and I tried to get to the bottom of during our research and recipe testing was why so many people have such an ambivalent relationship with vegetables:

they know they should eat more of them – they want to eat more of them – but they find preparing them a bit of a bore and, more often than not, mired in meat-centric food habits, they can't think of interesting vegetable dishes to cook. Other people worry that it just won't feel like a properly filling meal without a bit of meat on the plate. If either of these concerns resonate, if you're interested in eating a more plant-based diet and are looking for new and exciting ways to cook them, then this book is for you.

We'd like to think that the recipes will also appeal to people who already know and love Middle Eastern food or to those who are interested in discovering more about it. Our previous cookbooks all contained significant numbers of vegetarian dishes (of course they did! As I've just outlined, vegetables are an important part of the Middle Eastern food canon) but, with a few exceptions, the recipes here are all completely new.

And what about those of you who have already embraced a meat-free way of life? As Lucy and I found out from our reading, being 'vegetarian' means different things to different people. Health issues aside, there are all kinds of reasons for eating less or no meat (ranging from political to ethical to environmental, spiritual or religious) and it seems that vegetarianism is a sort of sliding scale, from the strictest regime whose adherents, like vegans, eschew any kind of animal-derived product at all, right through to the 'selective vegetarian', who won't touch red meat or poultry, but will happily eat seafood, and the even wobblier 'flexitarians' who consider themselves vegetarian but will occasionally tuck into a steak or bacon sandwich. Whichever kind of vegetarian you are, we hope you'll find recipes here that will be exciting and inspirational additions to your repertoire. They are all entirely meat-free, although some use dairy and eggs. If you are a vegan, or a vegetarian with vegan leanings, you'll want to make use of the range of vegan-friendly dairy and egg substitutes. You'll probably already be very familiar with what's on offer.

So here it is: our collection of modern Middle Eastern-inspired vegetarian recipes. With very few exceptions, you'll find that they are all easily achievable in a home kitchen. As I get older I'm leaning more and more towards a simple life and no longer feel the need to flex my cheffy muscles with elaborate, complicated creations. So these recipes are not about technique, but instead they are about celebrating the intrinsic flavour and freshness of glorious fresh produce.

And this, I think, is the key: whatever the motivations for wanting to change one's diet, for us, first and foremost, food has to be about pleasure. (For this reason alone, we've included a generous number of sweet dishes – although we suggest you adopt the Middle Eastern approach of eating them sparingly as the occasional treat, rather than as a daily indulgence.) But if nothing else, we hope to show you just how many things there are to do with vegetables, other than simply to boil them and stick them on a plate with a lamb chop. As you'll discover from this collection, austerity and denial have no place in the Middle Eastern approach to eating – with its emphasis on sharing, and on combining a variety of dishes of varying textures and tastes it is exciting and satisfying on all kinds of levels. However humble the ingredients, Middle Eastern food is always bold and celebratory, fresh and vital and, above all, has an emphasis on flavour and on generosity of spirit.

Finally, a word about availability. It's a very different world now, from when Lucy and I wrote our first cookbook, fifteen years ago. Then, Middle Eastern ingredients were hard to hunt down; now, you can buy preserved lemons, harissa, flower waters and spice blends in the average suburban supermarket. And while there are a few specific Middle Eastern herbs and vegetables that aren't yet being grown commercially in the West, let's not forget that we live in a world of abundance. To be sure, it's not an abundance that is evenly distributed, but most of us have easier and better access to quality fresh ingredients than ever before. Markets and farm shops are falling over themselves to encourage us to buy fresh local produce grown, in the main, by people who care. Even supermarkets are responding to consumer demand for greater variety and more information about provenance. Vegetable box schemes can expand one's vegetable horizons, too. They encourage us to experiment with whatever is currently in season – and it's delivered right to the front door.

Really, it's all there for the taking and the making and so we encourage you to join us in trying a New Feast.

GREG & LUCY MALOUF

HOW TO USE THIS BOOK

Middle Easterners have a very relaxed and fluid approach to eating. Unlike the European table, where dishes are formally divided into starters, main courses and desserts, a Middle Eastern meal is about sharing a selection of smaller dishes that are put out to eat all at the same time. It's how we always eat, and we love the way this unstructured approach allows us to experience so many complementary tastes and textures in the course of one meal.

Other than breakfast (which is clearly a meal in its own right) all the other recipes in the book can pretty much be eaten at any meal or any time of the day (although we do enjoy some of the breakfast dishes at other mealtimes too!). It seems natural, then, to group them by the type of dish they are, rather than by course. The twenty small sections that follow also demonstrate just how versatile vegetables are: instead of just being roasted or boiled, you'll see they can go into soups, stews or salads (warm or cold), they can be stuffed, baked into pastries, turned into fritters or dips or preserved by pickling. We've also included sections for the essential breads that accompany every Middle Eastern meal, as well as a few delicious things for spreading.

There are four sections to satisfy the sweet tooth (because vegetarians eat puddings, too, don't they?) and most of these are based upon fruits, with a selection for each season. You'll notice that we make good use of cream and sugar in our recipes because, frankly, this isn't a diet book. However when it comes to the sweet course, we do suggest that you reserve these treats for special occasions. In Middle Eastern countries, people rarely eat desserts, but end their meals with fresh fruit, and we heartily recommend such an approach for day-to-day eating.

We firmly believe that vegetables lend themselves extremely well to this flexible, democratic style of eating. With meat, there's always one dish that seems to cry out to be the hero. Vegetables are more unassuming. They tend to bump along very comfortably with each other, which means you shouldn't have to stress overly when it comes to menu planning.

Ultimately, we want life to be simple and you probably do too. So, with a few exceptions in the case of things like cakes and tarts, we've designed all the recipes to serve four people as part of a selection. But most of them can be happily scaled up or down. If you are serving larger numbers of people, then either increase the number of dishes or scale up a recipe. Most are very forgiving!

Other than that, we'd encourage you to put dishes together as you will. There are really no rules and you'll probably instinctively want to create a varied meal that combines, for instance, a dip with a pie and, perhaps a salad, or a tagine with a grain and a tangy relish (whereas combining a grain, couscous and lentil dish in the same meal would not be ideal).

While our overall intention is for you to embrace the Middle Eastern way of eating, we don't want to be overly prescriptive! With that in mind, remember that many of the recipes would easily make lovely side dishes for a more conventional meat-centred meal, if you wish. Or, if you don't fancy a mezze-style meal, you can always serve them in a more structured way, choosing a lighter recipe or a soup to start, a more substantial dish to follow and your choice of ice cream, sweet pastry or other dessert to end. Ultimately, it's entirely up to you!

The contents on pages 4–5 lists all the recipes in one complete spread. We'd encourage you to use it as a reference when you're planning your meals. Cast your eyes over the sections and pick out dishes that you're drawn to. Use your instincts to pull together items that you think would work well together. There are no rights or wrongs but, to get the ball rolling, over the page are some suggestions to inspire you.

MENU IDEAS

Lazy weekend brunch
Griddled flatbreads 36
Home-made crème fraîche butter 52
Spicy red hummus 71
Turkish eggs with spinach, chilli & yoghurt
cream 26
Baked beans with Turkish spices & crunchy
crumbs 202
Summer berry salad with ginger, lime & labneh 18
Blackberry sour-cream crumble cake 258
Crème fraîche ice cream 223

Friends for a summer barbecue
Fennel-Turkish chilli flatbreads 36
Turkish-style carrot labneh 73
Tunisian-style vegetables roasted on embers 167
Toasted quinoa with coriander, lime &
crunchy pumpkin 180
Shankleesh salad with parsley & pomegranate 140
Celeriac remoulade with tahini & golden raisins 134
Banana ice cream with salted date caramel 225

Family weekend picnic
Crushed hazelnut-rosemary flatbread 36
Home-made shankleesh 72
Summer vine leaves with tomatoes, pine nuts
& dill 108
Sweet pumpkin sambusek with oregano 128
White zucchini omelette with mint & melting
gouda 29
Potato salad with peas & Persian spices 157
Bitter chocolate-hazelnut cake with
candied grapefruit 257

Mid-winter Sunday lunch
Tomato & bean soup with harissa & honey 95
Turkish milk bread rolls with yoghurt glaze 40
Classic labneh in oil 73
Spicy red hummus 71
Chocolate muhallabeya with Turkish coffee
granita 239

Friday night family dinner
Jerusalem artichoke 'wedges' with green olive
aioli 115
Middle Eastern pizzas 46
Shredded bitter leaves with roasted grapes, almonds
& avocado 135
Stracciatella with orange peel 226

Middle-of-the-week working lunch
Semolina bread with aniseed & sesame 43
Artichoke & lemon labneh 73
Baked tomatoes with saffron, bulgur & barberries 106
Shankleesh salad with parsley & pomegranate 140
Lemon posset with fennel shortbread thins 234

Cocktail party nibbles
Feta cheese straws with Turkish chilli 130
Crushed broad beans 66
Fatima's fingers with goat's cheese, lemon, tarragon
& thyme 127
Sweet pumpkin sambusek with oregano 128
Hazelnut falafel & tahini-whipped crème fraîche 114
Spiced currant sfiha 250
Orange baklava cigars 252

Friends over for casual dinner
Charred corncobs with almond-saffron butter
Tomato & eggplant baked with tarragon-yoghurt
custard 173
Mixed spring greens with golden raisins &
couscous 217
Pear sorbet with Prosecco, cardamom & lime 229

High tea
Za'atar biscuits 129
Crushed broad beans 66
Teta's pie – dandelion, leek & barrel-aged feta 122
Slow-roasted eggplant with saffron-lemon
    cream 171
Beignets with bay leaf sugar 246
Spiced currant sfiha 250

Romantic dinner for two
Za'atar biscuits 129
Zucchini blossom & preserved lemon risotto
    with ricotta & parmesan 198
Persian soft herb salad with fresh figs &
    labneh 136
Negroni sorbet with blood orange &
    pomegranate 231

Autumn dinner party
Potato salad with peas & Persian spices 157
Roasted tomato & chickpea curry with coconut
    & coriander 209
Long-grain rice with lemon & toasted almonds 193
Coconut-date griddled flatbreads 36
Spicy carrot pickle 84
Labneh 73
Glazed apple-raisin fritters 24
Crème fraîche ice cream 223

Light, healthy springtime dinner
Mushroom soup with fresh za'atar 97
Honey-roasted carrots with dates, dandelions &
    Moroccan dressing 160
Cucumber, quinoa & tarragon-yoghurt salad 178
Buttermilk sorbet with bay leaf & lemon 228
Fennel shortbread thins 259

Lingering birthday lunch
Vegetable 'fritto misto' in saffron-yeast batter 116
Goat's cheese-za'atar flatbread 36
Harissa butter 55
Braised artichokes, preserved lemon & fingerling
    potatoes with basil crème fraîche 158
Turkish bread & roasted vegetable salad 150
Toasted nuts, seeds & grains with smashed cherries,
    herbs & goat's curd 185
Pavlova 'flowers' with apple jelly, raspberries &
    vanilla labneh 236

Pull-the-stops-out celebration dinner
Feta cheese straws with Turkish chilli 130
Wild garlic, leek & currant fritters with honey 113
North African eggplant pie with pimento sugar 124
Baby carrot tagine with yoghurt & honeyed
    pine nuts 174
Wedding couscous with herbs & flowers 219
Citrus salad with red radicchio &
    pomegranate dressing 139
Persian saffron tart with passion fruit curd &
    mascarpone mousse 247

Breakfast

SUMMER BERRY SALAD WITH GINGER, LIME & LABNEH ... 18

BLOOD ORANGES IN SPICY CARAMEL SAUCE WITH ASHTA ... 20

BREAKFAST COUSCOUS WITH NUTS, SEEDS & BLUEBERRIES ... 21

MIDDLE EASTERN GRANOLA WITH POMEGRANATE, SOUR CHERRIES & PISTACHIOS ... 23

GLAZED APPLE-RAISIN FRITTERS ... 24

TURKISH EGGS WITH SPINACH, CHILLI & YOGHURT CREAM ... 26

WHITE ZUCCHINI OMELETTE WITH MINT & MELTING GOUDA ... 29

EGYPTIAN BREAKFAST BEANS WITH FETA, LEMON OIL & GREEN CHILLI RELISH ... 30

Many years ago, before embarking on our travels around the Middle East we were both a bit ho-hum about breakfast, often skipping it altogether or downing a latte on the run. But now it is one of our favourite meals of the day.

When we are in Lebanon, Greg's top breakfast dish is *knafeh bi jibn*, a wicked pastry made of crisp, buttery, finely shredded filo, filled with soft white cheese and doused in orange flower syrup. (Warning: eat with a very strong black coffee!) For Lucy, it's a Persian-style breakfast of oversized flatbreads, warm from the bakery, smeared with saffron jam and clotted cream and washed down with copious cups of strong tea.

Sadly, such indulgence is not always practical, so the first meal of the day usually revolves around yoghurt and a selection of fresh or poached fruit, depending on what's in season. We'll sometimes also have a hard-boiled egg sprinkled with cumin salt or griddled flatbread with dips or a piece of fresh white cheese, like feta, with crunchy cucumbers, tomatoes and olives. Lucy's also a big fan of granola, and we've developed a fabulous low-sugar Middle Eastern version, chock-full of sour cherries and pistachios and a dash of rosewater.

At the weekends we often make time for something more substantial. The Middle East provides plenty of inspiration for hearty breakfast fare – dishes thick with beans and pulses are essential for seeing workers through to lunchtime, especially in the bitter winters and where people have physically arduous jobs. We've also included our favourite egg dishes, as well as glazed apple fritters for a sweet treat. And, because bread is such a vital part of breakfast (indeed, every meal of the day), it has its very own chapter, following on from this one (pages 32-49). You might also want to dip into Butters & Preserves, and Dips and Spreads (pages 50-63 and 64–75).

Summer berry salad with ginger, lime & labneh

A lovely summer breakfast fruit salad using perfectly ripe berries in a light delicately perfumed syrup. Use any combination of soft berries that you like; stone fruits, such as nectarines or white peaches are also delicious.

The quantities given for the syrup and labneh will make more than you need. However they can both be made ahead of time and will keep well in the fridge for up to 24 hours. You can also fancy-up the labneh by beating in 2 tablespoons of honey, a capful of orange flower water and the lightly crushed seeds from 4 cardamom pods before draining. Serve with fresh berries, use to fill the Pavlova 'Flowers' on page 236 or serve as accompaniment to all kinds of syrupy cakes or puddings instead of cream. It would be delicious with Orange Baklava Cigars (page 252), Spiced Currant Sfiha (page 250) or the Blackberry-Sour Cream Crumble Cake (page 258).

SERVES 4

450 g (1 lb) summer berries (your choice of raspberries, blackberries, blueberries, strawberries, red or white currants)

⅓ cup finely shredded baby mint leaves

sprigs of elderflower (optional)

Ginger-lime syrup

150 g (5 ½ oz) caster (superfine) sugar

150 ml (5 fl oz) water

4 cardamom pods, crushed

4 thin slices fresh ginger

strip of peel and juice from 1 lime

Vanilla labneh

1 tablespoon honey or maple syrup

1 vanilla pod, split and seeds scraped (or 1 teaspoon vanilla extract)

500 g (1 lb 2 oz) natural yoghurt

To make the ginger-lime syrup, put the sugar, water, cardamom pods, ginger and lime peel in a small saucepan. Bring to the boil, then simmer gently for about 5 minutes. Remove from the heat. When cool, add the lime juice then chill the syrup until ready to use. Strain and remove the aromatics just before serving.

For the soft-strained vanilla labneh, mix the honey and vanilla seeds into the yoghurt and scrape into a clean tea towel (a muslin square or new J-cloth will also do nicely). Tie the four corners together to form a hanging bag. Twist firmly to give it a good squeeze and kick-start the draining process. Suspend the bag from a wooden spoon set over a deep bowl and allow it to drain in the fridge for at least 4 hours or, preferably, overnight. The longer you hang it, the thicker it will be, but you can always thin it to a looser consistency, if necessary, with a little fresh yoghurt or cream.

Combine all the fruit in a mixing bowl with the mint and elderflower sprigs, if using, and pour on the chilled syrup. Toss gently, then divide between four serving bowls and serve with the labneh.

Blood oranges in spicy caramel sauce with ashta

After you've tried these spicy oranges, you'll never go back to the ordinary ones; they are seriously addictive! They keep well in the fridge and can be served chilled or warmed through gently. If you don't have the time or inclination to make the ashta, then serve them with strained or thick Greek-style yoghurt or with crème fraîche. And while we love them as a palate-enlivening breakfast, they also make a simple but effective dessert.

SERVES 4

4 medium–large blood oranges
    (or ordinary oranges)
100 g (3 ½ oz) caster (superfine)
    sugar
2 teaspoons leatherwood honey
3 star anise
½ teaspoon cardamom seeds,
    crushed to a powder
¼ teaspoon black peppercorns,
    crushed to a powder
½ small cinnamon stick
2 teaspoons orange flower water
    (or to taste)
squeeze lemon juice

Peel the oranges, then use a very sharp knife to slice the orange segments out of their skin casings (take care to remove all trace of pith and membrane) and set aside. Do this over a bowl to catch the juices and measure out 100 ml (3 ½ fl oz) of juice. (If there is not quite enough, make up the difference with water.)

Combine this orange juice with the sugar and honey in a small saucepan and heat gently until the sugar dissolves, swirling the pan occasionally. Add the star anise, cardamom, peppercorns and cinnamon and bring to the boil. Lower the heat to a vigorous simmer and cook for 8–10 minutes until it darkens to a deep reddish-brown (or until it reaches 130°C (250°F) on a candy thermometer). Remove from the heat straight away and stir in the orange flower water, lemon juice and orange segments (be careful, the caramel will spit and splutter). Stir gently, then remove from the heat and cool. Add a squeeze of lemon juice, then chill until ready to serve.

Ashta

Ashta (or kaymak) is a type of clotted cream that is delectably rich – around 60 per cent butterfat – and has a slight lactic tang. It is popular in many Middle Eastern countries, and particularly in Turkey, where it is eaten at breakfast with honeycomb or fresh fruit preserves. Ashta is often made from water buffalo milk or, otherwise, from cow's milk. It's produced commercially, but many households still make their own, as it's easy to do, requiring little skill but only time.

MAKES AROUND 300 ML (10 ½ FL OZ)

250 ml (9 fl oz) pure (double or
    heavy) cream
50 ml (1 ¾ fl oz) sour cream
40 ml (1 ¼ fl oz) mild-flavoured
    honey
finely grated zest of 1 orange
1 teaspoon orange flower water

Combine all the ingredients in a saucepan and very, very slowly bring to the boil. As soon as the mixture starts to bubble, lower the heat and keep it at a low simmer for 10 minutes. Tip into a shallow bowl (not plastic) and leave overnight, outside the refrigerator, wrapped in a blanket. Refrigerate until required. It will keep for 3–4 days.

Breakfast couscous with nuts, seeds & blueberries

Couscous lends itself surprisingly well to breakfast and you can make this alternative 'cereal' – which is a bit like a soft granola, chock-full of seeds, nuts and dried fruit – ahead of time, as it keeps well in the refrigerator for several days. We'd suggest sprinkling on the nut praline at the last minute, though, for maximum crunch.

SERVES 4

150 ml (5 fl oz) water

150 ml (5 fl oz) orange juice

1 tablespoon caster (superfine) sugar

200 g (7 oz) couscous

zest of 1 orange or lemon

1 teaspoon vegetable oil

35 g (1 ¼ oz) dried apricots (preferably organic), chopped to raisin size

35 g (1 ¼ oz) golden raisins

35 g (1 ¼ oz) currants

1 teaspoon ground cinnamon

1 tablespoon sunflower seeds

1 tablespoon pumpkin seeds

1 tablespoon sesame seeds

splash of orange flower water

200 g (7 oz) blueberries

your choice of hot or cold milk or buttermilk, with yoghurt or cream, to serve

Mixed nut praline

The nut praline can be made in advance and stored in the freezer. Take it out around an hour before you want to eat.

50 g (1 ¾ oz) caster (superfine) sugar

50 ml (1 ½ fl oz) water

20 g (¾ oz) hazelnuts

10 g (¼ oz) pine nuts

10 g (¼ oz) almond slivers

10 g (¼ oz) pistachio slivers

To make the mixed nut praline, combine the sugar and water in a small saucepan over a low heat. Tilt and gently shake the pan from time to time to help the sugar dissolve evenly.

Once the sugar has dissolved completely, increase the heat to medium and simmer for about 5 minutes, or until it reaches the 'thread' stage*, which is 110°C (225°F) on a candy thermometer.

Add the hazelnuts, pine nuts and almonds to the syrup and stir well. Lower the heat and cook, stirring continuously, for around 2 minutes until the sugar crystallizes. Don't panic! Keep everything moving around in the pan and the sugar will slowly redissolve to a liquid and begin to colour. At this stage, add the pistachio nuts. Stir over the heat for a further 4–5 minutes until the sugar is caramelized to a lovely golden brown. Tip out onto a tray lined with baking paper and spread the mixture out roughly. Leave to cool then bash to coarse crumbs with a rolling pin. Store in the freezer.

To prepare the couscous, combine the water and orange juice in a small saucepan and stir in the sugar. Bring to the boil then lower the heat and simmer for 5 minutes.

Meanwhile, mix the couscous with the orange zest and oil, using your fingers to rub in the oil as evenly as you can. Add the dried fruit and cinnamon, then pour in the hot syrup and stir everything together. Cover with a tea towel and leave for 10 minutes, stirring with a fork from time to time to prevent the couscous from clumping together.

When the couscous is cool, use your fingers to break down any small clumps and to ensure it is all flowing freely. Stir in the seeds, transfer to a sealed container and store in the fridge.

Remove from the fridge about 20 minutes before breakfast and spoon into cereal bowls. For each serving, stir in a few drops of flower water (don't over do it) and top with blueberries and a tablespoon of the nut praline. Serve with hot milk on the side, or zap in the microwave and serve with a dollop of cold buttermilk, yoghurt or thick cream.

*Note: If you don't have a candy thermometer, the 'thread' stage is reached when a drop of syrup falls from a spoon in a long, unbroken thread.

Middle Eastern granola with pomegranate, sour cherries & pistachios

Home-made granola is unbeatable, not least because it allows you to manage the level of sweetness (which can be frighteningly high in store-bought varieties) and to add your own favourite ingredients. This recipe has a Middle Eastern slant, incorporating tangy pomegranate molasses, exotic rosewater, dried sour cherries and pistachios (but why not also try chopped apricots and dates with coconut, hazelnuts and orange flower water?).

The base recipe uses apple purée, which is a Nigella Lawson suggestion (from *Feast*), which she, in turn, credits to Andy Rolleri. It is a terrific idea, as it allows you to reduce the amount of oil in the recipe and makes for an extra-crunchy granola. Other fruit purées work well, too, so feel free to experiment. And if you don't want to make your own purée (we used 1 large Granny Smith for this recipe), substitute with a good-quality, organic, unsweetened brand.

MAKES AROUND 800 G (1 LB 10 OZ) BUT THE AMOUNTS CAN EASILY BE MULTIPLIED, IF YOU PREFER TO DO THINGS IN BULK

Granola base

250 g (9 oz) rolled oats

60 g (2 ¼ oz) sunflower seeds

60 g (2 ¼ oz) sesame seeds

150 g (5 ½ oz) whole blanched almonds, roughly chopped

60 g (2 ¼ oz) light muscovado sugar

½ teaspoon sea salt

1 teaspoon ground cinnamon

½ teaspoon ground ginger

100 g (3 ½ oz) unsweetened apple purée

50 g (1 ¾ oz) honey

40 ml (1 ¼ fl oz) pomegranate molasses

1 tablespoon vegetable oil

Extras

100 g (3 ½ oz) pistachios, roughly chopped

100 g (3 ½ oz) dried sour cherries (or use ordinary dried cherries, but not glacé cherries)

80 g (2 ¾ oz) currants

2 teaspoons rosewater, or to taste (optional)

1 ½ tablespoons dried rose petals (optional)

Preheat the oven to 150°C (300°F).

In a large mixing bowl, combine the rolled oats, sunflower and sesame seeds, almonds, sugar, salt and spices.

In a small jug whisk the apple purée with the honey, pomegranate molasses and the oil. Tip into the dry ingredients and use your hands to mix everything together very thoroughly.

Tip the granola mixture into a large roasting tin and spread out into an even layer. Bake until it's coloured a deep golden brown, which will take anywhere from 45–60 minutes, depending on your oven. You'll need to stir the granola around every 20 minutes or so, to ensure it colours evenly. Pay special attention to the edges. Add the pistachios towards the end, so that they toast for about 10 minutes.

Remove from the oven and leave to cool briefly, then stir in the cherries, currants, rosewater and rose petals (if using). Store in an airtight container.

Glazed apple-raisin fritters

These are a knockout, and a firm favourite for a lazy weekend brunch ... or for afternoon tea ... or a late night snack. And they make an impressive last-minute dessert, too, if you dress them up with ice cream or crème fraîche.

MAKES AROUND 20

140 g (5 oz) plain (all-purpose) flour
1 ½ teaspoons baking powder
30 g (1 oz) caster (superfine) sugar
pinch ground cinnamon
½ teaspoon salt
1 large egg
140 ml (4 ¾ fl oz) milk
3 large apples (choose a good tart-sweet variety)
2 tablespoons golden raisins, very roughly chopped
sunflower or vegetable oil, for deep-frying

Apple glaze
140 g (5 oz) icing (confectioners') sugar
40 ml (1 ¼ fl oz) apple cider (or apple juice or, at a pinch, lemon juice)

Sift the flour and baking powder into a mixing bowl. Add the sugar, cinnamon and salt and whisk together briefly.

In a different bowl, whisk the egg with the milk. Tip into the dry ingredients and whisk everything together well to make a smooth batter. Set aside while you prepare the apples.

Peel the apples. Cut them into halves and remove the core (this is easiest with a melon baller). Cut into 5 mm (¼ in) thick slices, then cut the slices into 5 mm (¼ in) matchsticks.

When ready to cook, pour vegetable oil into a heavy-based saucepan or a deep-fryer to a depth of 5 cm (2 in) and heat to 170°C (325°F).*

Add the apple matchsticks and raisins to the batter and mix well. Drop small spoonfulls of batter into the oil ensuring you include a few raisins and 4–5 pieces of apple. You could also use a fork to do this. Don't worry about the shape – the more free-form, the better! Add more fritters to the pan, but do not overcrowd it. Fry for around 5 minutes, turning the fritters around in the oil from time to time, until they are evenly golden brown and crisp. Use a slotted spoon to lift them onto a plate lined with kitchen paper to drain.

Whisk the sugar and cider together to make a fairly thick glaze. Drizzle onto the fritters while they are still hot. Serve straight away.

*Note: The key thing when cooking these fritters is not to heat the oil to too high a temperature, so it's best to use a candy thermometer. If you don't have one, the oil will have reached the correct temperature when a cube of bread browns lightly in about 30 seconds. Any faster and it will be too hot.

Turkish eggs with spinach, chilli & yoghurt cream

Softly oozing eggs combine with spinach and a tangy yoghurt cream to make an unbeatable breakfast dish. It's important not to overcook the eggs, so the baking time will somewhat depend on the idiosyncrasies of your oven.

SERVES 4

2 bunches spinach, stalks removed, or 500 g (1 lb 2 oz) frozen spinach, defrosted

50 g (1 ¾ oz) butter, plus extra to grease

3 large shallots, finely sliced

2 cloves garlic, finely chopped

½ teaspoon ground cinnamon

1 teaspoon salt

½ teaspoon freshly ground black pepper

1 teaspoon Turkish red chilli flakes

4 extra-large eggs

Yoghurt cream

200 g (7 oz) Greek-style yoghurt

80 ml (2 ½ fl oz) pure (double or heavy) cream

½ teaspoon sweet paprika

salt and freshly ground black pepper

Preheat the oven to 180°C (350°F).

Blanch small batches of the spinach leaves in plenty of boiling salted water for 10 seconds. Refresh in cold water and then squeeze out as much moisture as possible. Loosen the clumps of spinach and chop it finely.

Heat the butter in a large frying pan. Add the shallots, garlic and spices and season with salt and pepper. Sauté over a medium heat until soft. Add the spinach and cook for 5 minutes, or until the spinach is soft.

Generously butter a medium ovenproof dish and spread the spinach mix evenly over the base. Make 4 little wells in the spinach and crack in the eggs. Bake for 12 minutes then check for doneness. The eggs should be starting to set, but still very runny.

Mix the yoghurt with the cream, paprika, salt and pepper. Spoon over the eggs and return to the oven for a further 3–4 minutes, or until the eggs are cooked to your liking. Serve immediately with warm crusty bread.

White zucchini omelette with mint & melting gouda

We learnt to make *kuku-ye sabzi*, one of Persia's best-loved omelettes, during our travels around Iran. It is similar in texture to a frittata, thick with herbs and leafy green vegetables (*sabzi* means 'greenery' in farsi), and sometimes comes garnished with walnuts or barberries. We love to add grated zucchini – especially white zucchini, which are more delicate and less bitter than the dark green variety – although either will do. Cheese is a deviation from the purist Iranian *kuku* but, hot from the oven, its melting softness is irresistible. Try to find a cumin-flavoured Gouda if you can.

A non-stick, ovenproof frying pan – no more than 20 cm (8 in) in diameter – is ideal for making *kuku*. We've also made this very successfully in a non-stick cake tin.

SERVES 4

100 ml (3 ½ fl oz) olive oil

1 onion, finely diced

1 teaspoon grated nutmeg

1 teaspoon dried mint

350 g (12 oz) white zucchini (courgettes) (about 3), coarsely grated

4 eggs

2 tablespoons self-raising flour

grated zest of 1 lemon

½ teaspoon salt

½ teaspoon freshly ground black pepper

200 g (7 oz) cumin-flavoured Gouda (or any other melting cheese), grated

Greek-style yoghurt, to serve (optional)

Preheat the oven to 180°C (350°F).

Heat half the oil in a frying pan over a low heat and fry the onion until it softens. Stir in the nutmeg and mint and fry for another minute. Remove from the heat and leave to cool.

Pour the remaining oil into a non-stick, ovenproof frying pan and heat in the oven for 5–10 minutes.

Squeeze the grated zucchini firmly to remove as much moisture as possible. Whisk the eggs until frothy in a large bowl. Whisk in the flour, lemon zest, salt and pepper, followed by the zucchini, onion mixture and cheese. The mixture will be quite sloppy.

Pour the mixture into the hot oil. Cover the pan with a lid or some foil and bake in the oven for 10 minutes or until nearly set. Remove the lid and cook for a further 10 minutes to brown the surface.

Cut into wedges and serve hot from the pan with thick yoghurt. Alternatively, drain on kitchen paper and cut into wedges when cold to serve with pickles or relish. The Spicy Carrot Pickle (page 84) or Eggplant Relish (page 82) would work very well.

Egyptian breakfast beans with feta, lemon oil & green chilli relish

The classic Egyptian breakfast dish – *ful medames* – is also popular in other Middle Eastern countries where you'll often find tiny hole-in-the-wall shops or stalls in the souks selling just this one dish.

Ful medames is intensely savoury and comforting and especially good on a cold winter morning. This version is quick and easy to make; no soaking required! The relish adds an extra chilli hit, and is based on a version of *ful* that Greg enjoyed during a trip to Jordan. For a heartier breakfast, serve with hard- or soft-boiled eggs, but, in any event, you'll want lemon wedges and lots of pita for scooping everything up.

SERVES 4

40 ml (1 ¼ fl oz) extra-virgin olive oil

grated zest and juice of ½ lemon

4 spring onions (scallions), finely chopped

1 clove garlic crushed with ½ teaspoon salt

400 g (14 oz) tin chickpeas, well rinsed and drained

300 g (10 ½ oz) tin broad beans (fava), well rinsed and drained

1 teaspoon ground cumin

¼ teaspoon Turkish red chilli flakes

¼ teaspoon freshly ground black pepper

2 medium vine-ripened tomatoes, diced

2 tablespoons shredded flat-leaf parsley leaves

soft white cheese, such as feta or fresh goat's cheese, crumbled

lemon wedges and pita, to serve

Green chilli relish

6 pickled green chillies, coarsely chopped

1 small clove garlic, very finely chopped

40 ml (1 ¼ fl oz) extra-virgin olive oil

squeeze lemon juice

salt and freshly ground black pepper

Mix the relish ingredients together and set aside.

In a medium saucepan, warm the oil with the lemon zest and juice. Add the spring onions and garlic paste and sauté over a gentle heat for 6–8 minutes, or until the spring onions have softened.

Mix in the chickpeas, broad beans and spices and cook gently for about 5 minutes until everything has warmed through. Stir in the tomatoes and cook for a further minute then taste and adjust the seasonings to your liking. Tip into serving bowls and top with parsley and cheese. Serve with the green chilli relish, lemon wedges and pita.

Breads

SESAME JOUJOU BREADS ... 34

GRIDDLED FLATBREADS: GOAT'S CHEESE-ZA'ATAR; COCONUT-DATE;

FENNEL-TURKISH CHILLI; CRUSHED HAZELNUT-ROSEMARY... 36

TURKISH MILK ROLLS WITH YOGHURT GLAZE ... 40

SEMOLINA BREAD WITH ANISEED & SESAME ... 43

SAFFRON FRUIT LOAF ... 45

MIDDLE EASTERN PIZZAS ... 46

The Middle East is justifiably renowned for its wonderful range of flatbreads. They are eaten with every meal and enjoyed as snacks throughout the day. Breads from this region are predominantly low-risen, but can be thick or thin, soft or firmer, white or wholemeal, sweet or savoury – or even baked into paper-thin crispbreads. In some areas, breads are sprinkled with seeds or the dough flavoured with spices before baking. Some have pockets and some come ready-stuffed. Some are baked on domed or flat metal griddles, others on hot stones or in wood-fired clay ovens, and others still in deep cylindrical tandoors.

Although flatbreads rule, you can also find higher-risen rolls and loaves. Turkish *simit* and Lebanese *kaak* are popular breakfast bread rings, similar to pretzels, and we've enjoyed rustic-style loaves made from fine or coarsely ground maize in both the north of Turkey and in North Africa.

In this section we've included a few of our favourites from around the Middle East. As well as the easy and endlessly versatile griddle breads, which you can cook in a hot wok or frying pan, there are tiny pocket joujou breads – like mini pita breads – which you can eat with just about everything, There is also the recipe for our lovely soft breakfast rolls that have a gorgeous glazed crust, and a rich, fruited saffron tea loaf. And we simply had to include a Lebanese *manoushi* dough recipe and a selection of tasty toppings. *Manoushi* are the Middle Eastern equivalent of Italian pizzas and, while strictly speaking they aren't bread, they are one of the most popular snack foods in the region.

Sesame joujou breads

The recipe below makes around 40 little joujou breads, but you can halve the quantities if you like. You can serve them as an accompaniment to just about anything, or alternatively you can chill the dough quite happily for up to 24 hours and it freezes very well indeed, for up to 4 weeks. Defrost at room temperature, then roll out and bake.

If you use 'instant' or 'dried active yeast', there's no need to activate it first in warm water, as you would with fresh yeast. However we do follow legendary baker Paul Hollywood's suggestion of keeping the salt and yeast on opposite sides of the bowl (salt can kill the yeast) before you mix everything together.

MAKES AROUND 40

625 g (1 lb 6 oz) strong (bread)
    flour
4 teaspoons dried active yeast
    (2 x 7.5 g / ¼ oz sachets)
450 ml (16 fl oz) warm water
40 ml (1 ¼ fl oz) extra-virgin
    olive oil
1 heaped teaspoon salt
150 ml (5 fl oz) milk
75 g (2 ½ oz) sesame seeds

Sift the flour into the bowl of a stand-mixer and add the yeast. Whisk the warm water with the oil and add it to the bowl. On the lowest speed, knead with the dough hook for 4 minutes. Add the salt then increase the speed to medium and knead for a further 4–6 minutes, or until the gluten has developed and the dough is smooth and satiny. Shape the dough into a ball and transfer to a large lightly oiled bowl. Cover with a tea towel and set aside in a draught-free spot for 45–60 minutes, until doubled in size.

Punch down the dough and knead again for a few minutes. Divide into 4 equal portions. At this stage you can wrap the dough pieces in cling film and chill or freeze.

When you're ready to bake, preheat the oven to its highest temperature.

On a floured work surface, roll out a ball of dough evenly to form a square about 3 mm (¹/₈ in) thick. Use a sharp knife to trim the edges neatly and then cut the dough into 8 cm (3 ½ in) squares or into little rounds. Brush lightly with milk then sprinkle on the sesame seeds evenly – each joujou bread should have a generous coating. Press the seeds gently into the dough then transfer each piece to a heavy-based baking sheet, taking care not to distort the shape. Leave for 10 minutes while you continue with the rest of the dough.

Bake the first lot of joujou breads for 4 minutes. They should colour lightly and puff up into lovely little pillows. Remove from the oven and tip into a clean tea towel or large napkin to keep warm while you bake the remaining joujou breads.

Griddled flatbreads

This is a wonderful all-purpose dough that suits both griddled and naan-style baked flatbreads, which are the most popular accompaniment for Middle Eastern meals. Use the basic recipe to make a batch of dough and fry them plain, or choose the filling that you fancy from page 39. The quantities of dough and fillings are sufficient for six large-ish flatbreads or eight smaller ones.

MAKES 6–8

450 g (1 lb) strong (bread) flour,
    plus extra for dusting
1 teaspoon baking powder
½ teaspoon salt
2 teaspoons dried active yeast
    (7.5 g / ¼ oz sachet)
2 teaspoons caster (superfine)
    sugar
150 ml (5 fl oz) hand-hot milk
30 ml (1 fl oz) vegetable oil
150 g (5 oz) natural yoghurt, lightly
    beaten
1 egg, lightly beaten
clarified butter, for brushing

Sift the flour and baking powder into the bowl of a stand-mixer. Add the salt to one side of the bowl and the yeast to the opposite side (salt can kill the yeast).

Dissolve the sugar in the hand-hot milk then add it to the bowl, along with the oil, yoghurt and egg. Mix briefly to form a ball.

Knead with the dough hook on a slow–medium speed for 10 minutes. You may need to scrape it up from the bottom of the bowl every now and then. Once the gluten has developed and the dough is smooth and satiny, shape it into a ball with lightly oiled hands and transfer to a large bowl. Cover with a tea towel and set aside in a draught-free spot for an hour, or until doubled in size.

Punch down the dough and knead by hand for a few minutes. Divide into 6 or 8 equal balls. At this point you can fry the breads as they are, or fill them with one of the stuffings, as outlined on page 39.

Keeping the rest covered, roll out one ball of dough onto a floured work surface, to a 30 cm (12 in) round for large breads or 23 cm (9 in) for smaller ones.

Heat a large, heavy-based frying pan over a very high heat. Fry the bread in the dry pan until large bubbles start to appear on the surface – it should only take 1–2 minutes. Flip over and fry for a further minute, or until lightly golden.

Brush with clarified butter while still warm and serve. Repeat with the rest of the dough.

Naans

Although these are usually baked on the sides of a tandoor oven, we've achieved reasonable success using a pizza stone, an unglazed roof tile or a heavy baking tray preheated in the oven at its highest temperature.

Divide the dough into 6 equal balls. Keeping the rest of the dough covered, roll out one ball of dough on a floured work surface into a tear-shaped naan, about 30 cm (12 in) long and 15 cm (6 in) at its widest point.

Slap onto the preheated baking tray and bake for 3 minutes. It should colour lightly and puff up. Flip over and bake for a further minute. Wrap in a tea towel while you bake the remaining naans. Brush with clarified butter while still warm and serve.

Goat's cheese-za'atar

(left)

Use the same dough to make a lovely, focaccia-style bread.

MAKES 2 LOAVES

50 ml (1 ¾ fl oz) extra-virgin olive oil
150 g (5 ½ oz) goat's cheese, roughly broken
2 teaspoons za'atar
1 teaspoon sumac
⅓ cup fresh oregano leaves
salt flakes and freshly ground black pepper

After punching down the dough, divide it in half and roll each portion into a flattish oval, about 30 cm x 18 cm (12 in x 7 in) and 2 cm (¾ in) high. Transfer to a heavy-based oven tray and set aside in a draught-free spot for around 30 minutes.

Brush the surface of each loaf liberally with extra-virgin olive oil. Make indentations in the surface and push in the pieces of crumbled goat's cheese. Sprinkle each loaf with za'atar and sumac and scatter on the oregano leaves. Season with salt and pepper and bake for 12–15 minutes, or until golden brown. The loaves should sound hollow when tapped on the base. Transfer to a wire rack and cool.

Coconut-date

MAKES 6-8

40 g (1 ½ oz) Medjool dates (about 3), stones removed, roughly chopped
50 g (1 ¾ oz) flaked almonds
20 g (¾ oz) desiccated coconut
½ teaspoon ground cumin
1 tablespoon crème fraîche
pinch sea salt

While the dough is rising, combine the ingredients in a food processor and whiz to form a paste. The consistency should be something like marzipan. Divide into 6 or 8 portions, depending on how many flatbreads you are going to make.

One ball at a time, flatten out the dough and make a shallow indentation with your thumb. Press in the ball of paste and carefully bring the dough up around it to seal. Flatten the ball on a floured work surface and roll it out to the desired shape. Fry the flatbreads, as instructed in the base method. Brush with clarified butter and serve warm. Repeat with the rest of the dough balls.

Fennel-Turkish chilli

MAKES 6-8

1 tablespoon fennel seeds
1 ½ teaspoons Turkish red chilli flakes
½ teaspoon sea salt

Set a small frying pan over high heat. Add the fennel and fry in the dry pan for a good minute, or until they start to pop and release their fragrance. Tip into a mortar and crush to a medium-coarse powder. Transfer to a small bowl and mix with the chilli and salt.

On a floured work surface, roll out each ball of dough to a thickish version of the desired shape. Scatter the spice mix over the surface evenly and then continue rolling it out thinly. Fry the flatbreads, as instructed in the base method. Brush with clarified butter and serve warm.

Crushed hazelnut-rosemary

MAKES 6-8

80 g (2 ¾ oz) hazelnuts
¼ teaspoon olive oil
½ teaspoon sea salt
1 tablespoon roughly chopped rosemary

Set a small frying pan over high heat. Add the hazelnuts, oil, rosemary and salt and fry for around 5 minutes, tossing the pan constantly, until the nuts are golden brown. Tip into a clean tea towel and use a rolling pin to crush the nuts roughly.

On a floured work surface, roll out each ball of dough to a thickish version of the desired shape. Scatter the nut mix over the surface evenly and then continue rolling it out thinly. Fry the flatbreads, as instructed in the base method. Brush with clarified butter and serve warm.

Turkish milk rolls with yoghurt glaze

These lovely breakfast rolls have a tender crumb and tasty crust. They keep reasonably well in a bread bin, and can be warmed through in the oven before serving. Serve them for breakfast with butter and jam, or as an accompaniment to your favourite soups or stews.

MAKES 6 ROLLS

425 g (15 oz) strong (bread) flour
1 teaspoon salt
3 teaspoons dried active yeast
　　(1 ½ x 7.5 g / ¼ oz sachets)
200 ml (7 fl oz) hand-hot milk
125 ml (4 fl oz) clarified butter
1 egg
butter, to grease

Yoghurt glaze
1 tablespoon natural yoghurt
1 tablespoon clarified butter
1 tablespoon nigella seeds
½ teaspoon salt flakes

Sift the flour into the bowl of a stand-mixer. Add the salt to one side of the bowl and the yeast to the opposite side (salt can kill the yeast).

Add the milk, butter and egg and mix briefly to form a ball. Knead with the dough hook on a slow–medium speed for 10 minutes, or until the gluten has developed and the dough is smooth and satiny. Shape the dough into a ball and transfer to a large lightly oiled bowl. Cover with a tea towel and set aside in a draught-free spot for 1–1 ½ hours, or until doubled in size.

Preheat the oven to 200°C (400°F) and lightly butter a small, deep-sided baking tin (no more than 15 cm x 20 cm / 6 in x 8 in).

Punch down the dough and divide into 6 even pieces. Roll each piece into a fat log and arrange in the prepared tin; they will expand to fill the space as the dough rises. Cover and set aside for another 30 minutes.

Meanwhile, to make the glaze, whisk the yoghurt with the clarified butter.

After the rolls have rested, brush them with the yoghurt glaze and use a fork to score the surface with fine lines. Sprinkle with nigella seeds and salt flakes and bake for 30–40 minutes, or until the rolls are golden brown. The bases should sound hollow when tapped. Cool on a wire rack.

Semolina bread with aniseed & sesame

With its glossy brown domed surface and unusual flavour, this North African bread is hugely appealing. It has a soft crumb and crunchy crust, with a hint of orange sweetness and aniseed.

MAKES 1 LOAF

225 g (8 oz) strong (bread) flour

225 g (8 oz) fine semolina

½ teaspoon salt

2 teaspoons dried active yeast (7.5 g / ¼ oz sachet)

½ teaspoon sugar

90 g (3 ¼ oz) butter, melted

grated zest of ½ orange

2 teaspoons aniseeds, lightly crushed

4 teaspoons sesame seeds

150 ml (5 fl oz) warm water

1 egg, lightly beaten

butter, to grease

1 egg yolk, beaten, to glaze

½ teaspoon salt flakes

Sift the flour and semolina into the bowl of a stand-mixer. Add the salt to one side of the bowl and the yeast to the opposite side (salt can kill the yeast).

Stir the sugar into the melted butter and add it to the bowl, along with the orange zest, aniseed, sesame seeds and half the water. Mix well. Add the egg and enough of the remaining water to form a soft dough. Knead with the dough hook on a slow–medium speed for 10 minutes, or until the gluten has developed and the dough is smooth and satiny. Shape into a ball and transfer to a large lightly oiled bowl. Cover with a tea towel and set aside in a draught-free spot for 1–1 ½ hours, or until doubled in size.

Preheat the oven to 180°C (350°F).

Place the dough on a lightly buttered baking tray and flatten it gently to a thickness of about 2.5 cm (1 in). Brush the surface with egg yolk, sprinkle with salt flakes and slash the surface with a sharp knife. Bake for 30–40 minutes, or until it is a glossy chestnut brown and sounds hollow when tapped on the base. Cool on a wire rack.

Saffron fruit loaf

A bit of a hybrid loaf: part cake, part bread. No matter, either way it's delicious for breakfast or teatime. It keeps fairly well, which is a blessing as we reckon it is even better a day after being made, toasted and slathered with Home-made Crème Fraîche butter (page 52) and jam.

MAKES 1 LOAF

20 saffron threads

300 ml (10 ½ fl oz) hot milk

500 g (1 lb 2 oz) strong (bread) flour

1 teaspoon salt

150 g (5 ½ oz) unsalted butter, diced, plus extra to grease

50 g (1 ¾ oz) soft brown sugar

2 teaspoons dried active yeast (7.5 g / ¼ oz sachet)

60 g (2 ¼ oz) currants

40 g (1 ½ oz) mixed dried fruit or mixed citrus peel

1 tablespoon plain (all-purpose) flour, for dusting

1 egg, lightly beaten

Stir the saffron strands into the hot milk and leave to infuse for 1–2 hours.

Combine the flour and salt in a mixing bowl. Rub in the butter with your fingertips to form fine crumbs. Stir in the sugar evenly then make a well in the middle of the dry ingredients.

Reheat the milk to blood temperature (there's no need to strain out the saffron threads as they look so pretty). Combine a few tablespoons of the milk with the yeast and mix to a slurry. Stir in the remaining warm milk and then tip all the liquid into the dry ingredients. Use your hands to work the mixture into a dough, then transfer to the bowl of a stand-mixer.

Knead with the dough hook on a slow–medium speed for 10 minutes, or until the gluten has developed and the dough is smooth and satiny.

Toss the dried fruit with the extra flour, which helps to prevent it sinking to the bottom of the loaf during baking. Add the fruit to the dough in two stages, kneading well after each addition.

Grease a 20 cm x 10 cm (8 in x 4 in) loaf tin with butter. Transfer the dough to the prepared tin and cover with a tea towel. Set aside in a draught-free spot for 1–1 ½ hours, or until doubled in size. Don't be tempted to speed up the proving time by sticking it on top of a radiator.

Preheat the oven to 180°C (350°F).

Once the dough has risen, brush with beaten egg and use a sharp knife to slash the surface, if you wish. Bake for 50–60 minutes, until the top is golden brown. The base of the loaf should sound hollow when tapped. Remove from the tin and cool on a wire rack. Allow the cake to rest for an hour before slicing and serving with butter (pages 52–57) or Ashta (page 20) and home-made jam (page 58).

Middle Eastern pizzas

You will find versions of these Middle Eastern-style pizzas all around the Middle East and Eastern Mediterranean where they're mainly eaten for breakfast or as a morning snack. We have included several of our favourite 'topping' recipes here, including za'atar, which is a more-ish combination of wild thyme, tangy sumac and sesame seeds. *Manoushi* – pizza breads smeared with oil and za'atar – are one of the most popular breakfasts in Lebanon and Greg craves them if he doesn't have them at least once a week!

This is one of the best pizza dough recipes we've found, and you can successfully freeze it for up to 4 weeks, which means it's worth making in fairly large amounts. You get the best results with home-made pizzas if you bake them on a pizza stone or even an unglazed roof tile. Preheat your oven and stone as high as you dare.

MAKES 4-6

600 g (1 lb 5 oz) strong (bread) flour, plus extra for dusting

10 g (¼ oz) salt

3 teaspoons dried active yeast (1 ½ x 7.5 g / ¼ oz sachet)

30 g (1 oz) caster (superfine) sugar

250 ml (9 fl oz) warm water

30 ml (1 fl oz) olive oil, plus extra to grease the bowl

2 eggs, lightly beaten

Sift the flour into the bowl of a stand-mixer. Add the salt to one side of the bowl and the yeast to the opposite side (salt can kill the yeast).

Dissolve the sugar in the warm water and then add it to the bowl, along with the oil and beaten eggs. Mix briefly to form a ball.

Knead with the dough hook on slow speed for 7 minutes, then increase the speed to medium and knead for a further 7 minutes. Once the gluten has developed and the dough is smooth and satiny, shape the dough into a ball and transfer it to a large lightly oiled bowl. Cover with a tea towel and set aside for an hour, or until doubled in size.

When you're ready to bake, preheat the oven to its highest temperature and preheat a pizza stone, unglazed tile or your heaviest baking sheet.

Punch down the dough and knead again for a few minutes. Divide into 4 or 6 equal balls. Keeping the rest of the dough covered, roll out one ball of dough thinly onto a floured work surface, to a 30 cm (12 in) round. Brush the surface lightly with olive oil, or spread with a flavoured butter (pages 55–56) as in the tip opposite. Add your favourite topping, remembering not to overload it. Bake for 4–6 minutes, until the pizza is risen and lightly browned. Serve piping hot.

Toppings

Really, these are limitless.

- For the classic *manoushi*, combine za'atar with sumac in a 3-to-1 ratio and mix to a thick, spreadable paste with olive oil. Smear evenly over the pizza bases and bake.

- Slow-roasted Tomatoes (page 79) are lovely with fresh oregano and creamy labneh (page 73), and perhaps black or green olives.

- Scatter on good-quality preserved artichokes (or use leftovers from page 158), break open a burrata, dot it over the surface and finish with finely chopped preserved lemon.

- Wilt chopped spinach and sauté it with garlic and shallot in a little butter. Mix in finely grated lemon zest and ½ teaspoon dried mint then spread over the pizza dough. Dot the surface with blobs of labneh (page 73), crack on an egg and bake until just set.

- For a three-cheese special, mix 180 g (6 oz) Home-made Shankleesh (page 72) with 180 g (6 oz) coarsely grated mozzarella, 100 g (3 ½ oz) coarsely grated parmesan, 1 teaspoon Turkish chilli flakes and 1 tablespoon extra-virgin olive oil. Smear it on thinly and bake.

- Spread the pizza bases with labneh (page 73) and top with thin slices of leftover boiled potatoes. Scatter on fresh za'atar or thyme leaves, finely diced preserved lemon and more blobs of labneh or goat's cheese.

- Mix-and-match thinly sliced vegetables (zucchini, mushroom, peppers, onion) – or use leftovers from the barbecued Tunisian-style Vegetables on page 167) and scatter on pieces of feta, mozzarella, labneh or Shankleesh (page 73 or 72).

- The Sweet Pumpkin and Oregano filling (page 128) also makes a delicious pizza topping.

- Rainbow chard, currants and pine nuts (page 155) make a great combination. Top with mozzarella and a sprinkling of Turkish red chilli flakes.

- Use any of the butters (pages 55–56) or Turkish Red Pepper Paste (page 69) to add instant flavour to the base, before adding toppings.

- Finally, if you have a sweet tooth, try one of the sweet butters as a flavour base (page 57), and top with figs or slices of your favourite summer stone fruits and sprinkle with brown sugar. Towards the end of the baking time, dollop with labneh (page 73) and bake for another minute until it starts to melt.

Butters & preserves

HOME-MADE CRÈME FRAÎCHE BUTTER ... 52

SAVOURY BUTTERS: PRESERVED LEMON; ALMOND-SAFFRON;

PERSIAN SABZI; HARISSA ... 55

SWEET BUTTERS: APPLE-WALNUT; APRICOT-CARDAMOM; PEAR-GINGER ... 57

RHUBARB, RASPBERRY & CARDAMOM FRIDGE JAM ... 58

GINGERED GRAPEFRUIT CURD ... 60

CANDIED CITRUS PEEL ... 63

We've included a lot of butters in this section as they're our new favourite thing! In truth, most Middle Eastern countries favour olive oil as their cooking medium and also for drizzling onto breads. However, there are some big exceptions. Butter is used in cakes and biscuits and, particularly, in their much-loved sweet and savoury pastries, where it is clarified and used for brushing between the layers of flaky filo to add richness and crunch. Butter is also frequently added to rice dishes at the end of cooking – especially in Iran – sometimes with a spoonful of saffron liquid, to add sheen and flavour. We eat – and relish – both olive oil and butter and each has its place in our kitchen and on our dining table.

Just recently we learnt how easy it is to make butter at home and so we've taken to whipping up regular and lactic butters at the drop of a hat. We also love making different flavoured butters to serve as effortlessly easy sauces. These have a particular affinity with simply cooked vegetables and add a quick flavour hit when dropped on top of hot grain- or pulse-based dishes. They also make a great base for more refined butter sauces, such as Hollandaise.

This section is not just about butter – it also includes a few of our favourite sweet preserves. Middle Easterners make amazing jams, largely because they have such wonderful produce growing all around them. If you have access to your own fruit, you'll perhaps already be a dab hand at maximizing the harvest. But, even if you don't, you'll understand that the aim is to capture the intense flavours of summer to dip into over the colder months.

Home-made crème fraîche butter

We've recently become entranced by the alchemy of butter making. It's quick and easy to do, and the result is so much better than the mass-produced stuff, you may never go back. An extra bonus of making your own butter is that, in a pleasing 'two-fer', you also end up with buttermilk! Not only is buttermilk the baker's friend (it adds a wonderful lightness and flavour to cakes, scones and pastry), but you can also whip it into potatoes for a delectable mash, whisk it into salad dressing or churn it into ice creams or sorbets (pages 220–231).

We began our butter adventures using double cream, which results in a lovely pale, glossy and fresh-tasting spread – a little softer than commercially produced butter. Then we graduated to using crème fraîche to make cultured butter – which is closer in flavour to the distinctive, faint sourness of good European butters. Home-made crème fraîche butter has a distinctive, lively, sweet tang and a true 'butter' flavour; best of all, it costs a fraction of what you'll pay for upmarket imported European versions.

The process really is incredibly quick and simple, but we've taken the trouble to describe it in some detail. Once you've done it once, you'll understand the process exactly.

If crème fraîche is expensive where you live, then you can easily make your own using the method described below.

MAKES AROUND 550 G (1 LB 3 OZ) BUTTER

1 kg (2 lb 4 oz) crème fraîche, at
    room temperature
1 teaspoon fine salt (optional)

Home-made crème fraîche

Seriously, this involves nothing more than adding a good dollop of cultured buttermilk to a bowl of cream, giving it a quick stir and then leaving it alone for 12–24 hours for the culture to work its magic. The longer you leave it, the thicker it will be and you'll get a more intense, complex flavour. We rarely bother about measuring, but you'll need roughly 50 ml (2 fl oz) buttermilk for every 500 ml (16 fl oz) pure (double or heavy) cream. Once you're happy with your crème fraîche, transfer it to the fridge where it will keep for about a week.

Prepare a large jug of iced water – you'll need at least 2 litres (64 fl oz).

Put the crème fraîche in the bowl of a food processor (or use a stand-mixer, but remember to cover the bowl with cling film to stop the buttermilk spraying everywhere). Turn it on and whiz for anywhere between 2–4 minutes (it takes 3 in our machine). It will thicken, like whipped cream, and then you'll see it stiffen and start to clump together and the colour will subtly change to the palest of creamy yellows. Keep processing until liquid – buttermilk – begins to splatter around the bowl. Tip everything into a sieve, pushing it gently to drain off the buttermilk. Return the butter to the processor and whiz it again until more liquid has been expelled, then drain this off too. Repeat a third time until all the liquid has been released.

The next stage is to wash the butter of any residual buttermilk. It's crucial to remove as much of this as you can as, otherwise, it will taint the flavour of the butter and it will 'spoil' faster.

Scrape the butter into a large bowl and add a good amount of the iced water. Use a couple of spatulas (we use the broad silicone type) to squish and squeeze the butter around in the water, lifting and turning it as you go. Tip off the cloudy water, add fresh iced water and continue with the pressing and turning. Work briskly to stop the butter warming up too much and repeat the process half a dozen times, or until the water runs clear.

At this point, change to using a fork to give the butter a final mash and pour away any last bits of liquid. Mash in the salt, if using, then divide the butter in half. Press it into containers, pat it into your preferred shapes, or roll it into logs. It will keep for 3–4 weeks in the fridge and for several months in the freezer.

Savoury butters

Preserved lemon

(second down, left)

MAKES 1 X 220 G (7 ¾ OZ) LOG OF BUTTER

175 g (6 oz) softened butter

1 preserved lemon, skin only, finely chopped

2 shallots, finely chopped

½ clove garlic, finely chopped

1 tablespoon finely chopped flat-leaf parsley leaves

1 teaspoon finely chopped thyme leaves

½ teaspoon sumac

Combine the ingredients in a mixing bowl and beat everything together well. Spoon onto a sheet of cling film or greaseproof paper and shape into a log. Roll up neatly, twist the ends, tie securely and chill until required. The butter will keep in a sealed container in the refrigerator for 2 weeks or up to 3 months in the freezer.

Almond–saffron

(third down, left)

MAKES 1 X 250 G (9 OZ) LOG OF BUTTER

40 g (1 ½ oz) whole blanched almonds

15 saffron threads (a generous pinch)

½ teaspoon salt

½ teaspoon extra-virgin olive oil

finely grated zest of 1 orange

splash orange flower water

125 g (4 ½ oz) unsalted butter, softened

Chop the almonds by hand fairly finely and evenly. You want to leave some body, not turn them into crumbs.

Toss with the saffron, salt and oil. Heat a small frying pan over a medium heat. Add the nut mixture and fry, stirring continuously for 1–2 minutes, just to warm everything through. It doesn't need to colour. Remove the pan from the heat and add the orange zest and flower water, stirring them in evenly. Leave to cool.

Add the mixture to the butter and beat everything together well. Spoon onto a sheet of cling film or greaseproof paper and shape into a log. Roll up neatly, twist the ends, tie securely and chill until required. The butter will keep in a sealed container in the refrigerator for 2 weeks or up to 3 months in the freezer.

Persian sabzi

(bottom, left)

For this recipe we recommend shredding the herbs, rather than chopping them. We find that chopping tends to bruise the delicate leaves and makes them 'bleed' into the butter, affecting the flavour and colour.

MAKES 1 X 225 G (8 OZ) LOG OF BUTTER

40 g (1 ½ oz) walnuts

125 g (4 ½ oz) unsalted butter, softened

40 g (1 ½ oz) feta, rinsed and finely crumbled

2 tablespoons snipped chives

2 tablespoons each of shredded tarragon, mint, Thai basil, dill and flat-leaf parsley leaves

¾ teaspoon sea salt

Preheat the oven to 180°C (350°F). Roast the walnuts for around 5 minutes until the skins start to colour. Tip into a clean tea towel and rub away as much of the skins as you can, then chop them roughly. Sieve to remove any excess dust and skin.

Add to the butter with the remaining ingredients and beat everything together well. Spoon onto a sheet of cling film or greaseproof paper and shape into a log. Roll up neatly, twist the ends, tie securely and chill until required. The butter will keep in a sealed container in the fridge for 2 weeks or up to 3 months in the freezer.

Savoury butters

Harissa butter

(page 54, top)

MAKES 1 X 140 G (5 OZ) LOG OF BUTTER

1 small shallot, finely chopped
1 clove garlic, finely chopped
¼ teaspoon salt
125 g (4 ½ oz) unsalted butter, softened
½ tablespoon Red or Green Harissa

Combine the shallot, garlic and salt in a mortar and pound to a paste. Add to the butter and harissa and beat everything together well. Spoon onto a sheet of cling film or greaseproof paper and shape into a log. Roll up neatly, twist the ends, tie securely and chill until required. The butter will keep in a sealed container in the fridge for 2 weeks or up to 3 months in the freezer.

Green harissa

MAKES ABOUT 250 ML (9 FL OZ)

125 g (4 ½ oz) large green chillies deseeded and shredded
1 clove garlic
100 g (3 ½ oz) spinach leaves, stalks removed
2 cups fresh coriander (cilantro) leaves
1 teaspoon caraway seeds
1 teaspoon coriander seeds
1 teaspoon dried mint
½ teaspoon chilli powder
60 ml (2 fl oz) olive oil
sea salt and freshly ground black pepper
vegetable oil, to seal

Combine all the ingredients, except for the oil, in the bowl of a food processor and whiz for 1 minute. With the motor running slowly, drizzle in the oil until the mixture is the consistency of pouring cream. Season with salt and freshly ground black pepper. Spoon the harissa into a clean jar and cover the surface with a thin film of flavourless oil. Store in the fridge where it will keep for up to 1 week.

Red harissa

MAKES ABOUT 200 ML (7 FL OZ)

1 red capsicum (pepper)
1 teaspoon cumin seeds
¾ teaspoon caraway seeds
10–15 dried long red chillies, rehydrated in boiling water for 10 minutes
10 small red chillies, deseeded
2 cloves garlic, crushed with ½ teaspoon sea salt
60 ml (2 fl oz) olive oil
vegetable oil, to seal

Preheat the oven to 200°C (400°F). Lay the capsicum on a foil-lined baking tray and roast for 15–20 minutes, turning every so often, until the skin blackens and blisters. Transfer to a bowl, cover with cling film and leave to steam for a further 10 minutes, which softens the capsicum and loosens the skin. Carefully peel away the skin and discard it with the stalk and seeds.

Heat the cumin and caraway seeds in a dry frying pan until lightly toasted and aromatic. Transfer to a mortar and crush to a powder. Combine all the ingredients in the bowl of a food processor and whiz together to make a paste. Taste carefully for seasoning – it is extremely hot – adding more salt if necessary. Tip into a saucepan and bring to the boil. Spoon the harissa into a sterilized jar and cover the surface with a thin film of flavourless oil. Store in the fridge where it will keep for up to 4 weeks.

Sweet butters

Apple–walnut

MAKES 1 X 240 G (8 ½ OZ) LOG OF BUTTER

40 g (1 ½ oz) walnuts

125 g (4 ½ oz) unsalted butter, softened

70 g (2 ½ oz) unsweetened apple purée (approximately 1 large apple)

1 teaspoon icing (confectioners') sugar

½ teaspoon ground coriander

¼ teaspoon ground cinnamon

Preheat the oven to 180°C (350°F). Roast the walnuts for around 5 minutes until the skins start to colour. Tip them into a clean tea towel and rub away as much of their skins as you can, then chop the nuts roughly. Use a sieve to remove any excess bits of dust and skin.

Add to the butter with the remaining ingredients and beat everything together well. Spoon onto a sheet of cling film or greaseproof paper and shape into a log. Roll up neatly, twist the ends, tie securely and chill until required. The butter will keep in a sealed container in the fridge for 2 weeks or up to 3 months in the freezer.

Apricot–cardamom

MAKES 1 X 220 G (7 ¾ OZ) LOG OF BUTTER

70 g (2 ½ oz) apricot leather (amardine), very finely diced

1 teaspoon icing (confectioners') sugar

125 g (4 ½ oz) unsalted butter, softened

1 teaspoon cardamom seeds, ground to a fine powder

2 teaspoons apricot jam

Toss the diced apricot with the icing sugar so that each tiny piece is coated. This will help keep them separate, rather than clumping together.

Add to the butter with the remaining ingredients and beat everything together well. Spoon onto a sheet of cling film or greaseproof paper and shape into a log. Roll up neatly, twist the ends, tie securely and chill until required. The butter will keep in a sealed container in the fridge for 2 weeks or up to 3 months in the freezer.

Pear–ginger

MAKES 1 X 200 G (7 OZ) LOG OF BUTTER

50 g (1 ¾ oz) dried pears, roughly chopped

2 teaspoons light muscovado sugar

125 ml (4 fl oz) water

125 g (4 ½ oz) unsalted butter, softened

1 teaspoon grated fresh ginger

1 teaspoon icing (confectioners') sugar

20 g (¾ oz) crème fraîche

Combine the pears, sugar and water in a small pan and bring to the boil. Lower the heat and simmer for around 15 minutes, until the water has evaporated and the pears are just starting to catch on the bottom of the pan. Remove from the heat and mash with the back of a spoon. Push through a fine sieve and leave to cool.

Add to the butter with the remaining ingredients and beat everything together well. Spoon onto a sheet of cling film or greaseproof paper and shape into a log. Roll up neatly, twist the ends, tie securely and chill until required. The butter will keep in a sealed container in the fridge for 2 weeks or up to 3 months in the freezer.

Rhubarb, raspberry & cardamom fridge jam

This is the kind of jam you turn to when you haven't got the energy to be faffing around with pectin and sterilizing jam jars. It's infinitely versatile: you can make it with almost any fruit, and in almost any quantities and you can liven it up with any herbs, spices or other flavourings that you like the sound of.

Fridge jam is better for you than the usual kind of store-bought jam, as it uses much less sugar. The general rule of thumb with jam is that you need somewhere between 55–70 per cent of the weight of the fruit in sugar to achieve a set; with fridge jam you use around 50 per cent, which also results in a much fruitier-tasting jam. The trade-off is that it doesn't last as long and you have to store it in the fridge, rather than the larder; no real hardship, though, as it's likely you'll have eaten it before any suspicious bits of green fuzz start to grow!

Another trick we use here is to macerate the fruit in sugar overnight, which releases the juices. Boiling the resulting syrup before you add the fruit gives a jam with a better texture, livelier colour and fresher flavour.

MAKES AROUND 600 G (1 LB 5 OZ)

750 g (1 lb 10 oz) rhubarb, cut into
    2.5 cm (1 in) pieces
510 g (1 lb 2 ½ oz) granulated sugar
grated zest and juice of 1 lemon
250 g (9 oz) raspberries
pinch salt
⅛ teaspoon ground cardamom
    seeds

Combine the rhubarb with the sugar, lemon zest and juice in a large mixing bowl. Cover with a clean tea towel and leave it overnight.

The next day, strain the syrupy juices into a large saucepan and bring to the boil slowly, stirring until any residual sugar has dissolved. Cook at a vigorously rolling boil for around 10 minutes, until it reaches 105°C (220°F) on a candy thermometer. If you don't have a thermometer, take it off the heat for a minute to allow the bubbles to subside and push the surface with a spoon. The surface should be thick and wrinkle slightly.

Add the rhubarb and return to the boil. Cook for 5 minutes, then add the raspberries to the pan. Boil for 10–12 minutes until the mixture is thick and 'jammy', stirring from time to time. Test with a cold plate (see *Note, below). When the jam is ready, remove the pan from the heat and stir in the salt and ground cardamom. Cool completely, then transfer to jars or a sealed container and store in the fridge or freezer. Eat within 4 weeks.

*Note: Put a large plate in the freezer when you start boiling your jam. To test if the jam is ready, drop a small amount onto the plate and return it to the freezer for a minute. It is ready if it forms a wrinkly skin when you push the surface with your finger. If it is too thin and runny, keep cooking the jam for a little longer and return the plate to the freezer so it's ready for you to test again.

Gingered grapefruit curd

Limes, clementines and citrus hybrids such as minneolas and tangelos all make delicious variations on the classic lemon curd, as do blood oranges, when in season. Here, we use pink grapefruit, which is one of our favourite citrus fruits of all, with its subtle sour-sweet bitterness and its vivid colour – so cheery on a dreary winter day. As with bitter marmalade, this curd probably appeals more to an adult palate, but we can't get enough of its bitter edge, tempered – but only just – by a creamy sweetness. The ginger adds a mild buzz of heat, but is entirely optional. Spread it on toast, swirl through yoghurt or into home-made ice cream and sorbet, or use it to fill beignets (page 246) or a cake for tea.

MAKES 350 G (12 OZ)

250 ml (9 fl oz) pink grapefruit juice (around 2 grapefruits), plus 1 tablespoon finely grated zest

3–4 tablespoons grated fresh ginger, or to taste (optional)

85 g (3 oz) caster (superfine) sugar

generous pinch salt

100 g (3 ½ oz) unsalted butter

2 eggs, plus 3 egg yolks

Put the grapefruit juice and zest with the grated ginger in a small saucepan and simmer until reduced by half. Set aside and leave to cool.

Transfer to a heatproof bowl and add the sugar, salt and butter. Set the bowl over a pan of simmering water (it shouldn't touch the water) and whisk gently until the butter melts and the sugar dissolves.

In a separate bowl, gently whisk the eggs and yolks together. Whisk in a good spoonful of the hot juice then tip into the saucepan and cook until the mixture thickens to a glossy custard. It should fall from the whisk in big dollops. Be patient, this can take anywhere from 10–20 minutes. Don't allow the curd to boil or the eggs will curdle.

Once thick, push the curd through a sieve, cool slightly, then spoon into sterilized jars and seal. Store in the fridge for up to 2 weeks. Once opened, eat within 3 days.

Candied citrus peel

You can use this technique with just about any citrus peel. Here we use grapefruits, which need to be blanched many more times than other citrus fruits as their skins are so bitter.

The peel will keep for several months and makes a lovely garnish for desserts (such as the Lemon Posset on page 234) and cakes (such as the Bitter Chocolate-Hazelnut Cake on page 257) Use the syrup for icings and cocktails.

MAKES AROUND 250 G (9 OZ)

2 pink, ruby or yellow grapefruits
caster (superfine) sugar
water

Use a very sharp knife to score through the grapefruit skin in quarters. Peel the skin and use the flat blade of the knife to slice away as much of the pith as you can.

Put the pieces of peel in a saucepan and cover with cold water. Bring to a vigorous boil then tip into a sieve to drain off the water. Because grapefruit peel is very bitter, you'll need to repeat this blanching process about 5 or 6 times. (Other citrus fruits will only need to be blanched 3–4 times.) After the final blanching, set the peel aside to drain and air-dry for a few minutes. Use a very sharp knife to shred the peel into fine strips.

Weigh the peel then transfer to a medium saucepan. Measure out double that weight of both sugar and water and add both to the pan with the peel. Heat gently until the sugar dissolves. Bring to the boil then lower the heat to a simmer. Add the shredded peel and simmer very gently for 1–1 ½ hours, until the peel is translucent. Cool then transfer the zest and syrup to a jar with a lid.

Make sure the peel is completely submerged in syrup or it may crystallize. If this does happen, transfer to a saucepan and heat gently until the sugar re-dissolves.

Dips & spreads

CRUSHED BROAD BEANS ... 66

PARSNIP SKORDALIA WITH GARLIC, LEMON & SCARMORZA ... 68

TURKISH RED PEPPER PASTE ... 69

PRESERVED LEMON GUACAMOLE ... 71

SPICY RED HUMMUS ... 71

HOME-MADE SHANKLEESH ... 72

LABNEH; TURKISH-STYLE CARROT; ARTICHOKE & LEMON; CLASSIC LABNEH IN OIL ... 73

Whether coarsely mashed or silkily puréed, vegetable and legume-based, dips and spreads are a stalwart of the Middle Eastern mezze table. The word 'mezze' derives from the Persian 'mazeh', which means 'to taste' and this, above all, is the bedrock of a good mezze spread. Small dishes – dips included – are intended to tempt and please the eye and to stimulate the palate, ready for the plates that follow. And, since mezze dishes are about contrasts of flavour and texture, dips are always accompanied by baskets of ultra-fresh crunchy vegetables, bunches of fragrant herbs and plenty of soft flatbreads for scooping and smearing.

Our previous books have all featured recipes for the most popular – and best-known – dips in the Middle East, so there is no baba ghanoush, muhammara or tzatziki in the following pages. But, fear not! Over the years, Greg, has created endless variations on these and on other popular dips, so this section features some of our current and slightly more unusual favourites.

Crushed broad beans

This garlicky paste appears in one of our earlier books (*Saha*). We created it as an accompaniment for flattened, char-grilled chicken, after enjoying a similar dish on one of our visits to Lebanon. We had such enthusiastic feedback that we offer it again here as a standalone dip or spread. Beware, it's fiendishly addictive.

SERVES 4

1 kg (2 lb 4 oz) fresh broad beans,
    about 200 g (7 oz) podded weight
1 clove garlic crushed with
    ½ teaspoon sea salt
1 shallot, very finely diced
¼ cup coriander (cilantro) leaves,
    finely chopped
50 ml (2 fl oz) extra-virgin olive oil
pinch cayenne pepper
freshly ground black pepper
juice of 1 lemon

To serve

4 slices sourdough toast
2 big handfuls mixed leaves (we like
    lambs lettuce, mizuna, purple
    basil or watercress)
pinch cayenne pepper
best quality extra-virgin olive oil

Bring a saucepan of salted water to the boil and blanch the broad beans for 2–3 minutes, although the time will somewhat depend on their size. Tip into a sieve to drain, then peel them and set aside to cool completely.

Pound the garlic and salt to a smooth paste. Next, add the broad beans and all remaining ingredients, one by one, to the mortar and pound to a rough, sludgy kind of paste. It's much easier to do this in a food processor, but take care you don't over-process. You definitely want to retain some texture.

When ready to serve, mound the beans onto slices of toasted sourdough and top with a mixture of leaves. Add a pinch of cayenne, then drizzle with extra-virgin olive oil and serve.

Parsnip skordalia with garlic, lemon & scamorza

Skordalia is a traditional Greek garlic sauce, usually made with mashed potatoes, stale white breadcrumbs or ground nuts. A number of years ago we developed a version of skordalia using parsnip, which gives a lovely sweet, mellow flavour. It works brilliantly and does double duty as a dip and as an accompaniment to grilled vegetables or meats. This is a riff on our earlier recipe, incorporating Italian scamorza cheese, which adds a smoky depth. If you can't find scamorza, use provolone instead, or even a smoked cheddar-style cheese.

MAKES 350 G (12 OZ)

450 g (1 lb) parsnips, trimmed, peeled and woody cores removed

300 ml (10 ½ fl oz) milk

1 clove garlic crushed with ½ teaspoon salt

juice of ½ lemon

50 ml (2 fl oz) olive oil

50 g (1 ¾ oz) scamorza cheese, coarsly grated

salt and freshly ground black pepper

Cut the parsnips into even-sized pieces. Place them in a saucepan with the milk and bring to the boil. Simmer briskly for 15–20 minutes, or until the parsnips are very soft and the milk has greatly reduced.

Carefully tip the hot mixture into a food processor, add the garlic paste and lemon juice and whiz for several minutes to a purée. Dribble in the oil very slowly, until it is all incorporated.

Return the purée to the saucepan then add the scamorza and stir in gently until it melts completely.

Serve at room temperature as a dip, with your favourite raw vegetables and warm pita. Skordalia also makes a lovely accompaniment to grills and barbecues.

Turkish red pepper paste

We first encountered this incredibly moreish pepper paste in a small pide restaurant on our first trip to Istanbul.

The first thing to arrive on the table was a small pot of spicy red pepper paste, a dish of butter and a plate of crumbled white Lor cheese. We ate these with big puffed-up rounds of flatbread, straight from the wood-fired oven, and thought we'd arrived in heaven. This is our version of the pepper paste – it is quite chilli-hot, so a little goes a long way. Serve it on warm flatbread with chilled unsalted butter and Lor cheese. If you can't get hold of Lor, then another crumbly white cheese, such as Wensleydale or a mature goat's cheese, will do nicely.

MAKES 350 G (12 OZ)

3 red capsicums (peppers), left whole

3 long red chillies, deseeded (or use smaller hot red chillies, if you're brave)

1 teaspoon pomegranate molasses

½ teaspoon dried mint

2 tablespoons shredded mint leaves

2 tablespoons extra-virgin olive oil

2 spring onions (scallions), finely diced

juice of 1 lemon

1 teaspoon sea salt

½ teaspoon freshly ground black pepper

vegetable oil, to seal

Preheat the oven to 200°C (400°F) and line a baking tray with foil.

Roast the capsicums for 10 minutes, by which time they should be starting to brown. Turn them over in the tray and add the long red chillies. Roast for a further 10 minutes, or until the skins of both capsicums and chillies are blistered and charred. Be careful not to let the chillies dry out too much. Remove from the oven and leave to cool.

When cool enough to handle, peel away the skins from the capsicums and pull out the seeds and membranes. Roughly chop the capsicums and tip into the bowl of a food processor. Use a sharp knife to scrape the flesh of the chillies away from their skins – this is easier than trying to peel them. Add the chilli flesh to the food processor, together with the remaining ingredients. Pulse, in short bursts, to a fairly smooth purée, then taste and adjust the balance of salt and lemon if necessary.

Spoon the paste into a sterilized jar and cover the surface with a thin film of flavourless oil. If you're not eating it straight away, store in the fridge where it will keep for up to 1 week.

Preserved lemon guacamole

This has been popping up on Greg's menus ever since he created it 20-odd years ago. It's from our first book (*Arabesque*) but we had to include it again here, as it's such an effective way of jazzing up boring old guacamole.

MAKES 400 G (14 OZ)

1 large ripe-but-firm avocado, cut into ½ cm (¼ in) dice

1 medium vine-ripened tomato, deseeded and cut into ½ cm (¼ in) dice

¼ small red onion, very finely chopped

1 long green chilli, deseeded, scraped and finely chopped

⅓ cup coriander (cilantro) leaves, chopped

½ preserved lemon, skin only, finely chopped

1 clove garlic crushed with ½ teaspoon salt

juice of 1 lime

salt and freshly ground black pepper

extra-virgin olive oil and sumac, to serve

In a large mixing bowl combine the avocado, tomato, onion, chilli, coriander and preserved lemon. Whisk the garlic paste into the lime juice and add to the bowl. Mix everything together very gently then taste and adjust the seasoning to your liking. Drizzle with extra-virgin olive oil and sprinkle with sumac before serving with pita.

Spicy red hummus

Adding spicy red pepper paste is a great way to liven up hummus. For the very best result, try to achieve as smooth a purée as you can. It's worth getting the blades of your food processor sharpened for this alone!

MAKES AROUND 450 G (1 LB)

400 g (14 oz) tin chickpeas, well rinsed and drained

30 g (1 ¼ oz) tahini, well stirred

30 g (1 ¼ oz) Turkish red pepper paste*

¼ teaspoon ground cumin

30 ml (1 fl oz) olive oil

2 ice cubes

¼ teaspoon salt

¼ teaspoon freshly ground black pepper

juice of 1–1 ½ lemons

In the bowl of a food processor, combine the chickpeas, tahini, red pepper paste and cumin. Whiz to as smooth a purée as you can. Dribble in the oil very slowly, until all is incorporated. Add the ice cubes and continue blending until they have melted. Add the salt, pepper and lemon juice, then taste, and adjust the balance of flavours. Add a little more red pepper paste, lemon juice or seasonings, as necessary.

*Note: Use good-quality Turkish red pepper paste, which is available from specialist food stores or make your own, using the recipe on page 69.

Home-made shankleesh

Unlike the broader repertoire of fresh white Middle Eastern cheeses, shankleesh is mould-ripened and aged, which gives it a very distinctive and pungent flavour. Essentially, it's labneh (page 73), taken to the extreme, by further drying, salting and adding a bacterial culture. After washing, the cheese is mixed with and then rolled in spices such as za'atar, aniseed, sumac, Aleppo pepper and very hot chilli flakes. The texture and flavour both develop with age: it becomes crumblier and dryer – some shankleesh are so pungent they can knock your socks off!

Shankleesh doesn't look like much, it's true – more like a grubby and misshapen baseball than anything you'd want to eat. But, rather like blue cheese, it's a taste that, once acquired, is hard to shake off. This is our homage to shankleesh and, although it's made by blending, rather than ageing, which gives it a creamier texture, we reckon it is surprisingly true to the spirit of the original. Shankleesh is usually eaten as a salad (see our version on page 140), but we eat it as we would any sharp blue cheese: with warm crusty bread or on toast, sprinkled onto soups or into salads, or even mashed with hard-boiled eggs or whipped up with mashed potatoes.

MAKES 4

100 g (3 ½ oz) French-style goat's
   cheese, roughly chopped
100 g (3 ½ oz) feta, crumbled
70 g (2 ½ oz) Greek-style yoghurt
1 tablespoon sumac
1 tablespoon za'atar
1 teaspoon Turkish red chilli flakes
1 teaspoon freshly ground white
   pepper
4 teaspoons dried oregano

Combine the goat's cheese and feta in a mixing bowl. Add the yoghurt and spices and mix together thoroughly. It should be fairly smooth, but retain a certain 'chunkiness'. Scrape into a bowl, cover and chill for around 12 hours, or until the mixture has firmed up.

Tip the mixture out onto a work surface and divide into 4 even portions. With lightly oiled hands, roll each into a rough ball and coat lightly in the dried oregano. Store in a sealed container in the fridge for up to 1 week.

Home-made shankleesh has a softer texture than the commercially made variety which means you break it into small lumps, rather than crumble it.

*Note: You can also buy vacuum-packed shankleesh in Middle Eastern stores.

Labneh

We can't imagine life without yoghurt. We both, independently, eat it by the tubful and at virtually every meal. We are totally convinced of its life-enhancing properties – not just because it is delicious – and love its versatility as both a savoury and sweet ingredient.

We are particularly fond of labneh, which is simply yoghurt that is strained through a cloth to remove the whey, which makes it thicker and more unctuous. There are degrees of thickness of course, depending on which yoghurt you start off with (some are thicker than others) and for how long it is strained. At the farthest end of the spectrum, you'll find yoghurt cheese that is virtually dry and has a strong, rather sour flavour. This type of labneh has been strained for several days and is then formed into little balls. These may be rolled in herbs and spices and are stored in olive oil, which means they will last for many months. Fresher labneh is strained for hours, rather than days, making it closer in consistency to a creamy spread. It has a mild, fresh flavour and may be eaten on its own, seasoned and drizzled with olive oil, or combined with other ingredients to make a dip, such as the universally popular tzatziki.

We've featured versions of tzatziki in several of our earlier books, so here we offer a base labneh method as well as some of our favourite – and slightly more unusual – labneh and yoghurt cheese recipes (overleaf).

MAKES AROUND 500G (1 LB 2 OZ)

Labneh: strained yoghurt

1 kg (2 lb 4 oz) natural yoghurt (don't use Greek-style, as this is already thick and some varieties have gelatine added to them)

Savoury labneh

1 clove garlic crushed to a paste with 1 teaspoon salt

2 tablespoons extra-virgin olive oil

Along with the garlic add 10 saffron threads or swirl in 1–2 tablespoons harissa or smoked paprika or any fresh herb purée to the yoghurt.

For sweet labneh

2 tablespoons honey

1 teaspoon orange flower water

Along with the honey, add 1 vanilla pod, split and seeds scraped (or 1 teaspoon vanilla extract) or sprinkle in the lightly crushed seeds from 4 cardamom pods, or swirl in 1 teaspoon orange flower water or rosewater.

Scrape the yoghurt and flavourings into a clean tea towel (a muslin square or new J-cloth will also do nicely). Tie the four corners together to form a hanging bag. Twist firmly to give it a good squeeze and kick-start the draining process. Suspend the bag from a wooden spoon set over a deep bowl and allow it to drain in the fridge for at least 4 hours or, preferably, overnight. This will give you soft-strained yoghurt, which is best used as a creamy accompaniment, similar to crème fraîche.

If you strain the yoghurt for 24–48 hours, you will produce a thicker, firmer labneh, similar in consistency to cream cheese. Use as an accompaniment to spicy dishes, such as tagines, Indian curries and most rice dishes. Combine with fresh herbs and/or vegetables to make dips or simply drizzle with extra-virgin olive oil and eat with crusty bread and a dish of olives.

Straining the yoghurt for 48–72 hours, will give you a much firmer yoghurt cheese. (After 72 hours it is very firm and dry indeed.) Remove it from the bag and, with oiled hands, roll into small balls. Place the balls in a jars with olive oil and the herbs of your choice.

Turkish-style carrot labneh

This might sound a little strange, but it is absolutely addictive. The sweetness of the braised carrots and the chilli-lime tang are a lovely counterpoint to the underlying creaminess of labneh.

MAKES 400 G (14 OZ)

20 g (¾ oz) unsalted butter

30 ml (1 fl oz) olive oil

150 g (5 ½ oz) carrots (1 ½– 2), coarsely grated

1 clove garlic, finely grated

½ teaspoon sea salt

½ teaspoon freshly ground black pepper

½ teaspoon Turkish red chilli flakes

finely grated zest of ½ lime

225 g (8 oz) Labneh, strained for 12 hours (see page 73)

1 tablespoon pure (double or heavy) cream or yoghurt

extra-virgin olive oil, to serve

Melt the butter with the oil in a wide frying pan over a medium heat. Add the grated carrots and garlic and sweat slowly for 5–7 minutes, until the carrots soften and turn a bright orange. Stir in the salt and pepper, chilli and lime zest. Remove from the heat and leave to cool down in the pan then tip into a bowl with the labneh. Beat into the labneh, together with the cream. Check the seasoning and serve with a good-quality extra-virgin olive oil.

Artichoke & lemon labneh

A dip that came about by accident after over-cooking artichokes braised in oil (page 158). You can use these, by all means, or use good quality artichokes in oil from a jar.

MAKES 350 G (12 OZ)

1 tablespoon olive oil

1 shallot, finely chopped

1 clove garlic, finely chopped

50 g (1 ¾ oz) good-quality artichokes in oil (or see page 158) cut into 1 cm (½ in) dice

¼ preserved lemon, skin only, finely chopped

finely grated zest of ½ lemon

salt and freshly ground white pepper

¼ teaspoon Turkish red chilli flakes

80 g (4 ¼ oz) Labneh, strained for 12 hours (see page 73)

extra-virgin olive oil, to serve

Heat the oil in a medium frying pan. Add the shallot and garlic and sauté gently for 5 minutes, or until translucent and starting to soften. Add the artichokes and break them apart in the pan with a wooden spoon. Sauté for another 15–20 minutes, until very soft. Stir in the preserved lemon, the zest, salt and pepper and chilli. Remove from the heat and cool completely. Tip into the bowl of a food processor, add the labneh and whiz to a purée. You want it to be fairly smooth, but still retain some texture. Check the seasoning and serve with a good-quality extra-virgin olive oil.

Classic labneh in oil

MAKES AROUND 500 G (1 LB 2 OZ)

1 kg (2 lb 4 oz) natural yoghurt, strained for 48–72 hours (see page 73)

½ cup chopped herbs (choose a selection or mixture of flat-leaf parsley, mint, chives, tarragon or dill), optional

½ tablespoon black peppercorns

olive oil

Remove the strained yoghurt from the bag and, with oiled hands, roll into small balls. Roll each ball in the herbs, if using, then put them into a jar with the peppercorns and enough olive oil to keep them completely submerged.

Pickles & relishes

SLOW-ROASTED TOMATOES WITH POMEGRANATE & THYME ... 79

BABY EGGPLANTS STUFFED WITH WALNUTS & CHILLIES ... 81

EGGPLANT RELISH ... 82

SWEET PEPPERS & SHALLOTS IN LEMON OIL ... 83

SPICY CARROT PICKLE ... 84

Middle Easterners are big on self-sufficiency. In the bountiful summer months they bottle, pickle and preserve all the fruit and vegetables they can lay their hands on (often home-grown) in preparation for the cold, dark winters.

Nowadays, there is no longer quite the same imperative to prolong the life of fresh produce, as most is so widely available throughout the year. So the art of preserving – whether pickling in brine or vinegar, packing in salt, storing in oil, or drying in the sun – is much more about the way these techniques transform the flavour and texture of ingredients. Think about the distinctive salty-sour tang of a Moroccan preserved lemon, the crisp crunch of a sweet gherkin or the intensely fruity chew of a sun-dried tomato.

Greg, like most Middle Easterners, has a deep love of sour and salty things, so he's a big fan of pickles. Whether it's a single 'hero' vegetable, packed into a herb-spiked vinegar, or a crunchy medley of spiced vegetables, cooked into a vibrant and tangy relish or deep, dark chutney, each has a place on the Middle Eastern table. They're a natural accompaniment to cheese, to rich soups and braises and to aromatic grilled meats and vegetables, and they are a quick and easy way to pep up filling, but bland starchy dishes of rice, pulses or grains.

None of the recipes in this section is technically challenging, and they don't require any special equipment (other than a large saucepan and some jars for storage), so don't be intimidated by the idea of turning your kitchen into a pickle factory! The pleasure you'll get from shelves full of gleaming jars of multi-coloured preserves that you created yourself is intensely satisfying.

Slow-roasted tomatoes with pomegranate & thyme

The recipe for these semi-dried tomatoes evolved from one in our earlier book, *Turquoise*. We developed it as a way of recreating the intensely flavoursome sun-dried tomatoes that proliferate in Turkey through the hot summer months. There, they are dried in the sunshine, along with capsicums and chilli peppers, but this slow oven-roasting method works almost as well. They are a stalwart of our pantry and we use them with abandon, as we would deli-bought sun-dried tomatoes: in salads, casseroles, pilafs and sauces – or just on their own as part of a mezze selection. The dried tomatoes keep for ten days, or for several months, if packed in oil in sealed sterilized jars.

MAKES AROUND 500 G (1 LB 2 OZ)

125 ml (4 fl oz) olive oil

60 ml (2 fl oz) sherry vinegar

40 ml (1 ¼ fl oz) pomegranate
    molasses

1 teaspoon good-quality harissa
    (or see page 56)

1 teaspoon sumac

a few sprigs of thyme

1 kg (2 lb 4 oz) medium vine-ripened
    tomatoes, halved lengthways

salt and freshly ground black pepper

Preheat the oven to 120°C (235°F).

In a large mixing bowl, whisk together the oil, vinegar, molasses, harissa, sumac and thyme. Add the tomatoes and toss gently so they are evenly coated in the mixture.

Arrange the tomatoes, cut side up, on metal racks set into baking trays (you'll probably need two). Bake the tomatoes for 3–5 hours, depending on how plump and juicy they are. They should become shrunken and shrivelled, but still be a little moist, rather than brittle and dry. You could even leave them in the oven overnight.

Remove from the oven and leave the tomatoes to cool on the racks. Arrange them in layers in a shallow container, separated by greaseproof paper and chill for up to a week. Alternatively, transfer the cold tomatoes to dry sterilized jars and fill with olive oil – they must be completely immersed and take care not to create any air pockets. Seal the jar and use within 3 months. Once opened, store in the fridge and eat within a month.

Baby eggplants stuffed with walnuts & chillies

These popular stuffed eggplants are one of our very favourite Lebanese pickles. They're eaten as part of a mezze spread and also feature on breakfast tables – a great way to wake up your tastebuds in the morning. Some versions include chopped chillies as part of the stuffing, which makes them even spicier. They are delicious with some sharp white cheese, crisp cucumber and tomatoes – and plenty of warm pita.

This recipe comes from Greg's sister-in-law, Amal Malouf, who is a brilliant cook. You'll need to source baby eggplants, which are fairly easy to find in areas with a large Middle Eastern, Asian or Mediterranean population.

MAKES 1 KG (2 LB 4 OZ)

1 kg (2 lb 4 oz) baby Lebanese eggplants (aubergines), no more than 5 cm (2 in) long

fine pouring salt

150 g (5 ½ oz) walnut halves, roughly chopped

2 tablespoons fresh oregano leaves

4 cloves garlic, thinly sliced

1 litre (35 fl oz) olive oil

2–3 small red chillies, split

Wash and dry the eggplants and cook them in boiling water for 5 minutes. Refresh them under cold water then drain in a colander. Split the eggplants in half lengthways to about 1 cm (½ in) from the stem. Open them up and rub salt into each side. Close them up again, stack them in the colander, weigh down with a heavy plate and allow to drain for 24–48 hours.

Rinse the eggplants and dry them thoroughly. Stuff each eggplant with a few walnut pieces, the oregano leaves and garlic slivers then pack them tightly into a large sterilized jar. Turn the jar upside down and sit it in a colander for 1 hour to allow more liquid to drain away.

Invert the jar and fill it with olive oil, taking care you don't create any air pockets. Poke in the handle of a wooden spoon to disperse any that do form. Push in the chillies, making sure that all the eggplants and chillies are completely immersed in oil, then seal the jar and leave in a cool place for 2 weeks before opening.

Unopened, the eggplants will keep up to a year. Once opened, keep in the fridge and eat within 6 weeks.

Eggplant relish

Another indispensable condiment that goes with just about anything, from grills and barbecues to couscous, pilafs and other rice- or grain-based dishes.

MAKES AROUND 350 G (12 OZ)

2 large eggplants (aubergines), peeled and cut into 2 cm (¾ in) cubes

salt

100 ml (3 ½ fl oz) olive oil

2 red onions, finely diced

1 clove garlic, peeled and finely sliced

1 teaspoon ground cumin

½ teaspoon turmeric

½ teaspoon sweet paprika

¼ teaspoon cayenne pepper

2 medium vine-ripened tomatoes, deseeded and diced

½ teaspoon salt

1 teaspoon sugar

juice of 1 lemon

175 ml (6 fl oz) water

¼ cup flat-leaf parsley leaves, finely chopped

¼ cup coriander (cilantro) leaves, finely chopped

¼ cup mint leaves, finely chopped

Put the eggplant cubes in a colander and sprinkle with salt. After 20 minutes, rinse them under cold water and pat them dry with kitchen paper.

Heat the oil in a frying pan and sauté the eggplant over a medium heat for around 10 minutes, turning the cubes from time to time, until they are light golden brown. Use a slotted spoon to transfer the eggplant to a colander to drain off excess oil.

Add the onions, garlic and spices to the pan and fry in the oil leftover from the eggplants over a gentle heat for 5 minutes, stirring from time to time.

Return the eggplant to the pan with the tomatoes, salt, sugar, lemon juice and water, and simmer gently for 8 minutes. Most of the liquid should have evaporated and the vegetables should be soft and almost jammy in consistency. Remove from the heat and stir in the fresh herbs. Serve at room temperature or refrigerate in a sealed container and eat within 5 days.

Sweet peppers & shallots in lemon oil

Use a long sweet variety of pepper (such as bull's horn or Hungarian) for this recipe and try to find a mix of colours, ranging from yellow to orange to variegated. Once roasted, both peppers and shallots are braised very gently in a lemon-spiced oil, to make a kind of confit. The recipe makes more oil than you'll need for this recipe, but it's hardly worth making in smaller quantities and, in any case, it is a lovely versatile oil that you can use in all kinds of dressings. Eat the peppers and shallots as you would peperonata: as a condiment, as part of a mezze selection or warmed through and served as a salad with peppery rocket leaves and soft creamy feta.

SERVES 4

8 long red capsicums (bull's horn
    or Hungarian peppers)
6 shallots, unpeeled
olive oil
strips of peel from 1 lemon

Lemon oil
250 ml (9 fl oz) Spanish olive oil
2 whole lemons, quartered
4 cloves garlic, unpeeled
1 tablespoon coriander seeds
1 tablespoon black peppercorns
3 star anise
2 bay leaves
1 cinnamon stick

To make the lemon oil, put the oil in a large saucepan and heat gently to blood temperature. Put the lemons, garlic, coriander seeds, peppercorns, star anise, bay leaves and cinnamon stick into a bowl and pour on the olive oil. Leave to infuse overnight.

Preheat the oven to 200°C (400°F) and line a baking tray with foil. Arrange the capsicums and shallots on the tray and drizzle with a little oil. Roast for 25 minutes, turning once, until the skins blister and char. Remove the capsicums from the oven and transfer them to a shallow bowl. Lower the oven temperature to 180°C (350°F) and continue roasting the shallots for a further 5–10 minutes then remove them from the oven.

When the vegetables are cool enough to handle, peel away and discard the skins from the capsicums and split them in half, leaving the stalks attached at the top to hold them together. Pull away and discard the seeds and membranes. Peel off the shallot skins and slice the flesh thinly.

Put the capsicums and shallots in a shallow dish and add the lemon peel. Strain the lemon oil then measure 100 ml (3 ½ fl oz) and pour it over the vegetables. (Decant the remaining oil into a sterilized bottle for use in salad dressings.) Place the dish in the oven and cook for 8 minutes.

Drain the vegetables well before serving. If you're not eating them straight away, store in a sealed container in the fridge where they will keep for up to 5 days.

Spicy carrot pickle

This much-loved pickle seems to go with just about everything. We think you'll find it's addictive; we've been known to finish a jar in one sitting.

MAKES AROUND 4 X SMALL-ISH (340 G/12 OZ) JARS

1 kg (2 lb 4 oz) carrots
2 teaspoons cumin seeds
2 teaspoons mustard seeds
6 fresh curry leaves (or dried will do at a pinch)
100 ml (3 ½ fl oz) apple juice
200 ml (7 fl oz) cider vinegar

Spice paste

2 teaspoons cumin seeds
3–4 small dried red chillies (depending on their heat)
1 teaspoon sea salt
5 cloves garlic, roughly chopped
50 g (1 ¾ oz) fresh ginger, peeled and roughly chopped
1 teaspoon turmeric
75 g (2 ½ oz) soft brown sugar
3 tablespoons vegetable oil

Cut the carrots into roughly 6 cm (2 ½ in) lengths, then cut into matchsticks. Set aside.

To make the spice paste, combine the cumin seeds and dried chillies in a mortar and grind to a fine powder. Add the salt, garlic and ginger to the mortar and continue to grind to a fairly smooth paste. Add the turmeric and sugar and mix in well.

Heat the oil in a wide casserole pan – a cast iron Le Creuset is ideal. Add the cumin and mustard seeds and fry for 10 seconds or until they just start to pop. Add the curry leaves and fry for 1–2 minutes, until they turn translucent. Add the spice paste and cook, stirring, for 2 minutes. Add the apple juice and vinegar and bring to a vigorous simmer. Add the carrots and stir well, so that they are all coated with the spicy liquid.

Lower the heat to a gentle simmer and cook for 15–20 minutes, stirring every few minutes to ensure they cook evenly. By the end of the cooking time the carrots should be soft, but still retain some texture and the liquid should have reduced by about one-third.

Leave to cool slightly then transfer to sterilized jars and store for up to 3 months. Once opened, store in the fridge and use within 5 days.

Soups

VEGETABLE STOCK ... 88

CHILLED YOGHURT SOUP WITH CUCUMBER, CURRANTS & WALNUTS ... 89

ASPARAGUS AVGOLEMONO ... 91

FRESH CORN SOUP WITH RICE, YOGHURT & SIZZLING MINT BUTTER ... 92

TOMATO & BEAN SOUP WITH HARISSA & HONEY ... 95

MUSHROOM SOUP WITH FRESH ZA'ATAR ... 97

LEMONY LENTIL SOUP WITH SAFFRON-SCRAMBLED EGGS ... 98

In the Western food world, soup is often viewed as a bit of a second-class citizen. In the Middle East, by contrast, it is truly celebrated. In many regions there are specialist soup shops that sell, not just soup, but often just one particular variety of soup. Soup is eaten for breakfast, lunch and dinner and, in some areas, it takes on huge symbolic significance. In Iran, there are soups to celebrate a child's first tooth or the start of a journey; in Turkey soups are eaten to celebrate a wedding – or to fix a hangover! Some soups are eaten at specific times during religious festivals – the famous Moroccan harira is eaten to break the daily fast during Ramadan – while others are elevated to national dish status, as seen in the leafy green Egyptian *melokheya*.

Whether comprising vegetables, grains or meat, thick or thin, hot or chilled, smooth and sophisticated or chock-full of legumes, noodles or dumplings, soups form some of our favourite meals throughout the year. The recipes in this section are all designed, with a Middle Eastern soul, to celebrate the best vegetables of the season.

Vegetable stock

Although it is perfectly possible to buy good-quality vegetable stocks these days, most supermarket varieties have a strong 'dried herb' flavour, which can overpower a dish. If you can, try to use a liquid stock, rather than cubes or powders but home-made is best!

This is a very low-fat stock with a delicate, fresh flavour. We make it in fairly large amounts and then freeze it in freezer bags in 500 ml (16 fl oz) batches. Saffron adds its usual distinctive flavour note and a lovely golden hue, but is entirely optional.

MAKES 4 LITRES (8 PINTS)

2 large onions, roughly chopped

2 leeks, well washed and roughly chopped

3 large carrots, roughly chopped

4 sticks celery, roughly chopped

1 head garlic, cut in half crossways

2 bay leaves

a handful thyme sprigs

1 teaspoon white peppercorns

15–20 saffron threads (optional)

Put all the vegetables into your largest pot. Cover generously with water, at least 4 litres (8 pints).

Bring to the boil, then lower the heat and simmer for an hour, skimming away any froth that rises to the surface, although this will be minimal.

Remove from the heat and cover the pot with cling film to make it airtight. By some magic, this helps to clarify the stock and seems to keep the vegetable essence in the stock. Leave to sit for 1 hour.

Remove the cling film. For the best and clearest stock, sit your sieve directly into the stock, gently submerging the vegetables, and ladle out the liquid. Don't be tempted to just pour it through the sieve as this makes it cloudy. Ladle the stock directly into a measuring jug and then freeze it in 500 ml (16 fl oz) portions for future use.

*Note: We don't use whole tomatoes for stocks as the seeds make it bitter, but if you have any tomato skins left over from another recipe (see pages 106 and 209) then add them to the pot. Similarly, a few mushrooms are also a good addition, but remove the gills as they discolour the stock.

Chilled yoghurt soup with cucumber, currants & walnuts

We make no secret of our yoghurt addiction and are completely in accord with the Middle Easterner's use of thinned yoghurt as a thirst-quencher on a baking hot summer's day.

As well as a drink, yoghurt is also used as a base for icy-cold summer soups – especially, we've found, in Iran and in Turkey. Some chilled versions are little more than garlicky purées of cucumber, yoghurt and herbs, while others are thickened with ground nuts or lavishly garnished with dried fruits and rose petals (see our recipe in our book, *Saraban*).

We find that chilled soups are somewhat diminished if they are puréed too finely so, to keep some body, in addition to the chopped walnuts and currants, we grate, rather than purée the cucumber. This soup is delicious served with warm or grilled bread. The garnishes look extremely pretty, but are all optional.

SERVES 4–6

3 Lebanese (short) cucumbers, peeled

1 small clove garlic crushed with 1 teaspoon sea salt

800 g (1 lb 12 oz) Greek-style yoghurt

2 tablespoons chopped tarragon leaves

2 tablespoons finely snipped chives

1 tablespoon chopped chervil sprigs

1 teaspoon dried mint

¼ teaspoon freshly ground white pepper

salt

40 g (1 ½ oz) finely chopped walnuts

2 tablespoons currants

up to 300 ml (10 ½ fl oz) icy-cold water

squeeze lemon juice

pistachio or radish slivers, rose petals, sumac or even a pinch of Turkish red chilli flakes, to serve (all optional)

Split the cucumbers lengthways and scoop out and discard the seeds. Grate the cucumber coarsely into a colander set on a plate, and refrigerate for 30 minutes.

Whisk the garlic paste into the yoghurt until evenly distributed, then whisk in the herbs.

Squeeze the grated cucumber firmly to remove as much moisture as you can, then stir into the yoghurt. Season with the pepper and salt and chill for at least 1 hour to let the flavours develop.

Just before serving, stir the walnuts and currants into the yoghurt and whisk in enough of the icy-cold water to achieve a soupy consistency – you may not need it all. Add a big squeeze of lemon juice, then taste and adjust the seasonings to your liking.

Sprinkle with pistachios, rose petals, radish or other garnishes as you please, and serve straight away.

Asparagus avgolemono

Egg and lemon soups and sauces are a distinctive feature of both Greek and Turkish cookery, dating back to medieval times. The appeal of *avgolemono* (as they are known in Greek) or *terbiye* (Turkish) sauces and soups is that they are rich and velvety-smooth, with a refreshing lemony flavour. It's a combination that perfectly complements new-season asparagus, without the high butter content of a Hollandaise sauce.

SERVES 4

1 tablespoon unsalted butter

1 small shallot, finely diced

200 g (7 oz) asparagus

75 g (2 ½ oz) orzo pasta

650–800 ml (22–28 fl oz) vegetable stock

salt and freshly ground white pepper

6 egg yolks

juice of ½ lemon

extra-virgin olive oil, to serve

Melt the butter in a medium saucepan. Add the shallot and sauté gently for a few minutes until it softens.

Peel the asparagus stalks. Cut off the tips and set them aside. Slice the stalks thinly on the diagonal. Add them to the pan and sauté for a few minutes. Stir in the orzo pasta, then add 750 ml (24 fl oz) of the stock to the pan and season with salt and pepper. Bring to the boil, then lower the heat and simmer gently for 8 minutes, or until the orzo is just tender.

Meanwhile, in a small mixing bowl, whisk the egg yolks with the lemon juice. Ladle a spoonful of the hot stock into the egg mixture and whisk together well. Pour this back into the barely simmering soup, whisking continuously. Cook at a gentle simmer, still whisking slowly, until the soup starts to thicken. Be sure not to let the soup boil or it will curdle. It should be a delicate pale lemon colour with a frothy, creamy consistency. If it seems too thick, thin it with the remaining stock.

Add the asparagus tips and simmer the soup gently for 3 minutes, or until they are just tender. Taste and adjust the seasonings if need be. Drizzle with a little extra-virgin olive oil as you serve.

Fresh corn soup with rice, yoghurt & sizzling mint butter

Using yoghurt as a base for hot soups is a slightly alien concept to Westerners, who still tend to think of it as a sweet dessert or as a base for cold dips. But hot yoghurt soups are very popular around the Middle East, where they are often thickened with rice, chickpeas, bulgur or barley, which makes them incredibly hearty and comforting.

This is one of our very favourite soups and we urge you to try it. Yoghurt's creamy sourness seems to have a natural affinity with sweet, fresh corn, and they combine to make a soup that is somehow both rich and refreshing. Whatever you do, don't miss out on the sizzling butter!

SERVES 4–6

1 tablespoon olive oil

1 knob of butter

2 shallots, finely chopped

2 cloves garlic, finely chopped

¼ fennel bulb, finely chopped

80 g (2 ¾ oz) short-grain rice

1 sprig thyme

1 bay leaf

½ small red bullet chilli, deseeded and finely chopped

¼ teaspoon freshly ground white pepper

juice of ½ lemon

1–1 ½ litres (35–52 fl oz) vegetable stock

100 g (3 ½ oz) fresh sweetcorn kernels (or use frozen)

300 g (10 ½ oz) Greek-style yoghurt

1 tablespoon cornflour (cornstarch)

20 ml (½ fl oz) water

1 egg yolk, lightly beaten

1 tablespoon chopped tarragon leaves

50 ml (2 fl oz) pure (double or heavy) cream

sea salt and freshly ground black pepper

Sizzling mint butter

40 g (1 ½ oz) butter

1 tablespoon dried mint

½ teaspoon hot smoked paprika

Heat the oil and butter in a large pot. Add the shallots, garlic and fennel and sauté for around 10 minutes, or until soft and translucent. Add the rice, herbs, chilli, pepper, lemon juice and 1 litre (35 fl oz) of the stock. Cook over a gentle heat for about 20 minutes, until the rice has broken down and is starting to thicken the soup. Add the corn kernels.

To stop the yoghurt splitting when you add it to the hot soup, tip it into a large bowl and stir until smooth. Mix the cornflour with the water and add to the yoghurt along with the egg. Stir well, then tip the stabilized yoghurt into the hot soup mixture. Lower the heat and cook at a bare simmer for about 10 minutes, stirring in one direction only. Be sure not to let the soup boil or it will curdle. If it seems too thick, add a little more stock.

When ready to serve, stir through the tarragon and cream, season with salt and pepper, then ladle the soup into warmed serving bowls. Quickly sizzle the butter in a small frying pan, then add the mint and paprika and heat until foaming. Swirl the sizzling butter into each bowl of soup and serve.

Tomato & bean soup with harissa & honey

Use a good-quality harissa paste (or see page 56) and balance the heat with a mild, not-too-floral honey. Served with all the 'extras' it makes a hearty and filling lunch or supper dish. Although we enjoy the temperature contrast of the chopped hard-boiled eggs and capers, this soup is also lovely served with a softly poached egg, which oozes, lava-like into the spicy soup.

We favour the robustness of chard here, but you could just as well use kale, cavolo nero or even spinach. You will only need the chard leaves for this recipe, so reserve the stalks for another dish (they are delicious roughly chopped, then sautéed in olive oil with a little lemon juice, allspice and cinnamon, or blanched, then tossed with olive oil, salt and pepper and drizzled with tahini).

SERVES 4–6

40 ml (1 ¼ fl oz) olive oil

1 leek, well washed and finely chopped

3 cloves garlic, finely chopped

1 teaspoon ground cumin

3 teaspoons good-quality harissa (or see page 56)

1 teaspoon honey

1 sprig thyme

400 g (14 oz) tin cannellini beans, drained and rinsed

400 g (14 oz) tin chopped Italian tomatoes

750 ml (24 fl oz) vegetable stock

½ teaspoon sea salt

¼ teaspoon freshly ground black pepper

75 g (2 ½ oz) (about 2 big handfuls) chard (silverbeet) leaves, stems removed

4 thick slices sourdough bread

1–2 tablespoons salted baby capers, well rinsed

2 cold, hard-boiled eggs, coarsely grated

extra-virgin olive oil, to serve

2 tablespoons coriander (cilantro) leaves, shredded

Heat the oil in a large saucepan and sauté the leek over a low heat for 8–10 minutes until soft and translucent. Add the garlic, cumin, harissa, honey and thyme and cook for a few more minutes, until the leeks are well coated and the spices are aromatic.

Add the cannellini beans, tomatoes, vegetable stock, salt and pepper and bring to the boil. Lower the heat and simmer gently for 15 minutes.

Shred the chard leaves and add them to the pan. Simmer for 5–8 minutes, or until they are wilted and soft.

When ready to serve, grill or toast the bread and place a slice in the base of each bowl.

Ladle in the soup and top each bowl with the capers and hard-boiled eggs. Drizzle with a little oil, garnish with coriander leaves and serve straight away.

Mushroom soup with fresh za'atar

Make this soup in season with any combination of wild mushrooms. For the rest of the year, it's equally good with readily available cultivated mushrooms, such as Swiss browns or large portobellos, as even the relatively small quantity of dried porcinis add a fabulous earthy depth of flavour.

Za'atar is wild thyme from the Middle East and is a flavour Greg grew up with. It's increasingly available elsewhere – especially if there is a Middle Eastern community – but if you can't find it use regular thyme or even oregano, both of which have a natural affinity with mushrooms.

SERVES 4-6

25 g (1 oz) dried porcini
    mushrooms
250 ml (9 fl oz) water
50 ml (2 fl oz) olive oil
40 g (1 ½ oz) butter
1 small leek, trimmed, well washed
    and sliced
4 shallots, finely chopped
2 cloves garlic, finely chopped
1 tablespoon chopped thyme leaves
½ teaspoon ground allspice
40 ml (1 ¼ fl oz) medium-sweet
    sherry
400 g (14 oz) mixed fresh
    mushrooms, cleaned and
    roughly chopped
1 litre (35 fl oz) vegetable stock
sea salt and freshly ground black
    pepper
2 generous tablespoons
    mascarpone
juice of ½ lemon
1 handful fresh za'atar leaves
    (or thyme or oregano), roughly
    chopped

Cover the porcini mushrooms with the water and leave to soak for 15 minutes.

Heat the oil and butter in a medium saucepan. Add the leek, shallots, garlic and thyme and sweat gently for about 10 minutes, or until soft.

Increase the heat, add the allspice and sherry and bubble vigorously for a few minutes to deglaze the pan. Add the fresh mushrooms and stir for a couple of minutes, until they start to release their liquid.

Fish the porcini mushrooms out of their soaking liquid and add them to the pan. Strain the liquid to remove any grit and add it to the pan too. Stir well and continue cooking for 20 minutes or so, until most of the moisture has evaporated.

Add the stock and bring to the boil, then simmer for 20 minutes. Season, to taste, then tip into a blender or food processor and blitz until quite smooth – although the soup will probably still retain some texture.

Return the soup to the pan and stir in the mascarpone, lemon juice and adjust the seasonings if need be. Sprinkle with fresh za'atar or oregano and serve straight away.

Lemony lentil soup with saffron-scrambled eggs

This is one of the most popular soups from Greg's early days at Melbourne's O'Connell's Restaurant and we can think of nothing better on a cold winter night. It is deliciously warming and subtly spiced, and the creamy scramble of eggs makes it comforting and filling.

SERVES 4-6

55 ml (1 ¾ fl oz) olive oil

1 onion, finely chopped

1 clove garlic, finely chopped

1 long green chilli, deseeded and
    finely chopped

250 g (9 oz) dried green lentils

1 teaspoon ground allspice

1 teaspoon honey

finely grated zest and juice of 1 lemon

1-1 ¼ litres (35-40 fl oz) vegetable
    stock or water

salt and freshly ground black
    pepper

1 cup coriander (cilantro) leaves,
    plus extra to garnish

extra-virgin olive oil, to serve

Saffron-scrambled eggs

4 eggs

10-15 saffron threads, lightly
    toasted and crushed*

80 ml (2 ½ fl oz) pure (double or
    heavy) cream

salt and freshly ground black pepper

40 g (1 ½ oz) butter

Heat the oil in a heavy-based pan and sweat the onion for 8-10 minutes until soft and translucent. Add the garlic and green chilli, and cook a further minute. Add the lentils, allspice, honey, lemon juice and zest, and then a litre (35 fl oz) of the vegetable stock. Bring to the boil, then skim, lower the heat and simmer for 45 minutes until the lentils are very tender. Season with salt and pepper, then add the coriander and remove from the heat.

Allow to rest, uncovered, for 10 minutes before blitzing to a purée in a blender or food processor. Taste and adjust the seasoning to your liking and thin with a little more stock if necessary.

When ready to serve, whisk the eggs gently with the saffron, cream and a little salt and pepper. Melt the butter in a frying pan and cook the eggs over a very gentle heat until they are very softly scrambled.

Bring the lentil soup to the boil, skim and pour into serving bowls. Top with a spoonful of the scrambled eggs, drizzle with a little extra-virgin olive oil and garnish with fresh coriander leaves.

*Note: To toast saffron threads, heat a small dry frying pan over a medium heat for about 30 seconds. Remove the pan from the heat, add the saffron threads and spread them out evenly. Cook for 1-2 minutes, until they dry out. Move them around in the pan from time to time to ensure they dry evenly and don't burn. Once dry, crush the threads to a powder with the back of a spoon.

Stuffed vegetables

ZUCCHINI BLOSSOMS WITH HALOUMI IN OLIVE-BRIOCHE CRUMBS ... 102

STUFFED ZUCCHINI COOKED IN YOGHURT ... 105

BAKED TOMATOES WITH SAFFRON, BULGUR & BARBERRIES ... 106

SUMMER VINE LEAVES WITH TOMATOES, PINE NUTS & DILL ... 108

A rather sophisticated category, demonstrating the technical skill of the Middle Eastern home cook. In fact, Middle Easterners (and people from the Eastern Mediterranean, and as far east as Armenia) seem to have an absolute passion for stuffing all kinds of vegetables with mixtures of rice with herbs, spices, meat or legumes. There's no denying that these dishes are fairly labour-intensive – especially the daintier ones that involve hollowing out or wrapping and rolling – meaning that making them is usually reserved for celebrations. But it provides a great opportunity for family members and friends to get together and help out! This is usually as much about socializing as it is about the food preparation, and we consider it one of life's great pleasures.

Food historians argue over the origin of stuffed vegetables – as do the Turks and the Greeks, both claiming them as their own! Arto de Hartourian, in his lovely book *Vegetarian Dishes from the Middle East* writes that the habit of wrapping minced meat or wheat and spices in vine, cabbage and fig leaves, and then cooking them in water flavoured with aromatics can be traced to the ancient Sassanian, Babylonian and Akkadian empires, as far back as the third millenium BC. With time, the practice was extended and developed beyond leaves to include vegetables, perhaps reaching a zenith in the elaborate banquets produced by the palace kitchens of the Ottoman Empire.

The most popular – and perhaps most iconic – stuffed items are vine leaves, known variously as *dolmades* or *sarma*. These are served hot, when they are traditionally filled with a mixture of rice and minced lamb, or at room temperature, when rice is flavoured with herbs and combinations of cinnamon, allspice and mint, with pine nuts, chickpeas or currants. The rolled leaves are then braised in an oil-rich braising stock, allowing the flavours to meld with the lemony backdrop of the vine leaf itself.

Other popular vegetables suitable for stuffing are eggplants, capsicums, tomatoes and zucchinis. In the following pages, we've provided our own modern interpretations of some of these, including a lovely vegetable version of the Lebanese favourite home-cooked meal, *kousa mahshi* (stuffed zucchini).

Zucchini blossoms with haloumi in olive-brioche crumbs

These crunchy, oozing deep-fried zucchini flowers are usually served as part of a mezze selection, but are sophisticated enough to act as a stand-alone starter if you're planning a formal dinner party. Try to find a good-quality brioche loaf; it makes excellent, super-crunchy golden crumbs.

SERVES 4

8 baby zucchini (courgettes) with
    blossoms attached
plain (all-purpose) flour, for
    dusting
2 eggs, lightly beaten with a little
    water
vegetable oil, for deep-frying
olive oil, for deep-frying
sea salt and freshly ground black
    pepper
purple basil leaves, to serve
    (optional)
lemon wedges, to serve

Olive-brioche crumbs

100 g (3 ½ oz) brioche
12 Kalamata olives, pitted, rinsed,
    dried and finely diced
1 teaspoon za'atar
1 teaspoon sesame seeds

Haloumi, mint and ginger stuffing

100 g (3 ½ oz) haloumi, grated
50 g (1 ¾ oz) mozzarella, grated
1 small clove garlic crushed with
    ½ teaspoon sea salt
generous pinch ground cardamom
generous grind black pepper
¼ teaspoon grated fresh ginger
2 tablespoons finely shredded
    flat-leaf parsley leaves
1 heaped teaspoon finely chopped
    mint leaves
½ teaspoon dried mint

To make the olive-brioche crumbs, put the brioche in the bowl of a food processor and whiz to fine breadcrumbs. Tip into a mixing bowl and stir in the remaining ingredients. Set aside.

To make the stuffing, combine the haloumi and mozzarella with the garlic paste, spices, fresh ginger and herbs.

Carefully open each zucchini blossom and pinch out the stamen. Roll a lump of the cheese stuffing into a thumb-sized sausage shape and gently stuff it into the blossom. Twist the top of the flower to seal. Repeat with the remaining zucchinis.

Set up a little production line of flour, egg wash and the crumb mixture. Dust each zucchini flower lightly with flour, then dip it into the egg and, finally, gently roll it in the crumbs to create an even coating.

When ready to cook, pour equal quantities of vegetable and olive oil into a deep-fryer or saucepan to a depth of around 8 cm (3 ¼ in) and heat to 190°C (375°F)*.

Fry the zucchini blossoms a few at a time for 2–3 minutes, or until the crumbs turn crisp and golden. Turn them around in the oil to ensure they colour evenly all over. Drain them on kitchen paper, season lightly, and serve piping hot with a sprinkling of salt and pepper, a handful of herbs and lemon wedges.

*Note: If you don't have a candy thermometer, the oil will have reached the correct temperature when it is shimmering, and when a small cube of bread sizzles up to the surface and turns a pale golden brown in about 20 seconds.

Stuffed zucchini cooked in yoghurt

This is a vegetable version of Greg's all-time favourite home-cooked meal, *kousa mahshi. Kousa mahshi* is, essentially, a hearty one-pot dish, where zucchinis (or baby marrows) are filled with a rice-and-meat mixture and braised in a hearty tomato sauce. This rather more refined version mixes the rice stuffing with dates, spices, flaked almonds and a splash of rosewater. The zucchinis are steamed (to cook the rice) before being finished off in a silkily smooth hot yoghurt sauce.

If you can, use white zucchini that are squat and bulbous, as they are easy to hollow out. We use a combination of a long, thin fish-filleting knife and a small melon baller!

SERVES 4

12 white zucchini or baby marrows
    (no smaller than 150 g / 5 ½ oz)

Stuffing
100 ml (3 ½ fl oz) olive oil
1 small onion, finely diced
250 g (9 oz) medium-grain rice
4 Medjool dates, pitted and cut
    into 1 cm (½ in) dice
around 400 ml (14 fl oz) vegetable
    stock
½ teaspoon ground allspice
¼ teaspoon ground cinnamon
1 teaspoon salt
2 bay leaves
40 g (1 ½ oz) flaked almonds
60 ml (2 fl oz) extra-virgin olive oil
3 tablespoons rose petals
splash rosewater

Hot yoghurt sauce
600 g (1 lb 5 oz) natural yoghurt
3 teaspoons cornflour (cornstarch)
60 ml (2 fl oz) water
2 egg yolks, lightly beaten
salt and freshly ground white
    pepper
½ teaspoon dried mint
extra-virgin olive oil, to serve

To make the stuffing, heat one-third of the olive oil in a medium-sized saucepan and fry the onion gently for about 5 minutes, just until it softens. Add the rice to the pan and stir well to coat all the grains in the oil and onion. Add the dates and pour on enough of the stock to cover the rice by one fingers' width. Add the spices, salt and the bay leaves, then cover the pan with a lid and simmer on a very low heat for 5 minutes, or until all the stock has been absorbed and the rice is just cooked.

While the rice is cooking, fry the almonds in the remaining olive oil until they colour a rich golden brown. They burn very easily, so stir them constantly.

When the rice is cooked, tip it into a mixing bowl, remove the bay leaves, and fork it through with 1 tablespoon of the extra-virgin olive oil. Stir in the nuts and 2 tablespoons of the rose petals and allow to cool completely before you stuff the zucchinis.

When completely cold, sprinkle on a splash of rosewater (don't overdo it: a couple of teaspoons should be ample).

Trim the zucchinis at the rounded end. With a melon baller or a long, thin knife, carefully hollow out the inside of each one. The idea is to have as thin a shell as possible, but without piercing the skin. Loosely stuff each zucchini to about three-quarters full, which leaves space for expansion during cooking.

Stack the zucchinis in a steamer set over a pan of simmering water and cook, covered, for 35–40 minutes, or until the rice is cooked.

While the zucchinis are steaming, prepare the sauce. Tip the yoghurt into a large bowl and stir briskly until smooth. Mix the cornflour with the water and add to the yoghurt with the egg yolks. Stir well then tip into a large saucepan. Lower the heat and cook, stirring in one direction only, for about 5 minutes, or until the sauce has thickened. Add the zucchinis to the pan and simmer gently for a further 5 minutes.

Serve with a sprinkle of dried mint and a drizzle of extra-virgin olive oil.

Baked tomatoes with saffron, bulgur & barberries

This is based on a simple meal that Greg's mum used to make with a mix of different-sized tomatoes from the garden. It's best made in full summer, when tomatoes are ripe and flavourful but if you don't grow your own, the best place to find a larger variety tomato for stuffing will be farm stores or farmers' markets. You should be able to find large beefsteak and oxheart varieties fairly easily and heritage varieties (such as the marmande) are increasingly widely available. At all costs, avoid the watery ones sold as 'slicing' tomatoes in some supermarkets.

SERVES 4

200 g (7 oz) small–medium vine-
    ripened tomatoes
80 ml (2 ½ fl oz) extra-virgin
    olive oil
sea salt
2 large shallots, thinly sliced
1 teaspoon Turkish red chilli flakes
80 ml (2 ½ fl oz) vegetable stock
15 saffron threads
4 large beefsteak tomatoes (or
    another large variety)
Greek-style yoghurt, to serve

Bulgur stuffing

120 g (4 ¼ oz) medium–coarse
    bulgur wheat
40 ml (1 ¼ fl oz) olive oil
2 small shallots, finely chopped
2 cloves garlic, finely chopped
2 tablespoons barberries
    (Barberries are available from
    Persian stores or some Middle
    Eastern stores. If you can't find
    them, use dried cranberries or
    cherries)
½ teaspoon ground cinnamon
½ teaspoon ground allspice
2 tablespoons pistachio slivers
½ teaspoon sea salt
½ teaspoon freshly ground black
    pepper

To make the stuffing, soak the bulgur wheat in boiling water for 20 minutes then tip into a sieve to drain. Use your hands to squeeze out as much water as you can then set aside.

Heat the oil in a small frying pan. Add the shallots, garlic, barberries and spices and sauté for a few minutes until the shallots soften. Add the bulgur wheat and pistachios and season with the salt and pepper. Stir to combine and set aside until ready to cook the tomatoes. It will keep in the fridge, covered, for up to 12 hours.

Preheat the oven to 180°C (350°F).

Arrange the vine-ripened tomatoes in a roasting tin. Drizzle on half the oil and sprinkle with salt. Roast for 10 minutes, or until the skins split. Peel away and discard the skins (or save for making stock, page 88). Add the shallots, chilli flakes, stock and saffron to the pan.

Working from the stalk end, carefully slice out the cores from the large tomatoes, then scoop out as much of the flesh as you can with a melon baller or teaspoon. With true 'stuffing' varieties, you'll find that the seeds are all clustered close to the centre, with a fair amount of space around them, making it easy to scoop them out. Chop the flesh finely and mix it into the bulgur stuffing mixture.* Divide the stuffing evenly between the tomatoes, packing it in tightly.

Sit the tomatoes on top of the vegetables in the roasting tin. Cover the tin with foil and bake for 30 minutes. Serve hot from the oven, or at room temperature, with Greek-style yoghurt.

*Note: In the winter, most large varieties of tomato have rather watery, tasteless flesh. We'd suggest discarding this, as it adds almost nothing in terms of flavour. Instead, double the amount of vine-ripened tomatoes and, after roasting and peeling, remove half the amount from the tin, chop them evenly and add this to the stuffing mix.

Summer vine leaves with tomatoes, pine nuts & dill

Versions of stuffed vine leaves can be found all around the Middle East and Mediterranean. This vegetarian version comes from Turkey (where they are known as 'sarma'). They are especially popular in the summer, when the appetite craves lighter, meat-free meals. Best served at room temperature, they are a stalwart of the mezze table or can even be eaten as a pre-dinner canapé.

SERVES 6–8

750 g (1 lb 10 oz) jar preserved
    vine leaves or about 500 g
    (1 lb 2 oz) fresh vine leaves
100 ml (3 ½ fl oz) olive oil
40 g (1 ½ oz) pine nuts
1 large onion, finely chopped
1 level teaspoon ground allspice
½ teaspoon ground cinnamon
1 level teaspoon dried mint
35 g (1 ¼ oz) currants
250 g (9 oz) short-grain rice
sea salt and freshly ground black
    pepper
250 ml (9 fl oz) vegetable stock
1 medium vine-ripened tomato,
    grated
2 tablespoons finely chopped dill
2 tablespoons finely chopped
    flat-leaf parsley leaves
1 lemon, sliced
200 ml (7 fl oz) hot water
juice of 1 lemon

If using preserved vine leaves, soak them for 10 minutes in plenty of cold water, then rinse and pat them dry. Fresh vine leaves should be washed, blanched in boiling water for 30 seconds and then refreshed in cold water.

To make the filling, heat half the oil in a heavy-based saucepan. Sauté the pine nuts for a few minutes over a medium heat until golden brown. Add the onion and sauté until softened, then add the spices, dried mint, currants and rice and season with salt and pepper. Stir well and add half the vegetable stock to the pan. Cook over a low heat, for 5 minutes, stirring occasionally. Add the remaining stock and cook for a further 5 minutes, or until all the stock has been absorbed. Remove the pan from the heat and stir in the grated tomato and fresh herbs.

Line the bottom of a heavy-based saucepan or flame-proof casserole with a few vine leaves and slices of lemon. Arrange the remaining leaves over a work surface, vein-side up, and cut away the stems. Place a spoonful of the filling across the base of the leaf. Roll it over once, then fold in the sides and continue to roll it into a neat sausage shape. The *sarmas* should be around the size of your little finger – don't stuff them too tightly or they will burst during the cooking. Continue stuffing and rolling until all the filling has been used.

Pack the stuffed vine leaves into the casserole dish, layering them with more lemon slices, then pour in the hot water, lemon juice and remaining oil. Sit a small plate on top of the *sarmas* to keep them submerged in the liquid, then simmer gently, covered, over a low heat for 30 minutes. Check whether the *sarmas* are ready: if there is still liquid in the dish, return to the heat and simmer for another 15 minutes, then check again.

Leave the *sarmas* to cool in the casserole dish. When ready to serve, turn them out onto a large platter.

Fritters

WILD GARLIC, LEEK & CURRANT FRITTERS WITH HONEY ... 113

HAZELNUT FALAFEL & TAHINI-WHIPPED CRÈME FRAÎCHE ... 114

JERUSALEM ARTICHOKE 'WEDGES' WITH GREEN OLIVE AIOLI ... 115

VEGETABLE 'FRITTO MISTO' WITH SAFFRON-YEAST BATTER ... 116

PUMPKIN KIBBEH STUFFED WITH FETA & SPINACH ... 118

Little fried rissoles and dumplings are enormously popular all over the Middle East and one of the best loved – falafel (or *ta'amia*) – has now reached iconic status in countries around the globe. However, this rise to fame has not been without controversy. Indeed, there are entire books and academic tracts devoted to the falafel! Both Egypt and Israel claim it as their national dish while in the West it's associated most strongly with Lebanese take-away shops. And it's not just their history that's contentious; the ingredients themselves are also part of a hot discussion. Egyptians favour large dried broad beans, Israelies, chickpeas, while in Lebanon and Syria they hedge their bets and use a combination of the two. Some recipes recommend using yeast as a rising agent, but most use bicarbonate of soda. As for texture, this varies from smooth and paste-like, to fairly coarse. But, what nearly all recipes agree on, is that falafel should be chock-full of green, herby goodness: a mixture of coriander (predominantly) and flat-leaf parsley. Once cooked, falafel are either dipped into tahini sauce, or stuffed into warm pita with plenty of salad, tahini and a good squeeze of lemon juice. Instead of repeating our traditional falafel recipe here (it featured in our first book, *Arabesque*), we've taken a few liberties and offer up a recipe for hazelnut falafel, which has proved very popular with Greg's dining customers over the years.

But this section is about more than just falafel. There are recipes for several of our favourite fried vegetables, including another Lebanese classic (the dish by which all Lebanese housewives are judged): the famous torpedo-shaped kibbeh. Kibbeh are usually made from spiced ground meat encased in a crunchy bulgur wheat shell, however vegetable versions are served during religious festivals when people cut down their meat consumption. We often make kibbeh with mashed potato but for something a bit different and for a splash of colour, try it, as here, with mashed pumpkin.

Hot and crunchy on the outside and soft and melting on the inside – what's not to love about fritters! Serve them as part of a mezze or with a cold glass of beer before your meal.

Wild garlic, leek & currant fritters with honey

Doughnuts and fritters are found all around the Middle East and Eastern Mediterranean, although this savoury version is based on Sicilian *zeppole*. With their crunchy exterior and soft, oozing centre they are fabulous with a pre-dinner drink, but you can also serve them as part of a mezze selection. Try alternating the flavours with fennel seeds and ricotta, Turkish red chilli flakes, snipped chives or even diced olives.

MAKES AROUND 24

100 g (3 ½ oz) unsalted butter, diced

½ teaspoon salt

300 ml (10 ½ fl oz) water

180 g (6 ¼ oz) plain (all-purpose) flour

3 large eggs (or 4 small-medium eggs)

150 g (5 ½ oz) soft, creamy feta, finely crumbled

2 tablespoons currants

⅓ cup thickly shredded wild garlic leaves (ramps)

vegetable oil, for deep-frying

2–3 tablespoons warmed honey, to serve

salt flakes, to serve

To make the fritters, combine the butter, salt and water in a medium saucepan and slowly bring to the boil so that the butter completely dissolves. As the liquid boils up, quickly add the flour in one go and mix vigorously with a wooden spoon to incorporate it into the liquid. Beat over a lower heat for 3–4 minutes, until the mixture is glossy and comes away from the sides of the pan in a smooth ball.

Tip the hot dough into the bowl of a stand-mixer. Beat for 1 minute on medium speed, then increase it to the maximum. Add the eggs, one at a time, then continue beating on maximum speed for 5 minutes, until the dough has cooled. Fold in the feta, currants and wild garlic leaves gently, taking care not to over mix.

When ready to cook, pour vegetable oil into a deep-fryer or saucepan to a depth of around 8 cm (3 ¼ in) and heat to 170°C (325°F)*.

Drop spoonfuls of the batter into the hot oil, taking care to incorporate some feta, currants and garlic shreds into each one. Fry in batches for 5 minutes, or until they transform into lovely golden brown puffs. Turn them around in the oil to ensure they colour evenly all over. Drain them on kitchen paper for a few seconds then serve while hot with a drizzle of warm honey and a sprinkling of salt flakes.

*Note: If you don't have a candy thermometer, the oil will have reached the correct temperature when it is shimmering, and when a small cube of bread sizzles up to the surface and turns a pale golden brown in about 40 seconds.

Hazelnut falafel & tahini-whipped crème fraiche

When it comes to falafel, every Middle Eastern country has its own very strong opinion. Egyptians claim them as their own and favour broad beans as the primary ingredient, while Israelies and Palestinians use only chickpeas. The Lebanese version (which is Greg's birthright) combines the two, with lots of chopped coriander and parsley for a vibrant green colour. The hazelnuts are completely unorthodox by anyone's standard, but they do add a lovely nutty flavour and an extra crunch!

MAKES AROUND 24 FALAFEL

150 g (5 ½ oz) dried, skinless broad
    beans (fava), soaked overnight
150 g (5 ½ oz) dried chickpeas,
    soaked overnight
1 teaspoon salt
1 small onion, finely chopped
2 cloves garlic, finely chopped
1 small red chilli, finely chopped
1 ½ cups fresh coriander (cilantro)
    leaves and stalks
½ cup flat-leaf parsley leaves,
    shredded
1 tablespoon ground coriander
1 tablespoon ground cumin
vegetable oil, for deep-frying
60 g (2 ¼ oz) hazelnuts, roasted,
    peeled and roughly crushed
1 teaspoon bicarbonate of soda
    (baking soda)

Tahini-whipped crème fraîche
180 ml (6 fl oz) crème fraîche
60 ml (2 fl oz) tahini, well stirred
juice of up to 1 lemon
1 clove garlic crushed with
    1 teaspoon sea salt, plus extra
    salt for seasoning

To make the sauce, combine the crème fraîche, tahini, lemon juice and garlic paste in a mixing bowl. Thin with a little water, if necessary – the sauce should have the consistency of runny honey. Taste and adjust the flavours with more salt or lemon juice. What you are aiming for is a balance of the sharp crème fraîche and lemon juice with nutty tahini and garlic. This sauce can be stored in the fridge in a sealed container for up to 3 days.

Drain the broad beans and chickpeas and rinse them well. Tip onto a clean tea towel and pat them dry.

Put them into the bowl of a food processor and add the salt. Whiz to the consistency of coarse, sticky breadcrumbs.

Add the onion, garlic, chilli, herbs and spices and whiz to a bright green paste. Take care not to over-process the mixture; it should be the consistency of fine crumbs, not a smooth paste. Chill for at least 30 minutes before frying.

When ready to cook, pour vegetable oil into a deep-fryer or heavy-based saucepan to a depth of around 8 cm (3 ¼ in) and heat to 180°C (350°F)*.

While the oil is heating, add the crushed hazelnuts and bicarbonate of soda to the falafel mixture. Heat a little oil in a frying pan and fry a teaspoon of the mixture to check the balance of seasoning. Adjust it to your liking, if need be.

Shape the mixture into little puck-shaped patties. Fry the falafel, a few at a time, for 6–7 minutes, or until they turn a deep golden brown. Turn them around in the oil to ensure they colour evenly all over. Drain them on kitchen paper and serve piping hot. Eat them with tahini-crème fraîche sauce for dipping, or stuff them into pita, with plenty of salad, a squeeze of lemon and a drizzle of sauce.

*Note: If you don't have a candy thermometer, the oil will have reached the correct temperature when it is shimmering, and when a cube of bread sizzles slowly to the surface and turns a pale golden brown in 30–40 seconds.

Jerusalem artichoke 'wedges' with green olive aioli

In our view, Jerusalem artichokes are sadly misunderstood and underused – which probably has something to do with their carminative reputation. However, they have a unique flavour that is extraordinarily versatile and lends itself well to both savoury and sweet dishes.

These 'wedges' came about during a spot of kitchen experimentation (aka mucking around!). When poached and then deep-fried, they develop a fantastic crunchy-chewy exterior and a melting interior. Serve them as a snack or mezze dish with a cold beer. They are brilliant with this green olive aioli, but equally good with a spicy relish (page 30) or with thick yoghurt swirled with Green Harissa (page 56) and a good sprinkling of salt.

SERVES 4

12 medium Jerusalem artichokes, peeled

olive oil, for frying

1 teaspoon sea salt

½ teaspoon ground cumin

Green olive aioli

2 egg yolks

1 teaspoon Dijon mustard

1 small clove garlic crushed with 1 teaspoon salt

1 teaspoon white wine vinegar

250 ml (9 fl oz) olive oil

juice of ½ lemon

1 tablespoon finely chopped green olives

1 tablespoon salted baby capers, well rinsed and chopped

salt and freshly ground black pepper

To make the aioli, whisk the egg yolks with the mustard, garlic paste and vinegar until light and creamy. Gradually add the oil, drop by drop, ensuring each amount is incorporated before adding more. When around half the oil has been added, you should have a thick glossy paste. Whisk in the lemon juice and then add the remaining oil in a slow, steady trickle. Mix in the olives and capers, then taste and adjust the seasonings to your liking. Keep chilled until ready to serve. It will keep up to 5 days in the fridge.

Sit the peeled artichokes in a steamer set over a pan of briskly simmering water. Depending on the size of your steamer, you may have to do this in two batches. Cover with a tight-fitting lid and steam for up to 15 minutes (but check after 10), until the artichokes are tender when pierced with the tip of a sharp knife. Remove from the heat and transfer the artichokes to a board for a few minutes to allow them to steam dry.

Meanwhile, pour olive oil into a small, heavy-based saucepan to a depth of around 4 cm (1 ½ in) and heat to 180°C (350°F)*.

Cut the artichokes in half lengthwise and fry in batches of 6–8. Fry them on a medium-high heat for around 10 minutes, moving them around in the oil to ensure they don't stick and that they colour evenly – don't be tempted to hurry the process! They will develop a lovely dark golden exterior, which is chewy-crisp, rather than super-crunchy.

Remove from the hot oil and drain them briefly on kitchen paper then transfer to a serving dish. Season generously with the salt and cumin and eat immediately, while still piping hot, with the green olive aioli for dunking.

*Note: If you don't have a candy thermometer, the oil will have reached the correct temperature when it is shimmering, and when a small cube of bread sizzles up to the surface and turns a pale golden brown in 30–40 seconds.

Vegetable 'fritto misto' in saffron-yeast batter

Deep-fried crunchy vegetables are always popular, especially when teamed with a spicy sauce. They are also good with the tahini sauce on page 114, aioli or even with a drizzle of honey and sprinkle of salt.

Here, we use a saffron-yeast batter, which is pleasingly untemperamental and robust enough to stand up to the spicy heat of the accompanying sauce. It needs to be made a few hours ahead of time, but you can leave it for up to 12 hours, which develops the flavours.

We've not given quantities of vegetables as you can probably figure out this out for yourself, depending on what you have to choose from in the fridge.

Choose from a selection of vegetables

eggplant (aubergine), pumpkin (squash), sweet potato, carrots, cut into 5 mm (¼ in) slices

cauliflower, broccolini, cut into small florets and sprigs

baby zucchini (courgette), okra, pattypan squash, cut into 5 mm (¼ in) slices

spring onions (scallions), cut into 3 cm (1 ¼ in) lengths

fine green beans, or flat beans cut into 2 cm (¾ in) pieces

capsicums (peppers), cut into strips

spinach leaves

vegetable oil, for deep-frying

1 tablespoon Zhoug (page 197)

200 g (7 oz) Greek-style yoghurt

a glug of extra-virgin olive oil

sea salt

Saffron-yeast batter

175 g (6 oz) plain (all-purpose) flour

3 teaspoons dried active yeast (1 ½ x 7.5 g / ¼ oz sachets)

250 ml (9 fl oz) warm water

75 g (2 ½ oz Greek-style yoghurt

saffron liquid (15–20 threads saffron steeped in 40 ml / 1 ¼ fl oz boiling water for 30 minutes)

½ teaspoon sea salt

To make the batter, sift the flour into a bowl. Sprinkle on the yeast then whisk in the warm water and yoghurt to form a batter. Stir in the saffron liquid and salt, then cover and leave to stand for at least 2 hours or up to 12 hours.

When ready to cook, pour vegetable oil into a small, heavy-based saucepan or a deep-fryer to a depth of 5 cm (2 in) and heat to 190°C (375°F)*.

Dip the vegetable slices, one kind at a time, into the batter then slip them straight into the oil. Fry until crisp and golden brown; the time will vary from seconds (in the case of leaves) to a few minutes for most of the vegetable. Drain on kitchen paper.

Stir the zhoug into the yoghurt and drizzle with the olive oil.

Serve the fritto misto piping hot, with a sprinkling of salt and the spicy sauce for dipping.

Note: If you don't have a candy thermometer, the oil will have reached the correct temperature when it is shimmering, and when a blob of batter sizzles up to the surface and turns a pale golden brown in about 20 seconds.

Pumpkin kibbeh stuffed with feta & spinach

This is a vegetable version of the famous torpedo-shaped kibbeh, so beloved by Lebanese restaurants. In Greg's family, as is common in Middle Eastern Christian communities, vegetable kibbeh are often served during Lent, when people reduce their meat consumption. They are most often made with mashed potato, but we find that butternut pumpkin (squash) works beautifully as well.

When it comes to the filling, be as imaginative as you like! Use the spinach mixture below as a base and add other flavours, depending on what you have to hand. We've been known to use feta, haloumi, goat's cheese or mozzarella, as well as nearly all the flavoured butters on pages 55–56 (but not all at the same time!).

MAKES 12

Kibbeh shell

450 g (1 lb) butternut pumpkin
    (squash)
salt and freshly ground black
    pepper
olive oil
100 g (3 ½ oz) fine bulgur wheat
½ small onion, finely chopped
1 tablespoon tahini, well stirred
1 tablespoon plain (all-purpose)
    flour
¼ teaspoon ground allspice
¼ teaspoon ground cinnamon
Greek-style yoghurt, to serve
extra-virgin olive oil, to serve

Feta & spinach filling

1 tablespoon olive oil
1 tablespoon butter
1 small onion, finely diced
100 g (3 ½ oz) spinach leaves,
    stalks removed
salt and freshly ground black
    pepper
feta or your choice of melting white
    cheese or savoury butter. We
    especially like Persian Sabzi
    Butter and Harissa Butter
    (pages 55–56)

Make the kibbeh shell first. Preheat the oven to 180°C (350°F). Cut the pumpkin into chunks and arrange in a small roasting tin. Toss with salt, pepper and a generous splash of olive oil. Cover with foil and roast for 25–30 minutes, or until very tender. Remove from the oven and leave to cool.

While the pumpkin is cooling, soak the bulgur wheat in warm water for 5 minutes. Tip into a sieve and, using your hands, squeeze out as much water as you can. Then tip into a tea towel and twist to extract even more water. When it's as dry as you can manage, tip it into a large mixing bowl.

Slice away the skin from the pumpkin and weigh out 250 g (9 oz) of flesh. Add it to the bowl with the bulgur wheat and mash the two together to form a smooth purée. Add the onion, tahini, flour and spices and season generously with salt and pepper. Knead with your hands until the mixture is thoroughly blended. Chill for at least 30 minutes, which will make the paste easier to work with.

To make the filling, heat the oil and butter in a medium frying pan and add the onion. Sweat for 5–10 minutes, until soft and translucent. Add the spinach leaves and stir over the heat, turning it around frequently, until it wilts. Remove from the heat and leave to cool. Season with salt and pepper then chop finely.

When you are ready to make the kibbeh, divide the shell mixture into 12 even portions. Take one portion in the palm of your left hand and roll it smooth with the other hand. Using the forefinger of your right hand, make an indentation in the ball and start to shape it carefully into a hollow shell. Try to make the shell as thin and even as you can. Wet your finger from time to time, to make it easier.

Fill the shell with a scant teaspoon of the spinach filling, together with a small cube of feta or your choice of flavoured butter. Add another pinch of spinach, then wet the edges of the opening and carefully pinch it closed. Make sure you don't trap any air inside. You are aiming to form a small torpedo-shaped dumpling, with slightly tapered ends. Repeat with the remaining mixture and filling.

Leave the stuffed kibbeh on a tray in the fridge, covered, for at least 30 minutes, or up to 4 hours, until you are ready to cook them.

When ready to cook, pour vegetable oil into a medium, heavy-based saucepan to a depth of about 6 cm (2 ½ in) and heat to 180°C (350°F)*. Fry the kibbeh, a few at a time, for 4–5 minutes, or until they turn a deep golden brown. Turn them around in the oil to ensure they colour evenly all over. Drain them on kitchen paper and serve piping hot with a dollop of yoghurt and a drizzle of extra-virgin olive oil.

Note: If you don't have a candy thermometer, the oil will have reached the correct temperature when it is shimmering, and when a cube of bread sizzles slowly to the surface and turns a pale golden brown in about 30–40 seconds.

Savoury pastries

TETA'S PIE – DANDELION, LEEK & BARREL-AGED FETA ... 122

NORTH AFRICAN EGGPLANT PIE WITH PIMENTO SUGAR ... 124

FATIMA'S FINGERS WITH GOAT'S CHEESE, LEMON, TARRAGON & THYME ... 127

SWEET PUMPKIN SAMBUSEK WITH OREGANO ... 128

ZA'ATAR BISCUITS ... 129

FETA CHEESE STRAWS WITH TURKISH CHILLI ... 130

As with their sweet cousins (pages 244–253), you can find endless varieties of savoury pies and pastries all around the Middle East, across the Mediterranean and over to North Africa and Moorish Spain. Their birthplace and the route they travelled have been somewhat blurred by the mists of time, but it's generally understood that they were spread, first by the Arabs and then the Persians and Ottoman Turks to all corners of the Islamic Empire. Similarities in name can be found in countries that are thousands of miles apart (Persian *sanbuseh* becomes *sambusek* in Lebanon and *samosa* in India, for instance), while sometimes, confusingly, the same name is given to a completely different kind of pie. Many of these crunchy little morsels play a hugely popular part on the mezze table, while others are enjoyed as snacks, and larger pies, such as the legendary Moroccan *bisteeya*, are much more substantial.

The range of shape, size and fillings for savoury pastries is endless. Some are made from crisp, tissue-thin filo, others from flaky kinds of puff pastry, and others still from denser yeast doughs. Some pastries are baked; others are shallow- or deep-fried. Little triangles, half-moons or fingers are some of the more common shapes you'll encounter, but you'll also come across rectangular parcels and some raised pies. And, you'll also find great coiled pastry 'snakes' that are cut into slices. The pastries can be filled with meat or seafood, but most commonly they are stuffed with a combination of vegetables and cheese – think of lemony spinach, pimento-spiced pumpkin or melting eggplant, with any one of myriad different white cheeses that melt to gooey goodness on cooking.

The savoury pastries in this section are slight twists on traditional favourites. The larger pies can be served as a more substantial part of a main meal, while the little crunchy morsels can be enjoyed as snacks, served as pre-dinner nibbles or can play a key role on a mezze table.

Teta's pie – dandelion, leek & barrel-aged feta

This recipe is similar to one that Greg remembers from his childhood, as cooked by his 'teta' (grandmother). His grandparents – like many Lebanese – were keen gardeners, and particularly loved growing produce that wasn't readily available in suburban Australia: purslane, za'atar (wild thyme) and the small white zucchini, essential for stuffing, were some of the favourites. Make this rustic, home-style pie using a variety of home-grown vegetables and herbs. And do have a go at the home-made filo, instead of always taking the easy route with store-bought. It is certainly less elegant than industrially produced filo, but the end result is crunchy and delicious, thanks to a generous brushing with butter as you assemble it.

SERVES 4–6

500 g (1 lb 2 oz) leeks, white and
    pale green parts only, well
    washed and finely sliced
80 g (2 ¾ oz) butter
1 onion, finely diced
55 g (2 oz) (2 generous handfuls)
    dandelion leaves*, well washed
    and very roughly chopped
1 teaspoon dried mint
½ teaspoon freshly grated nutmeg
2 eggs, lightly beaten
180 g (6 ¼ oz) barrel-aged Greek feta
50 g (1 ¾ oz) Grana Padano, grated
½ teaspoons freshly ground black
    pepper
sea salt, to taste
100 g (3 ½ oz) unsalted butter,
    clarified
Turkish red chilli flakes, to sprinkle

Home-made filo pastry
1 egg
1 tablespoon extra-virgin olive oil
100 ml (3 ½ fl oz) water
100 ml (3 ½ fl oz) milk
½ teaspoon salt
400 g (14 oz) strong (bread) flour

To make the pastry, mix together the egg, oil, water, milk and salt in a large bowl. Sift in the flour and use your hands to knead it briskly into a pliable dough. Don't overwork it or the pastry will become tough. Divide into 12 walnut-sized pieces and leave them to rest under a clean damp cloth for 30 minutes.

Meanwhile, bring a large saucepan of lightly salted water to the boil. Add the leeks and poach for 3–5 minutes, or until tender. Tip into a sieve and drain well.

Melt the butter in a large frying pan and sauté the onion gently for around 8–10 minutes, or until soft and translucent. Add the leeks to the pan, together with the dandelions, dried mint and nutmeg and continue cooking for a further 5 minutes. With the heat on low, tip in the eggs and whisk them gently into the leek mixture. Add the cheeses and pepper. Taste and season with salt if need be, which will depend on the saltiness of your cheeses.

When ready to bake your pie, preheat the oven to 160°C (320°F) and brush a rectangular baking tray (around 22 cm x 26 cm / 8 ½ in x 10 ½ in) with clarified butter.

Roll out each portion of pastry dough as thinly as you can. Each sheet should be roughly the same dimension as the baking tray.

Lay 8 sheets of pastry in the tray, brushing each with clarified butter as you go. Add the filling and smooth it over evenly. Top with the remaining 4 sheets of pastry, again brushing with butter as you go. Finish with a sprinkling of red chilli flakes, then bake for 50–60 minutes, or until golden brown.

*Note: Spring is the best time to pick dandelions, when the leaves are small and sweet. As the flowers and 'clocks' develop, the leaves become increasingly bitter – although this is the attraction for true dandelion fans. If you can't find dandelions then use chicory, wild rocket or peppery watercress instead.

North African eggplant pie with pimento sugar

This vegetarian take on the famous Moroccan 'bisteeya' is wonderfully effective. The eggplant, while not at all traditional, melds beautifully with the herbed custard to create a luscious and rich filling, that is just as satisfying and impressive as the traditional game birds. It is true that it is somewhat time-consuming to prepare the component parts, but the finished result makes such an impressive party-piece – and is so delicious – that it is worth the effort.

SERVES 4

280 g (10 oz) eggplant (aubergine), peeled and diced into 2 cm (¾ in) cubes

salt

200 ml (7 fl oz) olive oil

1 large onion, finely diced

1 clove garlic, finely diced

1 small red chilli, deseeded and finely diced

1 teaspoon grated fresh ginger

15 saffron threads

1 teaspoon ground cumin

½ teaspoon ground cinnamon

½ teaspoon ground ginger

splash good-quality dry sherry

600 ml (20 fl oz) vegetable stock

freshly ground white pepper

4 large egg yolks

¼ cup shredded coriander (cilantro) leaves

¼ cup shredded flat-leaf parsley leaves

100 g (3 ½ oz) unsalted butter, clarified

3–4 sheets filo pastry (store-bought or see page 122), depending on how thin they are

80 g (2 ¾ oz) flaked almonds, fried in oil until golden

pinch ground allspice (pimento)

20 g (¾ oz) icing (confectioners') sugar

Layer the eggplant cubes in a colander, sprinkling generously with salt as you go. Sit a plate on top and leave them in the sink for 30 minutes to draw out moisture. After degorging, rinse the eggplants and pat dry with kitchen paper.

Heat around 3 tablespoons of the oil in a large frying pan. Add the onion, garlic, chilli, ginger and spices and sauté for around 10 minutes, or until the onions are soft and translucent. Add the sherry and bubble vigorously for a few minutes, stirring well. Tip into a bowl and set aside.

Add the rest of the oil to the frying pan and fry the eggplant for 4–5 minutes over a medium-high heat, until evenly coloured and a rich golden brown. Tip into a sieve to drain, then blot with kitchen paper.

Tip the eggplant into a heavy-based saucepan or a flame-proof casserole, along with the spicy onion mixture and the stock. Season with salt and pepper. Bring to the boil over a medium heat then lower the heat and simmer gently for 10–15 minutes, or until the eggplant is tender.

Remove from the heat and tip into a sieve, reserving both the cooking stock and the eggplant filling. Set the eggplant aside in a bowl and return the stock to the pan. Simmer vigorously until reduced to around 200 ml (7 fl oz).

Beat the egg yolks in a mixing bowl. Add a splash of hot stock and beat well. Tip the eggs into the rest of the hot stock and cook over a low heat as you would a custard, stirring continuously, until creamy and thick. Strain through a sieve and chill for about an hour, until cold.

Fold the eggplant gently into the cold custard. Add the shredded herbs and check the seasonings. The filling can be chilled for up to 12 hours, until you are ready to bake the pie.

Preheat the oven to 180°C (350°F). Brush a 20 cm (8 in) ovenproof frying pan or sturdy cake tin with a little of the clarified butter.

Place a sheet of filo in the pan and brush with a little more butter. Top with the remaining filo sheets, buttering as you go, and arranging them at different angles to each other.

Scatter the almonds in an even layer then spoon in the eggplant filling. Brush the exposed ends of the filo pastry with more butter and bring them all up and over the filling to enclose it entirely. Gently press flat and brush all over with more butter to seal the pastry. Bake for 15–18 minutes, or until golden brown.

Remove the pie from the oven and use kitchen paper to blot away any excess grease from the surface of the pie. Invert it carefully onto a flat baking sheet then slide it back into the frying pan, right side up. Return to the oven for another 5 minutes, or until evenly browned all over. Remove from the oven and cool for a few minutes.

Mix the allspice with the icing sugar. To serve, dust the pie with an even layer of sugar using a pretty stencil, or use a hot metal skewer to mark the surface with a trellis pattern.

Fatima's fingers with goat's cheese, lemon, tarragon & thyme

These pastries are also popularly known as 'cigars', and are nearly always included as part of a Middle Eastern mezze spread. You can make them with filo pastry, but we find spring roll wrappers work very well and hold up better to deep-frying.

We include tarragon in the filling, which adds a lovely aniseed note that goes well with the goat's cheese. Feel free to experiment with your own choice of soft cheese and fresh herbs.

MAKES 16

200 g (7 oz) rindless goat's cheese, crumbled

1 small onion, grated

2 tablespoons shredded tarragon leaves

1 tablespoon chopped fresh thyme leaves

finely grated zest of ½ lemon

1 egg yolk

salt and freshly ground black pepper

1 heaped teaspoon cornflour (cornstarch)

3 tablespoons water

16–20 spring roll wrappers

1 teaspoon extra-virgin olive oil

vegetable oil, for deep-frying

Green Chilli Relish (page 30), to serve

Combine the cheese, onion, herbs, lemon zest and egg yolk in a bowl, then season with salt and pepper and mash thoroughly with a fork.

When ready to assemble, mix the cornflour and water together to make a paste.

Work with one spring roll wrapper at a time, placing it on the work surface so that there is a corner pointing towards you (rather than a flat edge). Place a spoonful of filling across the corner closest to you, about a quarter of the way in. Roll this corner up and over the filling, and then for another couple of turns. Bring the two side corners in so they meet in the centre, then continue rolling, like a cigar. Brush the remaining corner with cornflour paste to seal. Repeat until all the filling and wrappers have been used. You're aiming to achieve neat fingers, around 13–14 cm (5–5 ½ in) long and about 1.5 cm (¾ in) thick.

To cook the pastries, pour vegetable oil into a medium, heavy-based saucepan to a depth of about 6 cm (2 ½ in) and heat to 190°C (375°F)*. Fry the pastries, a few at a time, for 2–3 minutes, or until they turn golden brown. Turn them around in the oil to ensure they colour evenly all over. Drain them on kitchen paper and serve piping hot.

*Note: If you don't have a candy thermometer, the oil will have reached the correct temperature when it is shimmering, and when a cube of bread sizzles up to the surface and turns a pale golden brown in about 20 seconds.

Sweet pumpkin sambusek with oregano

Sambusek are one of the best-loved Middle Eastern pastries, eaten as a snack or as part of a mezze spread. Typically, they are half-moon shaped, with a pretty pinched edge. They are usually filled with cheese, spinach or minced lamb, but we like to ring the changes with other spiced vegetables. We are very fond of this rather Greek-inspired pumpkin filling, but also make sambusek with the recipe for Potato Salad with Peas and Persian Spices on page 157, which turns them into something closer to an Indian samosa.

MAKES AROUND 16

1 tablespoon olive oil

1 tablespoon butter

1 large shallot, very finely chopped

400 g (14 oz) butternut pumpkin (squash) flesh, grated

1 teaspoon salt

1 ½ tablespoons golden caster (superfine) sugar

freshly ground black pepper

1 egg, beaten

80 g (2 ¾ oz) feta, finely crumbled

1 tablespoon shredded oregano leaves

egg wash made from 1 egg and 1 teaspoon water

Pastry

200 g (7 oz) self-raising flour, plus extra for dusting

30 g (1 oz) butter, cubed and chilled, plus extra for greasing

¼ teaspoon salt

pinch sugar

50–100 ml (2–3 ½ fl oz) warm water

To make the pastry, combine the flour, butter, salt and sugar in the bowl of a food processor and whiz until the mixture is the consistency of fine breadcrumbs. Gradually add enough warm water for the mixture to just come together into a dough. Tip onto a work surface and shape it into a round. Wrap in cling film and rest for 30 minutes before using.

Heat the oil and butter in a large frying pan. Add the shallot and sweat gently for 5–10 minutes, until soft and translucent. Increase the heat to medium, add the grated pumpkin and sauté for around 10 minutes, stirring from time to time, until the pumpkin is soft. Stir in the salt, sugar and pepper. Remove from the heat and leave to cool. When cold, mix in the egg, feta and oregano.

When ready to make the sambusek, preheat the oven to 180°C (350°F) and lightly grease a large baking sheet.

On a floured work surface, roll out the pastry to a thickness of about 3 mm (⅛ in) and cut out 16 circles with an 8 cm (3¼ in) pastry cutter. Place a spoonful of filling on one half of the circle and brush the other half with a little egg wash. Fold the pastry over the filling to make a half-moon shape and pinch or crimp the edge to seal. Brush with more egg wash and repeat with the remaining pastry and filling.

Carefully lift the sambusek onto the prepared baking sheet and bake for about 15 minutes, or until golden brown. Transfer to a wire rack and allow to cool briefly.

Za'atar biscuits

Za'atar is the Arabic word for 'wild thyme', and also for a herby seasoning mix made of dried thyme, sour red sumac and sesame seeds. In Lebanon, this mix is perhaps most commonly combined with olive oil to make a paste, and brushed onto the pizza-style flatbreads called *manoushi*, which are turned out in their thousands by bakeries, big and small, every morning. If you've travelled in Lebanon, you'll know only too well that it is impossible to walk past one of these bakeries without stopping to buy a *manoushi*; not surprisingly, they are the most popular snack food in the country.

Za'atar makes a wonderfully effective addition to our favourite little cheese biscuits. They keep quite well in a sealed container, not that they're likely to last long.

MAKES AROUND 30

100 g (3 ½ oz) unsalted butter, diced and chilled, plus extra for greasing
100 g (3 ½ oz) plain (all-purpose flour), plus extra for dusting
½ teaspoon Turkish red chilli flakes
50 g (2 oz) cheddar, finely grated
50 g (2 oz) parmesan, finely grated
1 egg, lightly beaten

Za'atar mix
3 tablespoons za'atar
1 tablespoon sumac

Mix together the za'atar and sumac.

Combine the butter, flour, 2 teaspoons of the za'atar mix, the chilli flakes and both cheeses in the bowl of a food processor. Whiz until the mixture starts to form crumbs, and then starts to clump together to form a ball.

Tip onto a floured work surface and, working briskly, bring the mix together to form a dough. Wrap in cling film and chill for 30 minutes.

When ready to bake, preheat the oven to 180°C (350°F) and lightly grease a baking tray.

On a lightly floured work surface, roll out the pastry to a thickness of about 3 mm (⅛ in). Use a small pastry cutter to cut out biscuits and transfer them carefully to the prepared baking tray, spacing them about 2 cm (¾ in) apart. Lightly knead and re-roll the trimmings until you've used up all the dough.

Brush the surface of each biscuit with a little beaten egg and sprinkle fairly densely with the za'atar mix. Bake for 10 minutes, or until they are golden brown. Remove from the oven and cool on the tray for a moment. Lift them carefully onto wire racks to cool and serve, if you can, while warm.

Feta cheese straws with Turkish chilli

A twist on the ever-popular cheese straw, these use sharp, salty feta and Turkish red chilli flakes, which give them an addictive spicy kick. Serve before dinner with a glass of chilled Fino sherry! They are best eaten on the day you bake them, but the dough freezes well for up to a month.

MAKES 30–40

150 g (5 ½ oz) plain (all-purpose) flour, plus extra for dusting

200 g (7 oz) feta, chilled and chopped

60 g (2 ¼ oz) butter, chilled and chopped, plus extra for greasing

½ teaspoon salt

1 teaspoon Turkish red chilli flakes

1 tablespoon crème fraîche (or sour cream), chilled

Combine all the ingredients, except for the crème fraîche, in the bowl of a food processor. Pulse briefly, 5 or 6 times, until the mixture resembles coarse breadcrumbs. Add the crème fraîche and process for 10–15 seconds, or until the mixture starts to clump together and form a ball.

Tip onto a floured work surface. Divide the mixture in half and shape into rounds. Wrap each piece in cling film and chill for 30 minutes.

When ready to bake, preheat the oven to 180°C (350°F) and lightly grease a baking tray.

Use a floured rolling pin to roll out a portion of the dough to as even a rectangle as you can manage. It should be about ½ cm (¼ in) thick and up to 25 cm (10 in) long. With a very sharp knife, cut into long strips, around 1 cm (½ in) wide – but a little randomness in both length and shape is good.

Lift the strips carefully onto the prepared tray (you may have to bake them in batches) and bake for around 15 minutes until a deep golden brown. Do make sure you don't undercook them, or they will be softish, instead of crisp and crunchy. Cool on the tray for a few moments, then transfer to a wire rack to cool further. They are at their very best just slightly warm but, in any event, should ideally be eaten on the day you make them.

Raw vegetable salads

CELERIAC REMOULADE WITH TAHINI & GOLDEN RAISINS ... 134

SHREDDED BITTER LEAVES WITH ROASTED GRAPES, ALMONDS & AVOCADO... 135

PERSIAN SOFT HERB SALAD WITH FRESH FIGS & LABNEH ... 136

CITRUS SALAD WITH RED RADICCHIO & POMEGRANATE DRESSING ... 139

SHANKLEESH SALAD WITH PARSLEY & POMEGRANATE ... 140

SHAVED ZUCCHINI WITH GRANA, BURRATA & BASIL ... 142

WINTER TABBOULEH ... 145

We've split our salads into two chapters: those made with raw vegetables and salad leaves, and those made with cooked vegetables, because in Middle Eastern countries the latter are often considered a category in their own right.

In truth, it's something of a fine distinction. But then the very term 'salad' is also a bit tricky. Most Middle Easterners make little distinction between dishes that we might otherwise call cold appetizers (such as dips), and salads. They are all just mezze! One thing that holds true though – be they raw or cooked – is that salads are nearly always considered dishes in their own right. They are rarely relegated to 'accompaniment' status, in the way that we tend to view them, somewhat dismissively, in the West, although they are usually served together with a selection of other dishes for sharing around the table.

As it happens, some of our very favourite meals are salads, and we love the endless permutations and combinations of texture and flavour that they offer. We firmly believe that salads can hold their own with any other kind of dish, especially when they incorporate generous handfuls of fresh herbs, toasted nuts and seeds, and all sorts of fruits and soft tangy cheeses.

The most important thing of all with raw vegetable salads is to use the freshest and finest ingredients. There is such an abundance of great produce nowadays, that there really is no excuse for resorting to a sad bag of limp lettuce leaves. If you are a vegetable gardener, then you'll already be tuned into the seasons, but otherwise, be led by what's on offer in farmers' markets and greengrocers.

None of the recipes that follow is strictly traditional, but they all borrow heavily from tradition and incorporate some of our favourite Middle Eastern flavours and ingredients. As with all the recipes in this book, they're designed to be eaten as part of a group of dishes, however several of these salads would also make a lovely light lunch just on their own – perhaps with some warm bread on the side.

Celeriac remoulade with tahini & golden raisins

We like to make this winter salad as an interesting variation on the French bistro classic. Although celeriac is not especially Middle Eastern, we love its nutty celery-sweetness and think it works really well with earthy tahini. If you don't have any golden raisins in the pantry, then use a grated apple instead, as you do need something with a sour-sweet tang to balance it out. Don't feel obliged to make your own mayo; a good-quality store-bought one will be fine too.

SERVES 4

60 ml (2 fl oz) apple juice
60 g (2 ¼ oz) golden raisins
½ medium celeriac
2 large gherkins, finely chopped
1 cup shredded flat-leaf parsley
    leaves

Tahini mayonnaise
1 large egg yolk
1 teaspoon Dijon mustard
1 teaspoon white wine vinegar
250 ml (9 fl oz) olive oil
juice of 1–1 ½ lemons
2 tablespoons tahini (well stirred)
salt and freshly ground white
    pepper, to taste

Boil the apple juice, then pour onto the raisins and leave for 5 minutes. (Alternatively, combine them in a small bowl and microwave on high for a minute.) Set aside.

Peel the celeriac and shred it finely. The least onerous way to do this is using a food processor with a fine-shred attachment or a mandoline – but at a pinch you can julienne it finely by hand.

Drain the raisins, reserving the juice. Add them to the celeriac, together with the chopped gherkins and shredded parsley.

To make the mayonnaise, whisk the egg yolk with the mustard and vinegar until pale and creamy. Gradually whisk in the olive oil, a few drops at a time, ensuring it is completely incorporated before adding more. When you've added about half the oil you should have a thick glossy paste. Loosen with a large splash of lemon juice, then add the rest of the oil in a slow trickle, whisking all the while. Season, to taste, with salt and pepper.

Measure out 100 ml (3 ½ fl oz) of the mayonnaise (store the leftovers in the fridge and use as you would any mayonnaise) and mix it with the tahini, and reserved apple juice. Add more lemon juice until you like the balance of nutty-tartness. Dollop onto the celeriac and toss everything together well. Season to taste with more salt and pepper.

Shredded bitter leaves with roasted grapes, almonds & avocado

Use your favourite combination of bitter salad leaves for this punchy salad. We love to throw dandelion leaves into the mix when they are in season, but you can use whatever is available – or even substitute peppery watercress or rocket. It makes a lovely accompaniment to heavier, richer dishes, such as the Slow-roasted Eggplant with Saffron-lemon Cream (page 171) or North African Eggplant Pie with Pimento Sugar (page 124).

SERVES 4-6

200 g (7 oz) black grapes
    (muscatels are lovely)
1 teaspoon extra-virgin olive oil
2 teaspoons sherry vinegar
1 teaspoon honey
sea salt
1 tablespoon vegetable or
    sunflower oil
50 g (1 ¾ oz) almond slivers
½ teaspoon sweet paprika
1 red witlof (Belgium endive),
    bases trimmed
2 handfuls rocket (arugula),
    stalks removed
2 handfuls watercress sprigs
2 handfuls frisée lettuce
1 avocado, diced
1 small shallot, sliced into very
    thin rings

Dressing
juice of ½ lemon
1 tablespoon extra-virgin olive oil
salt and freshly ground black
    pepper

Preheat the oven to 200°C (400°F). Put the grapes in a mixing bowl and toss them with the oil, vinegar and honey. Tip into a small ovenproof frying pan and roast for 8 minutes. Transfer to the stovetop over a high heat. Add a pinch of salt and sauté, shaking the pan from time to time, until the liquid caramelizes to a sticky glaze. Remove from the heat and set aside.

Heat the vegetable or sunflower oil in a small frying pan. Add the almonds to the pan and sprinkle on the paprika and a pinch of salt. Fry for 3–4 minutes, shaking constantly, until they start to colour. Remove from the heat and tip into a metal sieve to drain. Transfer to kitchen paper and pat dry.

Slice the red witlof leaves very finely. Transfer them to a large mixing bowl, along with the remaining greens, the avocado and shallot. Add the roasted grapes, reserving the glaze liquid for the dressing.

To make the dressing, whisk the glaze liquid with the lemon juice and oil and season well. Pour onto the salad and use your hands to toss everything together very gently.

Persian soft herb salad with fresh figs & labneh

One of the great pleasures of our travels around Iran a few years ago was the way each and every meal began with a basket of fresh herbs – called *sabzi* – along with soft white cheese and warm flatbread. It's a habit that we've continued to this day, as it's a brilliant appetite-sharpening way to begin any meal. This refreshing salad is really just a more refined variation on the *sabzi* theme: it's all about the freshness of the herbs and leaves that you choose – and feel free to experiment with your own selection. Similarly, try replacing the figs with cherries, white peaches or nectarines, when they are in season. Eat, Persian-style, with Griddled Flatbreads (page 36) or as an accompaniment to rich or filling dishes.

SERVES 4-6

12 leaves red witlof (Belgium
    endive), bases trimmed
1 cup watercress leaves and
    flowers
⅓ cup chervil leaves
⅓ cup snow pea tendrils
¼ cup basil leaves
¼ cup Thai or purple basil leaves
¼ cup chocolate mint leaves
4 firm, but ripe, figs, peeled and
    quartered
3 French cocktail radishes,
    halved lengthways
200 g (7 oz) Labneh, strained for
    12 hours (page 73)
edible flowers, such as borage, or
    nasturtiums, to garnish (these
    are pretty, but entirely optional)

Hazelnut dressing
50 ml (2 fl oz) hazelnut oil
a few drops of sesame oil
50 ml (2 fl oz) olive oil
30 ml (1 fl oz) champagne or
    good-quality white wine
    vinegar
50 ml (2 fl oz) water
salt and freshly ground black
    pepper

To make the dressing, tip the oils into a bowl and whisk in the vinegar, then the water. Season with salt and pepper.

For the salad, combine all the ingredients, except the labneh, in a serving bowl. Lightly season with salt and pepper and pour in as much dressing as required. Use your hands to mix everything together gently. Add blobs of labneh and flowers, if using, and serve.

Citrus salad with red radicchio & pomegranate dressing

Citrus fruits come into season just when our bodies and souls need them most, and this lovely refreshing salad is the perfect dish to cheer up a dreary winter's day. Here, we use a mixture of ruby grapefruit, oranges and mandarins, but when blood oranges are in season, we tend to make them the solo star.

Barberries have a fabulous sour-sweet flavour. They are available from Persian stores or some Middle Eastern stores, but if you can't find them, use dried cranberries or cherries instead.

SERVES 4

3 blood oranges (or use ordinary oranges, ruby grapefruit or a mix of your favourite citrus fruit)

generous handful of red radicchio leaves, shredded (or use red witlof (Belgium endive), bases trimmed and leaves separated and shredded)

2 baby fennel, or 1 medium fennel, very finely sliced

1 shallot, finely sliced

2–3 handfuls rocket (arugula) leaves

1 tablespoon tarragon leaves

2 tablespoons shredded flat-leaf parsley leaves

2–3 tablespoons pomegranate seeds

Almond-barberry labneh

25 g (1 oz) almonds (skins on)

1 knob of butter

1 ½ tablespoons barberries, soaked in water for 2 minutes, then drained and patted dry

Labneh, strained for 48–72 hours (page 73)

Pomegranate dressing

½ teaspoon pomegranate molasses

1 tablespoon red wine vinegar

1 teaspoon thyme leaves

60 ml (2 fl oz) extra-virgin olive oil

salt and freshly ground black pepper

To make the almond-barberry labneh, chop the almonds evenly to the consistency of very coarse breadcrumbs. Heat the butter in a small frying pan and fry the almonds for around 2 minutes, stirring constantly, until they are golden brown. Add the barberries to the pan and fry for a further 2 minutes, stirring constantly. Drain on kitchen paper and leave to cool completely. Roll the labneh balls carefully in the cold almond-barberry mixture so they are evenly coated and then set aside.

To make the salad, use a very sharp knife to peel the oranges, taking care to remove all the pith. Holding the fruit over a large mixing bowl to catch the juice, carefully slice each segment out of its skin casing and into the bowl.

Combine the dressing ingredients in a small bowl. Add the collected citrus juice and whisk everything together. Adjust the seasoning to your liking and set aside.

Add the remaining salad ingredients to the bowl with the orange slices and pour in enough dressing to coat lightly. Mix everything together very gently and tip onto a serving platter. Scatter on the pomegranate seeds, then tuck the labneh balls in among the salad and serve straight away.

Shankleesh salad with parsley & pomegranate

This is our version of a traditional shankleesh salad. You can find shankleesh – a rather pungent, spiced cheese, with something of a blue-cheese quality about it – in Middle Eastern grocers, usually vacuum packed in the chill-cabinet. Store-bought shankleesh varies in texture and flavour, depending on its age and the spices used. These range from za'atar to Aleppo pepper and even very hot chilli flakes. Our own home-made version (page 72) is very quick and easy to whip up and is so moreish that it never seems to last long. But whether you buy it or make your own, shankleesh provides a brilliant spicy counterpoint to this refreshing, crunchy salad. The pomegranate seeds are not traditional, but add an intermittent pleasing sweet crunch.

SERVES 4

1 Lebanese (short) cucumber, peeled and cut into cut into small chunks

3 medium vine-ripened tomatoes, chopped

¼ small red onion, finely sliced

2 handfuls roughly torn bitter leaves (we like young dandelion leaves, but you can also use rocket (arugula), radiccio, watercress or endive (witlof))

½ cup flat-leaf parsley leaves

¼ cup purslane leaves (or use winter purslane)

1 tablespoon roughly torn oregano leaves

salt and freshly ground black pepper

⅓ cup pomegranate seeds

1 ball Home-made Shankleesh (page 72)*, broken into small pieces, or use 80g (2 ¾ oz) of a good commercial one

30 ml (1 fl oz) Saffron Vinaigrette (page 148), or use extra-virgin olive oil and lemon juice

Combine the cucumber, tomatoes, onion, leaves and herbs in a large mixing bowl. Season lightly and add the pomegranate seeds. Add enough vinaigrette to coat lightly and mix everything together very gently. Crumble the shankleesh over the top of the salad; store-bought cheese will be firmer than our home-made version. Eat with plenty of warm bread.

*Note: You can also buy vacuum-packed shankleesh in Middle Eastern stores.

Shaved zucchini with grana, burrata & basil

This is such a pretty salad, and lovely for a hot summer's day. It surprises us that zucchinis are often overlooked as a raw salad vegetable, as they make a lovely alternative to cucumber. Use good-quality Grana Padano or parmesan for this dish and make sure you find a really top-notch burrata. You'll want one that oozes creamily into the salad, softening the tangy parmesan and lemon and the pungent pepperiness of the salad leaves.

SERVES 4

2 medium zucchinis (courgettes)

2 handfuls of rocket (arugula)
  leaves, stalks removed

1 handful lambs' lettuce

½ cup purple basil leaves (or use
  ordinary basil)

juice of ½ lemon

45 ml (1 ½ fl oz) extra-virgin
  olive oil

2 tablespoons finely grated Grana
  Padano or parmesan

1 teaspoon finely grated
  lemon zest

salt and freshly ground black
  pepper

4 small burrata

Trim the ends from the zucchinis then slice them thinly lengthways; a mandoline makes this easy.

Transfer the zucchini slices to a large mixing bowl and add the rocket, lambs' lettuce, basil, lemon juice and 2 tablespoons of the oil. Sprinkle on half the Grana or parmesan and half the lemon zest and season to taste with salt and pepper. Use your hands to mix everything together gently.

Divide between 4 plates and tuck a burrata in the centre of each salad. Sprinkle on the rest of the Grana or parmesan and lemon zest. Drizzle the remaining oil over the burrata and serve.

Winter tabbouleh

This is a winter version of tabbouleh that incorporates tiny crunchy florets of raw cauliflower to the other familiar ingredients for a lovely refreshing salad. Serve as you would a traditional tabbouleh, with baby cos lettuce leaves for scooping. The hazelnut oil is optional, but its toasty flavour does work brilliantly with the cauliflower.

SERVES 4

60 g (2 ¼ oz) fine bulgur wheat

80g (2 ¾ oz) tiny cauliflower florets

1 green tomato, deseeded and cut
 into 1 cm (½ in) dice

1 vine-ripened tomato, deseeded and
 cut into 1 cm (½ in) dice

1 Lebanese (short) cucumber, peeled,
 halved lengthways, deseeded and
 cut into 3 mm (⅛ in) dice

2 spring onions (scallions), finely
 sliced

1 cup flat-leaf parsley leaves,
 shredded

¼ cup mint **leaves, shredded**

½ teaspoon ground allspice

½ teaspoon ground cinnamon

juice of 1 lime

80 ml (2 ½ fl oz) extra-virgin olive oil

salt and freshly ground black pepper

a drizzle of hazelnut oil, to serve
 (optional)

baby cos lettuce leaves, to serve

Soak the bulgur wheat in cold water for 15 minutes. Tip into a tea towel and twist to extract as much moisture as you can, then scrape into a large mixing bowl.

Add the remaining vegetables, herbs and spices and pour in the lime juice and oil. Use your hands to mix everything together thoroughly then taste and season with salt and black pepper. Drizzle with hazelnut oil, if using, and serve with baby cos lettuce leaves.

Cooked vegetable salads

BABY LEEKS IN SAFFRON VINAIGRETTE WITH HAZELNUT CRUMBS ... 148

TURKISH BREAD & ROASTED VEGETABLE SALAD ... 150

FRESH BORLOTTI BEANS WITH TOMATO & POMEGRANATE DRESSING ... 152

GREEN BEANS WITH CHERMOULA, SHALLOTS & FETA ... 153

RAINBOW CHARD WITH SOUSED CURRANTS & PINE NUTS ... 155

POTATO SALAD WITH PEAS & PERSIAN SPICES ... 157

BRAISED ARTICHOKES, PRESERVED LEMON & FINGERLING POTATOES

WITH BASIL CRÈME FRAÎCHE ... 158

HONEY-ROASTED CARROTS WITH DATES, DANDELIONS & MOROCCAN DRESSING ... 160

In this chapter we offer recipes for cooked vegetables that are served cold or at room temperature, as a kind of salad. This is a hugely popular way of preparing vegetables in nearly all Middle Eastern countries, as well as in the Eastern Mediterranean and across North Africa. As with the raw vegetable salads of the previous chapter, these dishes are intended to be served along with several others, as part of a mezze selection.

The Turks are, perhaps, the greatest champions of this type of cooked salad. They have an entire category of dishes known as *zeytinyagli* in which vegetables, along with a range of aromatics, are braised in olive oil. (As with stuffed vegetables, such as the vine leaves on page 108, dishes that are to be eaten at room temperature are always cooked in olive oil, as it doesn't set hard as it cools, as butter would.) It's a technique that the Turkish are believed to have invented when they first settled in Anatolia in around the eleventh century and encountered olive trees along the Mediterranean and Aegean shorelines.

As well as a few of our favourite *zeytinyagli*-style dishes, we've also included some poached and roasted vegetable salads and a couple that could be served in a more Western way, as accompaniments to a main meal.

Baby leeks in saffron vinaigrette with hazelnut crumbs

There are few things nicer on a warm day than tender poached leeks in a tangy mustard vinaigrette with lots of crusty bread for mopping the plate clean. In this Middle Eastern-inspired version, a robust saffron-and-spice-spiked vinaigrette is definitely king, flooding the plate with liquid gold, while the crunchy breadcrumbs are the crowning glory.

SERVES 4

a handful of hazelnuts
400 g (14 oz) baby leeks (or
      8 small-medium leeks)
1 clove garlic
a few sprigs of thyme
a handful of hazelnuts
3 generous tablespoons butter
50 g (1 ¾ oz) coarse fresh
      breadcrumbs (sourdough,
      if possible)
big pinch Turkish red chilli flakes
salt and freshly ground black
      pepper

Saffron vinaigrette

10–15 saffron threads
2 tablespoons champagne or
      good-quality white wine vinegar
1 tablespoon white wine
1 teaspoon honey
2 spring onions (scallions), very
      finely diced
1 clove garlic crushed to a paste
      with ½ teaspoon salt
big pinch Turkish red chilli flakes
1 sprig thyme, leaves only
½ teaspoon coriander seeds
¼ teaspoon fennel seeds
¼ teaspoon white peppercorns
125 ml (4 fl oz) extra-virgin olive oil
juice of ½ lemon
¼ teaspoon salt, or to taste

To make the saffron vinaigrette, combine the saffron, vinegar, wine and honey in a small saucepan. Heat gently until the honey has dissolved, then add the spring onion, garlic, red chilli flakes and thyme leaves. Pour into a jar with a lid and leave to cool.

Combine the coriander and fennel seeds and the peppercorns in a small dry frying pan and cook over a medium heat for 3–4 minutes, until lightly toasted and aromatic. Crush roughly in a mortar then add them to the saffron infusion, along with the olive oil and lemon juice. Shake vigorously then taste and adjust the seasoning to your liking.

In the same pan, dry-fry the hazelnuts for 4–5 minutes, or until the skins darken and they start to smell toasty. Tip into a tea towel and rub away the skins. Chop the nuts roughly and set aside.

Trim and clean the leeks well, making sure you wash away any lingering bits of soil. Bring a large pan of salted water to the boil and add the leeks, garlic and thyme. Poach for 4–5 minutes (8–10 if they are larger), or until tender. Drain well then pat them dry with kitchen paper.

Transfer the leeks to a serving platter and, while they are still hot, spoon over enough saffron vinaigrette to moisten, but not drown them*. Leave them to cool to room temperature.

Toast the hazelnuts in a dry frying pan for 4–5 minutes over a medium heat, then chop them finely and set aside. Heat the butter in the same pan and, when it's sizzling, add the breadcrumbs and chilli flakes and fry until they are golden brown and crunchy. Add the chopped hazelnuts and fry for another minute. Season, to taste, then tip the hot crumbs over the leeks and serve straight away.

*Note: Leftover vinaigrette will keep in a sealed container in the fridge for 3–4 days. It makes a delicious dressing for cooked vegetables salads – especially artichokes or asparagus – and adds a classy touch to a humble potato salad.

Turkish bread & roasted vegetable salad

We are big fans of 'fattouche' salads, which tumble torn pieces of Arabic bread into a mix of chopped garden vegetables. The bread is usually toasted or, better still, fried, which adds an appealing crunch factor. This recipe uses Turkish bread, fried in a spicy paste, which is more substantial and adds pleasing bulk and texture to the roasted vegetables. If you're concerned about the calories, then toast the bread in the oven, instead of frying it.

SERVES 4

4 long red capsicums (bull's horn
    or Hungarian peppers), choose
    a mixture of red, orange and
    yellow ones, if you can
8 shallots, unpeeled
8 cloves garlic, unpeeled
80 ml (2 ½ fl oz) olive oil
2–3 tablespoons butter
4 baby zucchini (courgettes) halved
    lengthways (or use 2 regular
    zucchini, sliced lengthways)
8 Roasted Tomatoes (page 79),
    optional (or use good-quality
    slow-dried tomatoes), roughly
    chopped
¼ loaf of Turkish bread (or a
    ciabatta), roughly torn into
    large chunks
salt and freshly ground black
    pepper
1 teaspoon Turkish red pepper
    paste (page 69)
80 ml (2 ½ fl oz) extra-virgin olive oil
2 tablespoons salted baby capers,
    well rinsed
2 teaspoons sherry vinegar
juice of ½ lemon
½ cup basil leaves, roughly torn
1 cup lambs lettuce or rocket
    (arugula) leaves
Greek-style yoghurt, to serve

Preheat the oven to 200°C (400°F). Arrange the capsicums, shallots and garlic on a foil-lined baking tray and rub with a little oil. Roast for 25 minutes, turning once, until the skins blister and char. Remove the capsicums from the oven and transfer them to a shallow bowl. Cover with cling film and leave to steam for 10 minutes, which loosens the skins and makes them easier to peel.

Continue roasting the garlic for another 5 minutes, then transfer it to a different bowl. Lower the oven temperature to 160°C (320°F) and continue roasting the shallots for a further 10 minutes then remove them from the oven and add to the bowl with the shallots.

When all the vegetables are cool enough to handle, peel away the skins from the capsicums and pull out and discard the seeds and membranes. Slice the peppers into wide strips, making sure you retain any of the roasting juices. Squeeze the garlic out of its skins and set aside to make the dressing. Peel away the shallot skins and slice the soft roasted flesh in half.

Transfer all the roasted vegetables, together with any juices, to a mixing bowl.

Heat a tablespoon of oil and a tablespoon of butter in a frying pan and sauté the zucchini slices over a medium–high heat for a few minutes, turning regularly, until they colour a deep golden brown. Transfer to the mixing bowl, along with the roasted tomatoes.

Add a little more butter and oil to the pan and heat to a sizzle. Add the Turkish bread and season with salt and pepper. Fry over a medium heat, turning regularly, until it starts to crisp and colour. Add the pepper paste and sauté for a further 3–4 minutes, until the bread has absorbed the paste and colours a reddish brown. Remove from the pan and set aside for a moment.

Lower the heat and add the extra-virgin olive oil to the pan. Add the reserved garlic and the capers and sauté for a minute or two, squishing the garlic to a paste. Don't allow it to brown. Add the sherry vinegar and lemon juice and increase the heat to a simmer. Let it bubble for a few minutes then pour onto the vegetables.

Add the bread to the bowl, along with the basil leaves and lambs lettuce, and toss everything together very gently. Taste and adjust the seasoning if need be, then serve warm or at room temperature with cool, creamy yoghurt.

Fresh borlotti beans with tomato & pomegranate dressing

We get very excited when raw borlotti beans reach the shops in the summertime. They are exquisitely pretty, with their cream and pink marbling and have a lovely creamy texture, especially when cooked. We enjoy eating them raw – popped out of their pods, just like broad beans – but they are absolutely delicious baked in this aromatic stock and served at room temperature as a vegetable salad.

SERVES 4

800 g (1 lb 12 oz) fresh borlotti beans, to yield 250g (9 oz) podded weight

150 g (5 ½ oz) vine-ripened tomatoes

3 shallots, quartered

3 cloves garlic, lightly crushed

⅓ cup thyme sprigs

2 bay leaves

40 ml (1 ¼ fl oz) extra-virgin olive oil

1 tablespoon good-quality harissa (or see page 56)

450 ml (16 fl oz) vegetable stock

½ teaspoon freshly ground black pepper

squeeze lemon juice

1 teaspoon sea salt

Tomato & pomegranate dressing

125 ml (4 fl oz) reserved poaching stock

juice ½ lemon

45 ml (1 ½ fl oz) extra-virgin olive oil

salt and freshly ground white pepper

1 medium vine-ripened tomato, deseeded and finely diced

2 tablespoons pomegranate seeds

Preheat the oven to 160°C (320°F).

Tip the podded borlotti beans into a medium-sized roasting tin and scatter on the tomatoes, shallots, garlic and herbs. Mix the oil with the harissa, then add it to the stock. Pour over the beans and season with pepper. Don't add any salt at this stage. Cover with a sheet of greaseproof paper, followed by a sheet of foil. Bake for an hour then add the lemon juice and salt and return to the oven, uncovered, for a further 45 minutes, or until the beans are very tender and most of the liquid has evaporated.

Remove from the oven and leave the beans to cool in the stock. Once cool, tip the beans into a colander, reserving the poaching stock. Pick out and discard the thyme and bay leaves from the beans.

To make the dressing, whisk 125 ml (4 fl oz) of the reserved poaching stock with the lemon juice and oil. Season with salt and pepper, then stir in the tomato and pomegranate seeds. Pour the dressing over the beans and serve with warm bread.

Green beans with chermoula, shallots & feta

We are always looking for interesting ways to serve green beans, and this salad is one of our favourites. If you've got chermoula already made, you can knock this up in a matter of minutes. Chermoula makes a great accompaniment to all sorts of dishes but, in all honesty, we sometimes just eat it alone with lots of warm bread and butter.

SERVES 4

1 tablespoon butter

2 shallots, finely sliced

1 medium vine-ripened tomato, chopped

1 teaspoon Chermoula (see below)

200 g (7 oz) fine green beans, trimmed and cut in half lengthways

1 teaspoon currants

200 ml (7 fl oz) vegetable stock or water

salt and freshly ground black pepper

big squeeze lemon juice

60 g (2 ¼ oz) feta, crumbled

Chermoula

2 tablespoons cumin seeds

1 tablespoon coriander seeds

1¼ tablespoons sweet paprika

½ tablespoon ground ginger

2 cloves garlic, roughly chopped

2–4 small red chillies (to taste), deseeded and finely chopped

juice of 2 lemons

100 ml (3 ½ fl oz) olive oil, plus more to top the chermoula

½ teaspoon salt

½ teaspoon freshly ground black pepper

vegetable oil, to seal

To make the chermoula, toast the cumin seeds in a dry frying pan over a medium heat for 2–3 minutes until aromatic. Grind to a powder. Repeat with the coriander seeds. Tip both into the bowl of a food processor, along with the remaining ingredients. Whiz to a smooth purée, then taste and adjust the balance of seasonings, if need be.

Spoon the chermoula into a clean jar and cover the surface with a thin film of flavourless oil. If you're not eating it straight away, store in the fridge where it will keep for up to 2 months.

Melt the butter in a pan and add the shallots, tomato and chermoula. Sauté gently for 4 minutes, until slightly softened, then add the beans, currants and stock. Cook over a low–medium heat for 10 minutes, or until the beans are tender. Season with salt, pepper and lemon juice. Serve at room temperature, sprinkled with feta.

Rainbow chard with soused currants & pine nuts

Chard, like silverbeet, gives you plenty of bang for your buck, with its differently textured stem and leaf. In fact many recipes call for them to be cooked separately (as each requires a different approach) but in this cooked salad they are braised together and served, Moorish-style, with tangy soused currants and crunchy pine nuts. Plain chard or other leafy greens, like cavolo nero or kale, work just as well.

SERVES 4

400 g (14 oz) rainbow chard, stems
    and leaves separated
50 ml (2 fl oz) olive oil
2 shallots, finely sliced
2 cloves garlic, very finely chopped
juice of 1 lemon
50 g (1 ¾ oz) pine nuts
salt and freshly ground black pepper
extra-virgin olive oil, to serve

Soused currants

80 g (2 ¾ oz) currants
¼ star anise
2 cloves
125 ml (4 fl oz) apple juice (or use
    pomegranate juice, for a change)

For the soused currants, combine the currants star anise and clove in a small bowl. Bring the apple juice to the boil then pour it over the currants and leave them for a good 20 minutes to plump up and cool. If not using straight away, store them in a sealed jar in the fridge for up to 2 weeks.

Chop the chard stems to 1 cm (½ in) lengths and shred the leaves thickly.

Heat the oil in a large saucepan or casserole. Add the shallots, garlic and chard stalks and sauté over a low–medium heat for 10 minutes, or until soft and translucent. Add the chard leaves and lemon juice and cook for a further 5–6 minutes, stirring everything around from time to time, until the leaves have completely wilted and the stems are soft. Remove from the heat and stir in the soused currants. Season, to taste, with salt and pepper then set aside to cool.

Just before serving, heat the pine nuts in a dry frying pan over a medium heat for around 3 minutes, stirring frequently, until lightly toasted. Tip them over the chard and serve at room temperature with a glug of extra-virgin olive oil.

Potato salad with peas & Persian spices

This is not your standard potato salad, drowned in gloopy mayonnaise. In fact it's a salad only inasmuch as we like to serve it at room temperature! But it's one of our very favourite quick-and-easy dishes. It's a treat for the eyes too, with its vibrant greens and yellows, and the palate-jolting flavours really pack a punch. It also makes a great stuffing for sambusek (page 128).

SERVES 4

500 g (1 lb 2 oz) small new potatoes
2 tablespoons vegetable oil
½ teaspoon mustard seeds
1 shallot, very finely chopped
2–3 cloves garlic crushed with
    ½ teaspoon salt
½ teaspoon turmeric
¼ teaspoon ground cumin
1 small dried red chilli, crumbled*
¼ teaspoon freshly ground black
    pepper
120 g (4 ¼ oz) fresh or frozen
    baby peas
⅓ cup shredded coriander
    (cilantro) leaves
lime wedges, yoghurt and warm
    flatbread, to serve

Boil the potatoes in salted water for 18 minutes, or until just tender. Drain in a colander and leave them to dry. When cool enough to handle, peel away and discard the skins. Cut the potatoes into 1 cm (½ in) dice.

Heat the oil in a small frying pan and fry the mustard seeds over a high heat for a minute or until they start to splutter. Add the shallot and garlic paste, followed by the spices, and cook for around 10 minutes, stirring every now and then, until the onion is soft and translucent.

Meanwhile, cook the peas in briskly boiling water for 2–3 minutes, then drain them well.

Add the potatoes and peas to the spicy onion mixture and stir everything together gently but thoroughly. Cook over a gentle heat for 2–3 minutes, then taste and adjust the seasoning if need be. Remove the pan from the heat and cool to room temperature. Stir in the coriander and serve with lime wedges, yoghurt and plenty of warm flatbread.

*Note: In truth, chillies are used rather sparingly in Persian cooking, and really only feature in the south of the country, where the Indian influence is stronger. Use more, or fewer, depending on your preference.

Braised artichokes, preserved lemon & fingerling potatoes with basil crème fraîche

There's no denying that preparing fresh artichokes is a labour of love, but every year, as spring rolls around, we find ourselves craving them. This dish uses one of our favourite Eastern Mediterranean cooking techniques, of braising vegetables slowly in an oil-rich, aromatic liquor. We let the artichokes' flavour sing through, sharpened with preserved lemon and paired with creamy-fleshed, new-season fingerling potatoes. Any small, stubby or heritage-style, waxy potato will work well here; try nutty kipflers or, if you live in the UK, sweet Jersey Royals. With its smooth basil cream topping this dish is lovely served hot, warm or even cold.

SERVES 4

1 lemon

4 large globe artichokes, or 250 g (9 oz) artichoke hearts

200 g (7 oz) small fingerling or kipfler potatoes, peeled if you like

½ preserved lemon, cut into chunks

8 small shallots, peeled

1 head garlic, cloves separated and peeled

2 bay leaves

generous handful thyme sprigs, roughly torn

2 sprigs rosemary, roughly torn

¼ teaspoon coriander seeds, roughly crushed

¼ teaspoon Turkish red chilli flakes

sea salt and freshly ground black pepper

100 ml (3 ½ fl oz) vermouth or dry white wine

400 ml (14 fl oz) vegetable stock

100 ml (3 ½ fl oz) extra-virgin olive oil

Basil crème fraîche

80 ml (2 ½ fl oz) crème fraîche

finely grated zest of ½ lemon

50 g (1 ¾ oz) grated parmesan

½ cup loosely packed basil leaves

Preheat the oven to 180°C (350°F).

Prepare a bowl of cold water, acidulated with the juice of 1 lemon. Trim the artichoke stems, leaving about 4 cm (1 ½ in), and peel away the tough outer layer. Remove the outer hard leaves until you get to the lighter coloured inner leaves. Cut through the artichoke crossways, just above the heart, to remove all the leaves. Use a sharp knife or melon baller to remove the choke. Cut the artichokes in half lengthways, then drop them into the lemon water.

Put all the vegetables in a medium roasting tin and tuck the herbs in among them. Scatter on the coriander and chilli flakes and season with ¼ teaspoon each of salt and pepper. Pour in the wine, stock and oil and cover the tin with a sheet of greaseproof paper, followed by a sheet of foil.

Bake for 30 minutes, then remove the foil and paper and return to the oven for a further 20 minutes.

While the vegetables are braising, combine the crème fraîche, lemon zest and parmesan in a small saucepan and heat gently until the parmesan melts.

Transfer the vegetables and some of the braising liquor to a serving dish and season with a little extra salt and pepper. Tear the basil leaves roughly and add them to the crème fraîche. Spoon over the vegetables and serve.

Honey-roasted carrots with dates, dandelions & Moroccan dressing

This salad is a little bit Moroccan in inspiration, with its emphasis on the underlying sweetness of roasted carrots, fudgy nuggets of Medjool dates and a splash of orange flower water in the spicy dressing. We like to use a mixture of different coloured heirloom varieties of carrot, when we can find them, but otherwise, we'll use smaller Dutch carrots that come with their greenery still intact.

SERVES 4

60 g (2 ¼ oz) hazelnuts

400 g (14 oz) baby carrots
      (heirloom varieties, ideally),
      with tops attached

1 teaspoon honey

1 teaspoon pomegranate molasses

2 tablespoons thyme leaves

salt and freshly ground black
      pepper

2 tablespoons olive oil

1 shallot, finely sliced

55 g (2 oz) (2 generous handfuls)
      dandelion leaves or watercress
      leaves, well washed and
      roughly sliced

6 Medjool dates, pitted and diced

80 g (2 ¾ oz) soft goat's cheese,
      roughly crumbled

Moroccan dressing

1 clove garlic crushed with
      ½ teaspoon sea salt

¼ teaspoon ground cinnamon

¼ teaspoon ground cumin

¼ teaspoon sweet paprika

¼ teaspoon Turkish red chilli
      flakes

juice of 1 lemon

drizzle of honey

2 tablespoons extra-virgin olive oil

splash of orange flower water
      (optional)

Preheat the oven to 200°C (400°F).

Scatter the hazelnuts into a small baking tray and roast in the oven for 8–10 minutes, or until the skins darken and they start to smell toasty. Tip into a tea towel and rub away the skins. Chop the nuts roughly and set aside.

Scrub (or peel) the carrots well, leaving the tops and wispy end bits attached. Make sure you winkle out any bits of soil that can lodge in and around the stalks. Arrange the carrots in a heavy-based roasting tin, drizzle with honey and pomegranate molasses, scatter on the thyme leaves and season well. Toss them with the oil and roast for 25–30 minutes, or until well browned and cooked through. A little crunchy caramelization around the skinny ends is a good thing. Remove from the oven and set aside.

While the carrots are roasting, make the dressing. Put all the ingredients in a clean jar with a lid and shake together.

In a large mixing bowl, combine the shallot, dandelion leaves, dates and hazelnuts. Add the warm carrots and enough dressing to coat everything lightly. Add the crumbled cheese and serve straight away, ideally while the carrots are still warm.

Hot vegetable dishes

PEAS WITH PEARL ONIONS & PRESERVED LEMON CREAM ... 165

GRIDDLED BROCCOLINI WITH ALMONDS & HARISSA BUTTER ... 166

TUNISIAN-STYLE VEGETABLES ROASTED ON EMBERS ... 167

CHARRED CORNCOBS WITH ALMOND-SAFFRON BUTTER ... 168

SLOW-ROASTED EGGPLANT WITH SAFFRON-LEMON CREAM ... 171

TOMATO & EGGPLANT BAKED WITH TARRAGON-YOGHURT CUSTARD ... 173

BABY CARROT TAGINE WITH YOGHURT & HONEYED PINE NUTS ... 174

As we hope is obvious from the other chapters in this book, vegetables often take centre-stage on the Middle Eastern table. With so many wonderful ways of preparing them – from baking and frying to stuffing, grilling, braising and pickling, serving in soups, in salads and as smaller morsels – vegetables can offer an enormous and endless variety of flavours and textures.

The dishes in this chapter, in the main, celebrate a single vegetable as their hero. Some are simplicity itself: lightly grilled or barbecued and served with a spiced butter or fragrant dressing – these are the dishes that would work well as a side dish in a more traditional Western-style meal. Others are a little more complex in flavour, made up of richer layers of aromatics and spices, although none is technically challenging. As with the other recipes throughout the book, all are designed to be served as part of a selection – to be mixed-and-matched, perhaps with a grain-based dish and a salad, dip or savoury pastry.

Whatever you choose to serve them with, they all benefit from using the freshest seasonal produce you can lay your hands on.

Peas with pearl onions & preserved lemon cream

Sometimes, all we want with our peas is a knob of good butter and a few fresh mint leaves. At other times, we feel they are worthy of so much more. In this recipe, we combine them with tiny onions and garlic, roasted to bring out their inherent sweetness, and top the lot with a silky-rich cream, sharpened with tiny bursts of lemon.

SERVES 4

240 g (8 ½ oz) pearl onions (use the really tiny ones, if you can find them)

1 whole head of garlic, cloves separated

1 teaspoon za'atar

1 teaspoon sumac

1 teaspoon sea salt

40 ml (1 ¼ fl oz) extra-virgin olive oil, plus extra to drizzle

100 ml (3 ½ fl oz) white wine

80 ml (2 ½ fl oz) water

150 g (5 ½ oz) fresh peas

extra-virgin olive oil, to serve

Preserved lemon cream

1 tablespoon olive oil

1 large shallot, finely diced

½ preserved lemon, skin only, finely diced

1 tablespoon medium sherry

150 ml (5 fl oz) pure (double or heavy) cream

big squeeze lemon juice

Preheat the oven to 200°C (400°F).

Trim the root ends from the pearl onions, but leave the skins on. Slice them in half, lengthways. Trim off the woody ends from the garlic cloves, but leave the skins on. Toss the onions and garlic with the za'atar, sumac, salt and oil then arrange in a roasting tin, cut-side up. Pour in the wine and water and roast for 20 minutes, stirring once or twice, until the liquid has evaporated and they are starting to caramelize.

Meanwhile, make the preserved lemon cream. Warm the oil in small pan. Add the diced shallot and preserved lemon and sweat very gently for 5–10 minutes. Turn up the heat and deglaze the pan with sherry. When it has nearly all bubbled away, add the cream and simmer for 3–4 minutes.

Cook the peas in briskly boiling water for 2–3 minutes, or until tender, then drain them well.

When ready to serve, combine the peas and the roasted onion mixture in a serving bowl. Add a drizzle of extra-virgin olive oil and toss everything together gently.

Add a squeeze of lemon juice to the cream and drizzle it over the peas. Add a drizzle of olive oil and serve straight away.

Griddled broccolini with almonds & harissa butter

Broccolini, broccoli and their purple-sprouting cousin all work beautifully here. They benefit from the light charring of a barbecue or griddle pan and from the spicy buttery sauce and hint of a crunch from the toasted almonds. But, in all honesty, sometimes we forget about the almonds, and just melt the butter and drizzle it over, or dip it, like we would asparagus.

SERVES 4

400 g (14 oz) broccolini or broccoli*
Harissa Butter (page 56), melted
30 g (1 oz) flaked almonds

Bring a large pan of salted water to the boil. Blanch the broccolini in batches for 1–2 minutes, or until barely tender (it will be cooked further on the griddle) then transfer to a bowl of iced water to stop the cooking and preserve the bright green colour. Drain in a colander and leave to air-dry.

While the broccolini is drying, heat a ridged cast-iron griddle pan over a high heat. When it is shimmering hot, sear the broccolini in batches for 4–5 minutes, turning the spears occasionally to ensure they char evenly with stripes from the griddle pan. Transfer to a warm dish and continue with the rest of the broccolini.

When ready to serve, toast the almonds in a dry frying pan and scatter over the broccolini. Serve with the melted harissa butter on the side.

*Note: If using broccoli, separate it into small florets before blanching. Purple-sprouting broccoli can have rather woody stems, which you will need to trim and peel, as well as cutting away some of the excess leaves. Whichever vegetable you use, the important thing is that it should all be of a similar size to ensure even cooking.

Tunisian-style vegetables roasted on embers

This fragrant Tunisian marinade is one of our all-time favourites and makes these roasted vegetables a fabulous non-meat option at a barbecue. Serve with warm flatbread or a fairly neutral grain-based dish, such as buttered couscous or rice. They would also be lovely with a bitterleaf salad alongside.

You can always roast the vegetables in the oven*, of course, although you won't get quite the same light charring and smoky depth. The quantities of vegetables given here are really just a suggestion; feel free to choose your own favourites.

SERVES 4

4 Dutch or heirloom carrots, scraped, but with 1 cm (½ in) stalk left attached

4 small onions, unpeeled

2 long red capsicums (peppers), halved lengthways and deseeded

2 baby fennel, halved lengthways

4 Swiss brown mushrooms, stalks removed

2 long red chillies, halved lengthways and deseeded

4 baby zucchini (courgettes), ends trimmed

¼ small butternut pumpkin (squash), skin left on, cut into thin wedges

Greek-style yoghurt, to serve

Tunisian marinade

1 teaspoon coriander seeds

½ teaspoon caraway seeds

½ cup flat-leaf parsley leaves

½ cup mint leaves

½ cup tarragon leaves

2 tablespoons dill fronds

125 ml (4 fl oz) olive oil

1 tablespoon good-quality harissa (or see page 56)

2 teaspoons finely chopped preserved lemon, skin only

1 teaspoon salt

Build your barbecue so as to create a hot area and a cooler area (or heat a gas barbecue accordingly). Allow the fiercest flames to die down, leaving white-hot embers.

To make the marinade, heat the coriander seeds in a dry frying pan over a medium heat for about 2 minutes, until lightly toasted and aromatic, then grind to a powder. Repeat with the caraway seeds. Tip both into the bowl of a food processor and add the herbs, oil, harissa, preserved lemon and salt. Whiz to a smooth purée.

Toss the prepared vegetables with a generous third of the marinade. They must all be well coated. Reserve the rest of the marinade to serve as a sauce after cooking.

Cook the vegetables in stages, starting with those that will take the longest to cook. Start the cooking over the hottest part of your barbecue to char them, then move them to lower heat. Don't move them constantly, but do make sure that they don't blacken. Once tender, transfer to a serving platter and keep warm.

Serve the roasted vegetables with the rest of the marinade for drizzling, as well as with warm flatbreads and lots of thick, Greek-style yoghurt.

*Note: To oven roast, first preheat the oven to 220°C (425°F). When the oven is hot, preheat two heavy-based roasting tins for 5 minutes. Carefully arrange the vegetables in the hot tins and roast for 25–30 minutes, shaking and turning them around a couple of times. When they are tender and have caramelized to a good, deep golden brown, remove from the oven.

Charred corncobs with almond-saffron butter

Whenever we visit the Middle East, we are drawn to the glowing coals of street-stand braziers. They proliferate along the waterfront promenades and are dotted along alleyways and city squares. At night-time the air is thick with smoke and the mingled aromas of grilling food. While little meat skewers are inevitably associated with Middle Eastern countries, grilled chestnuts (in the winter) and corncobs (in the summer) often appeal to us more.

Charring adds a lovely smokiness to sweetcorn cobs, and they are wonderful on a hot summer's night. If you don't want to light a barbecue, then parboil the corn in salted water (which should take between 3–10 minutes, depending on the size and freshness of the corn), and finish them off on a hot griddle pan. Serve with any of the savoury butters on pages 52–56, although the almond-saffron butter is one of our favourites.

SERVES 4

4 corncobs
up to 125 g (4 ½ oz) Almond-saffron
    Butter (page 55)
olive oil
salt and freshly ground black
    pepper
lime wedges, to serve

Peel back the husks from the corncobs and pull away and discard the silks. Submerge the husks (but not the cobs) in a bowl of water for 15–20 minutes, which will prevent them burning on the barbecue. At the same time, soak 4 lengths of string in water, too.

Smear each corncob with a generous tablespoon of the butter, then shake off excess water from the husks and pull them back up around the corn. Tie in place with the wet string. Place the cobs on a charcoal grill and cook for 15–20 minutes, or until tender, turning regularly so they cook evenly.

Alternatively, brush the corncobs generously with olive oil and cook them on the barbecue using the husks as a nifty sort of handle. This method gives the corn a lovely rustic charring. Then smear generously with the butter as you serve them.

Season, to taste, and serve with more almond-saffron butter and lime wedges.

Slow-roasted eggplant with saffron-lemon cream

This dish is luscious and undeniably rich, but proves to be an absolute winner whenever we prepare it. The long, skinny Japanese eggplants work best here, but if you can't find them, then use two regular ones instead. The vine leaf garnish is very pretty, but certainly optional. It does make for a lovely presentation on special occasions.

SERVES 4

3 Japanese eggplants (aubergines) (around 650 g / 1 lb 7 oz)

2 large onions, cut into large dice

2 cloves garlic, sliced

2 long red chillies, cut on the diagonal into 1 cm (½ in) pieces

1 teaspoon ground cumin

1 teaspoon ground coriander

1 teaspoon Turkish red chilli flakes

juice of 1 lemon

200 ml (7 fl oz) olive oil

200 ml (7 fl oz) water or vegetable stock

salt and freshly ground white pepper

2 vine leaves, to garnish (fresh, pickled or vacuum-packed, see page 265)*

Saffron-lemon cream

450 ml (14 fl oz) pure (double or heavy) cream

20 saffron threads

juice of ½ lemon

salt and freshly ground white pepper

Preheat the oven to 200°C (400°F).

Peel the eggplants then quarter them lengthways. If using regular eggplants, cut them into fat wedges.

Combine the eggplant, onion, garlic and chillies in a mixing bowl. Add the spices, lemon juice and oil and mix everything together thoroughly.

Tip into a roasting tin and pour in the water or stock. Season generously then roast for 35 minutes, uncovered. Shake the tin every now and then, and gently turn the vegetables around in the spicy liquid so they cook evenly.

While the eggplant is roasting, make the saffron-lemon cream. Pour the cream into a small saucepan and bring to the boil. Add the saffron, lemon juice and a generous pinch of salt and pepper. Simmer for 2 minutes then remove from the heat.

After the eggplants been cooking for 25 minutes, or when they are tender and starting to brown, pour on the saffron-lemon cream. Cook for a further 10 minutes. Take the baking dish to the table and serve the eggplants hot or warm.

*Note: If using fresh vine leaves, blanch them in boiling water for 30 seconds and refresh in cold water. Pickled or vacuum-packed vine leaves should be soaked for 10 minutes then thoroughly dried. Brush the dried leaves all over with olive oil and arrange on a flat baking tray lined with baking paper. Cover with a second layer of paper and weight with another tray. This keeps them flat. Bake in the oven preheated to 160°C (315°C) for 8–10 minutes, or until crisp and translucent.

Tomato & eggplant baked with tarragon-yoghurt custard

With its creamy topping of herby yoghurt custard, this comforting dish is reminiscent of a Greek moussaka and makes a lovely supper dish with a simple salad alongside.

SERVES 4

1 kg (2 lb 4 oz) eggplants (aubergine), about 3 large eggplants

salt

40 ml (1 ¼ fl oz) olive oil

1 large onion, finely chopped

2 cloves garlic, finely chopped

1 teaspoon ground allspice

700 g (1 lb 9 oz) vine-ripened tomatoes, roughly chopped (or use 2 x 400 g / 14 oz tins chopped Italian tomatoes)

freshly ground black pepper

150 ml (5 fl oz) vegetable oil

300 ml (10 ½ fl oz) crème fraîche

1 ⅛ teaspoons cornflour (cornstarch)

2 tablespoons water

150g (5 ½ oz) Greek-style yoghurt

1 egg

¼ cup flat-leaf parsley leaves, finely chopped

2 tablespoons finely snipped chives

1 tablespoon finely chopped tarragon leaves

50 g (1 ¾ oz) cheddar or parmesan, grated

Slice the eggplants into thick rounds. Layer them in a colander, sprinkling generously with salt as you go. Sit a plate on top and leave them in the sink for 30 minutes to draw out moisture. After degorging, rinse the eggplants and pat each slice dry with kitchen paper.*

Meanwhile, heat the olive oil in a heavy-based saucepan. Add the onion, garlic and allspice and sweat for about 10 minutes, or until they have softened. Add the tomatoes, season with pepper, then simmer gently for about 15 minutes, or until the tomatoes are very soft.

Add a good glug of vegetable oil to a clean frying pan over a medium heat. Add slices of eggplant to the pan, without overcrowding it, and fry over a medium–high heat for 5–10 minutes, turning them around in the oil so they colour evenly. They should become soft and a rich golden brown. Drain on kitchen paper while you continue with more oil and eggplant slices.

Preheat the oven to 180°C (350°F). Arrange a layer of eggplant slices over the bottom of a medium-sized casserole (a 23 cm / 9 in Le Creuset is ideal). Spread a layer of the tomato mixture on top. Continue layering, finishing with a layer of tomato.

Put the crème fraîche in a small saucepan and bring to a boil. Simmer for 5 minutes then remove from the heat. Meanwhile, mix the cornflour with the water and add it to the yoghurt along with the egg. Beat well, then tip into the crème fraîche. Stir in the chopped herbs and half of the grated cheese then pour over the tomato-eggplant mix and spread out evenly.

Bake for 25 minutes, then sprinkle on the remaining cheese and return to the oven for a further 10 minutes, or until the topping is puffed and golden. Once cooked, remove from the oven and allow to rest for 10 minutes before serving.

*Note: Some people tell you not to bother with salting (degorging) eggplants as nowadays they are cultivated to be less bitter than they were in the past. When you're frying them, however, we think it's important not to omit this step, as it has less to do with the flavour than in drawing out moisture and thereby reducing the amount of oil absorbed. It also helps to fry at a fairly high temperature, as this also reduces the absorption.

Baby carrot tagine with yoghurt & honeyed pine nuts

This unusual, subtly sweet and spicy carrot tagine is made wonderfully rich and tangy with the last-minute addition of yoghurt. Serve it with plain buttered couscous, Wedding Couscous (page 219) or Mixed Spring Greens with Golden Raisins & Couscous (page 217). It is also delicious with Long-grain Rice with Lemon & Toasted Almonds (page 193).

SERVES 4

40 ml (1 ¼ fl oz) olive oil

a generous knob of butter

1 large onion, finely grated

1 large carrot, finely grated

2 cloves garlic, finely grated

1 teaspoon ground cumin

1 teaspoon ground coriander

½ teaspoon turmeric

½ teaspoon finely ground black
   pepper

1 tablespoon honey

400 g (14 oz) tin chickpeas, well
   rinsed and drained

400 g (14 oz) baby (or Dutch-style)
   carrots, with tops attached

600 ml (21 fl oz) vegetable stock

200 g (7 oz) natural yoghurt

1 tablespoon cornflour (cornstarch)

1 egg yolk

⅓ cup coriander (cilantro) leaves

Honeyed pine nuts

1 tablespoon butter

1 teaspoon honey

60 g (2 ¼ oz) pine nuts

good pinch salt

Preheat the oven to 180°C (350°F).

Heat the oil and butter in a large flame-proof casserole. Add the grated onion and carrot, the garlic, spices and honey. Sauté over a low heat for about 10 minutes, or until the onion is soft and translucent and the carrot is meltingly soft.

Add the chickpeas and whole baby carrots, then pour in the stock. Bring to the boil, then lower the heat, cover the pan and cook in the oven for 30 minutes.

Remove the tagine from oven and transfer it to the stovetop over a medium heat.

In a small bowl, whisk the yoghurt with the cornflour and egg yolk. Add a big spoonful of the tagine cooking liquid to the yoghurt and stir it in well. Tip the yoghurt into the tagine, bring to a simmer and cook, stirring, until the sauce thickens slightly.

Heat the butter and honey over a medium heat in a small frying pan. When the butter has melted, add the pine nuts and salt and fry for around 2 minutes until they turn golden brown.

Stir the coriander leaves into the tagine. Drain the pine nuts and sprinkle on top of the tagine as you serve it.

Grains

CUCUMBER, QUINOA & TARRAGON-YOGHURT SALAD ... 178

TOASTED QUINOA WITH CORIANDER, LIME & CRUNCHY PUMPKIN ... 180

GOLDEN BULGUR WHEAT WITH APPLE, RAISINS & YOGHURT ... 182

SPICY TURKISH KISIR ... 183

TOASTED NUTS, SEEDS & GRAINS WITH SMASHED CHERRIES, HERBS & GOAT'S CURD ... 185

FARRO WITH SLOW-ROASTED TOMATOES, ARTICHOKES, OLIVES & OREGANO ... 187

FREEKEH PILAF WITH SPICED ROAST PUMPKIN & SHALLOTS ... 188

If there is one foodstuff than can be said to be a universal staple it must, surely, be the plant group called grains. Staple cereal grains, such as wheat, rice and corn, have been cultivated for many thousands of years, with some historians even arguing that it was this very act that civilized humankind, forcing us to abandon our wandering ways and settle down to farm.

In the countries of the Middle East, wheat and rice (which has a chapter all of its own following this one) are the main staples, with wheat tipping the scales as the main grain of choice. This is possibly because rice is not an indigenous crop, while wheat originates in the region (in the Fertile Crescent between the Tigris and Euphrates rivers).

Wheat is a hugely versatile grain that can be eaten in many different ways. The whole grains (with the husk and outer bran still intact) are used in pilafs and stuffings and as a base for cold salads. Refined grains have their outer husks removed, making them faster cooking, and ideal for creamy, porridge-like dishes. Both these types of whole grain are frequently paired with beans, pulses or dairy (or animal protein) for a more complete meal. Milled grains are those that are flattened into flakes, ground into meal or, at the furthest extreme, into flour for our daily bread (see pages 32–43).

The grain that is most readily identifiable as Middle Eastern is probably burghul – or bulgur wheat – thanks to its use in the ubiquitous salad, tabbouleh. Bulgur wheat is cracked and roughly ground, making it quicker to cook and giving it a lovely nutty, earthy flavour. In addition to being a main part of all kinds of cold salads, we also love to use it in patties, stuffings and hearty pilafs.

In this chapter we also offer Middle Eastern-inspired recipes for ancient strains of wheat, such as farro and freekeh, and for the tiny seeds called quinoa (although the latter originates in South America!). These starchy grains are all at their best when used as a blank canvas for carrying stronger flavours. Whether in hot, hearty dishes or in cool salads, we like to team them with punchy olives, the acid sharpness of tomatoes and citrus, vibrant herbs and palate-provoking spices, finishing with a generous slick of olive oil. This approach brings their more subtle flavour to life and enhances their robust, chewy texture.

Cucumber, quinoa & tarragon-yoghurt salad

We are huge fans of quinoa. Botanically speaking, quinoa is a relative of leafy vegetables like spinach and beets, and not cereal grains like wheat. Its tiny seeds are nutritional super-foods, with high levels of protein, fibre, iron and other essential elements. Best of all perhaps, it is amazingly quick and easy to prepare. It works well as a gluten-free substitute in dishes where you might otherwise use couscous or cracked wheat, but has its own delicate flavour and texture. As a bonus, its near-translucent pearly sheen is very pretty. This quality is shown off to great advantage in this light summer salad with its refreshing aniseed flavours of fennel and tarragon.

SERVES 4

100 g (3 ½ oz) quinoa

350 ml (12 fl oz) boiling vegetable stock or water

1 Lebanese (short) cucumber, peeled, deseeded and cut into 5 mm (¼ in) dice

½ small fennel, cut into 5 mm (¼ in) dice

a handful of nasturtium leaves (optional)

a handful of edible flowers (optional)

3 tablespoons chopped tarragon leaves

2 tablespoons chopped flat-leaf parsley leaves

2 tablespoons snipped chives

1 teaspoon dried mint

50 g (1 ¾ fl oz) Greek-style yoghurt

40 ml (1 ¼ fl oz) extra-virgin olive oil

juice of ½ lemon

salt and freshly ground black pepper

100 g (3 ½ oz) soft, creamy feta, crumbled

Put the quinoa into a pan and cover generously with boiling stock or water. Simmer for 10 minutes then tip into a sieve and leave to drain for 10 minutes or so, stirring with your fingers every now and then to help drain away any excess moisture. Pat dry with kitchen paper.

Tip the cooled quinoa into a large mixing bowl. Add the cucumber, fennel, leaves, flowers and fresh and dried herbs. Pour on the yoghurt, oil and lemon juice and season with salt and pepper. Finally, add the crumbled feta and mix everything together gently. Check the seasoning and chill for 10–15 minutes until ready to serve.

Toasted quinoa with coriander, lime & crunchy pumpkin

This is a more robust dish than the salad on page 178 and, as such, we think the quinoa benefits from a light toasting before cooking, to bring out the nutty flavour.

It is rather common to use fried onion as a crunchy garnish for Middle Eastern dishes (see page 194) and we've recently started applying the same treatment to shredded pumpkin (squash), which also has a sweet base note. It works brilliantly! Serve this dish, which is full of spicy, tangy flavours, warm or at room temperature.

SERVES 4

100 g (3 ½ oz) quinoa

350 ml (12 fl oz) vegetable stock
    or water

150 g (5 ½ oz) peeled pumpkin
    (squash), grated

250 ml (9 fl oz) vegetable oil

½ teaspoon ground cumin

½ teaspoon sea salt

3 spring onions (scallions),
    trimmed and finely diced

4 vine-ripened cherry tomatoes,
    diced

1 ½ cups coriander (cilantro)
    leaves, shredded

¼ cup purple basil leaves (or use
    ordinary basil)

1 teaspoon Turkish red chilli
    flakes

Lime-sumac dressing

juice of ½ lime

30 ml (1 fl oz) extra-virgin
    olive oil

1 teaspoon sumac

½ teaspoon ground cumin

salt and freshly ground black
    pepper

Heat a small saucepan and dry-fry the quinoa for 2–3 minutes, stirring to ensure it colours evenly. Add the stock or water – it will bubble vigorously and then settle down. Bring to the boil then simmer for 10 minutes. Then tip into a sieve and set aside.

Put the grated pumpkin in a tea towel and squeeze to extract as much moisture as you can.

Heat the vegetable oil in a small frying pan until it starts to shimmer. Add the pumpkin to the oil and cook for 4–5 minutes over a medium heat, moving it constantly in the oil to ensure it colours evenly. You may need to do this in batches. Drain in a sieve and then on kitchen paper. Sprinkle with cumin and salt and set aside.

To make the dressing, whisk all the ingredients together in a bowl and set aside.

Tip the quinoa into a serving bowl and toss through the spring onions, tomatoes, coriander, basil and chilli flakes. Add the dressing and stir well. Top with the fried pumpkin and serve straight away.

Golden bulgur wheat with apple, raisins & yoghurt

Bulgur – or cracked wheat – is hugely popular in the Middle East where, in many countries, it's a far more prevalent staple than rice. Fine-grade bulgur wheat is used as a flavour-carrying base for herb-laden salads such as Tabbouleh (page 145), and for the crisp outer shell of Kibbeh (page 118). Medium and coarse bulgur is more commonly used for pilafs and stuffings and it has a lovely nutty, earthy flavour.

One of the great virtues of bulgur wheat is that you don't need to cook it. Fine-grade bulgur, in particular, only needs a 15 minute soak in warm water to plump and soften it. The medium and coarse versions need a little longer, but their slight chewiness is part of the appeal.

SERVES 4

200 g (7 oz) fine bulgur wheat

1 teaspoon ground cumin

1 teaspoon ground coriander

½ teaspoon turmeric

½ teaspoon Turkish red chilli
    flakes

1 star anise, ground to a powder

100 ml (3 ½ fl oz) olive oil

juice of 1 lime

30 g (1 oz) golden raisins, roughly
    chopped

1 Granny Smith apple, peeled and
    chopped

40 g (1 ½ oz) roasted hazelnuts,
    chopped

½ small preserved lemon, skin
    only, finely chopped

¼ cup shredded coriander
    (cilantro) leaves

1 teaspoon sea salt

½ teaspoon freshly ground black
    pepper

Greek-style yoghurt, to serve

Soak the bulgur wheat in warm water for 15 minutes. Tip into a sieve and, using your hands, squeeze out as much water as you can. Then scrape into a tea towel and twist to extract even more water. When it's as dry as you can manage, transfer to a large mixing bowl.

Stir the spices into the oil and lime juice then tip into the bulgur wheat. Add the golden raisins, chopped apple, hazelnuts, preserved lemon and coriander and toss everything together gently. Add the salt and pepper, then taste and adjust the balance of flavour to your liking. Add more lime juice, oil or salt and pepper if needed. Serve straight away with lots of yoghurt.

Spicy Turkish kisir

In Lebanon and Syria they have tabbouleh; in Turkey they have *kısır*. The ingredients in *kısır* vary from town to town, but in the south-east of the country it is usually pepped up with spicy red pepper paste and pomegranate molasses. While Arab versions of tabbouleh are, in essence, herb salads flecked with bulgur, Turkish *kısır* is staunchly grain based. Both salads, though, make a great addition to a mezze table, and are best eaten scooped up in little lettuce leaves.

Don't be tempted to increase the amount of boiling water here: it doesn't look like a lot of liquid, but the bulgur will soften further in the juice from the tomatoes and the dressing.

SERVES 4

200 g (7 oz) fine bulgur wheat

125 ml (4 fl oz) boiling water

1 tablespoon tomato paste

1 teaspoon Turkish red pepper paste*

juice of 1 lemon

1 teaspoon pomegranate molasses

60 ml (2 fl oz) extra-virgin olive oil

1 long green chilli, deseeded and finely chopped

3 large vine-ripened tomatoes, chopped

5 spring onions (scallions), finely chopped

1 cup flat-leaf parsley leaves, chopped

1 cup mint leaves, chopped

sea salt and freshly ground white pepper

baby lettuce leaves, to serve

Soak the bulgur in the boiling water for 15 minutes, then tip into a large bowl. There's no need to squeeze out the water, as you want it to keep absorbing moisture.

Add the pastes, lemon juice, molasses and oil to the bulgur. Use clean hands to work the grains so that the pastes and liquid are evenly distributed and the bulgur is tinted a pretty pale pink. Add the chilli, tomatoes, spring onions and herbs and mix well. Taste and adjust the seasoning by adding salt and pepper and more lemon juice or pomegranate molasses if required.

Mound the salad onto a serving platter and garnish with baby lettuce leaves. Alternatively, use wet hands to form the mixture into walnut-sized balls and serve them nestled in the lettuce leaves.

*Note: You'll find Turkish red pepper paste in Middle Eastern grocers and some specialist food stores. Alternatively, use the recipe on page 69.

Toasted nuts, seeds & grains with smashed cherries, herbs & goat's curd

We love the speckled combination of bulgur and red quinoa in this fabulous mixed salad. It's all about the marriage of varying textures – the bite of the grains, the crunch of the nuts and the juicy cherries – with intense bursts of flavour. Don't skimp on the dressing (which is fabulously zingy), as the bulgur and quinoa will drink it up.

SERVES 4

100 g (3 ½ oz) medium-coarse bulgur wheat

50 g (1 ¾ oz) red quinoa

70 g (2 ½ oz) pecan nuts

2 tablespoons sunflower seeds

2 generous handfuls watercress or rocket (arugula) leaves

1 large shallot, very finely sliced

1 long green chilli, deseeded and finely shredded

½ cup shredded mint leaves

½ cup shredded flat-leaf parsley leaves

salt and freshly ground black pepper

12 plump cherries, pickled and lightly smashed*

100 g (3 ½ oz) soft goat's curd or feta, crumbled

Lime-ginger dressing

45 ml (1 ½ fl oz) lime juice

30 ml (1 fl oz) pomegranate molasses

160 ml (5 ¼ fl oz) olive oil

½ teaspoon grated fresh ginger

¼ teaspoon Turkish red chilli flakes

Salt and freshly ground black pepper

Soak the bulgur wheat in boiling water for 25–30 minutes. Tip into a sieve and, using your hands, squeeze out as much water as you can. Then scrape into a tea towel and twist to extract even more water. When it's as dry as you can manage, transfer to a large mixing bowl.

While the bulgur wheat is soaking, heat a small saucepan and dry-fry the quinoa for 2–3 minutes, stirring to ensure it toasts evenly. Cover generously with boiling water – it will bubble vigorously and then settle down. Simmer for 10 minutes then tip into a sieve and leave to drain for 5 minutes or so, stirring with your fingers every now and then to help drain away any excess moisture. Tip onto a shallow tray and pat as dry as you can with kitchen paper. Add the cooled quinoa to the bowl with the bulgur wheat.

Heat a frying pan and dry-toast the pecan nuts for 2–3 minutes, stirring to ensure they colour evenly. Chop them roughly then add to the mixing bowl, along with all the remaining ingredients, except for the goat's curd.

Shake all the dressing ingredients together in a jar then pour on to the salad – you may not need all of it, but the bulgur and quinoa will soak it up quite thirstily. Mix everything together gently, then taste and add more salt and black pepper if necessary. Gently mix in the crumbled goat's curd and serve straight away.

*Note: When fresh cherries aren't in season use 100 g (3 ½ oz) dried cherries as an equally delicious variation.

Farro with slow-roasted tomatoes, artichokes, olives & oregano

We are relatively new converts to farro, which, like spelt and kamut, is another ancient variety of wheat. Farro – also known as emmer wheat – was one of the earliest crops to be domesticated in the Fertile Crescent and it has a lovely nutty, chewy quality. Farro is sometimes accused of being a little bland, but we find it helps enormously to cook it with plenty of aromatics before you add any other ingredients. This makes it so comfortingly delicious that we have been known to eat it on its own – albeit with lots of butter, salt and freshly ground black pepper.

We often treat farro like bulgur wheat, couscous and other starchy grains and use it cold, as a base for salads but it also works superbly well in hot dishes. We like to pair it with robust flavours, such as the olives, chilli and slow-roasted tomatoes in this Mediterranean-inspired pilaf.

SERVES 4

150 g (5 ½ oz) farro
500 ml (16 fl oz) water
1 tablespoon cider vinegar
½ tablespoon Turkish red pepper paste* (or use tomato paste)
½ teaspoon salt
½ stick celery
1 bay leaf
1 sprig thyme, plus ½ tablespoon thyme leaves
30 ml (1 fl oz) olive oil
60 g (2 ¼ oz) parmesan
30 g (1 oz) pitted black olives
2 good-quality artichokes in oil (or see page 158), torn apart
6 Slow-roasted Tomatoes (see page 79)
¼ cup chopped fresh oregano leaves
salt and freshly ground black pepper
big squeeze lemon juice
Labneh, strained for 12 hours (page 73), to serve

Put the farro in a medium saucepan with the water, vinegar, pepper paste, salt, celery, bay leaf and thyme. Bring to the boil, then lower the heat and simmer for around 30 minutes, without stirring. The liquid will absorb as it cooks, but add a little more water if it gets too dry. When all the liquid has absorbed and the farro is tender (it will still have a slight chewy bite), tip into a sieve and fish out and discard the aromatics.

Transfer the farro to a large mixing bowl and stir in the olive oil and half of the parmesan. Fold in the olives, artichokes, slow-roasted tomatoes and oregano and taste for seasonings. Add salt and pepper if need be, then add a big squeeze of lemon juice, top with labneh, the rest of the parmesan and serve straight away.

*Note: You'll find Turkish red pepper paste in Middle Eastern grocers and some specialist food stores. Alternatively, use the recipe on page 69.

Freekeh pilaf with spiced roast pumpkin & shallots

Although it's a relative newcomer to Western kitchens, freekeh has been used around the Middle East and in Turkey for millennia and we love it for its intense savoury flavour. To make freekeh, wheat grains are harvested while still immature and green. They are then set on fire, which burns away the chaff, leaving the young kernels intact and imparting an intense, smoky flavour. In this hearty pilaf, freekeh pairs beautifully with the sweetness of the roasted pumpkin and shallots. It would make a wonderful meal on a cold winter's night.

SERVES 4

200 g (7 oz) freekeh

60 ml (2 fl oz) olive oil

1 teaspoon allspice

½ teaspoon ground cinnamon

1 teaspoon Turkish red chilli flakes

2 cloves garlic, peeled but left whole

10 shallots, 2 halved and 8 left
    whole

1 bay leaf

2 sprigs thyme

750 ml–1 litre (24–35 fl oz)
    vegetable stock

400 g (14 oz) butternut pumpkin
    (squash), peeled and cut into
    2 cm (1 in) cubes

2 teaspoons pomegranate
    molasses

½ teaspoon salt

½ teaspoon freshly ground black
    pepper

lemon wedges and natural yoghurt,
    to serve

Pick through the freekeh to remove any debris or grit, then rinse it thoroughly under running water and leave to drain.

Heat half the oil in a heavy-based flame-proof casserole. Add the freekeh, allspice, cinnamon and half the chilli flakes and stir well to coat with the oil. Add the garlic and the 2 halved shallots, together with the herbs and 750 ml (24 fl oz) of the stock. Bring to the boil then lower the heat and simmer very gently for up to an hour. Resist the temptation to stir, as this makes the freekeh gluggy, but check every 20 minutes or so to make sure it's not catching on the bottom of the pan. Add a little more stock if necessary.

While the freekeh is cooking, preheat the oven to 200°C (400°F).

Combine the remaining 8 shallots and the pumpkin cubes in a large mixing bowl. Add the other ingredients, including the remaining oil and chilli flakes, and toss everything together well.

Separate out the shallots and transfer them to a small roasting tin. Roast for 10 minutes, by which time they should be starting to soften and brown around the edges. Add the pumpkin and roast for a further 10 minutes, then test to see if the pumpkin is tender. If not, lower the heat to 180°C (350°F) and roast for another 10 minutes.

When the freekeh is cooked (it will still be a little chewy at the centre), check to see if all the liquid has evaporated. If not, turn up the heat for a few minutes until it is all absorbed. Remove from the heat and fish out the bay leaf and thyme if it bothers you. The onion and garlic will have cooked down into the pilaf, so give it a good stir and taste for seasonings. Add extra salt and pepper if need be.

Gently fold in the roasted pumpkin and shallots and serve straight away with lemon wedges and natural yoghurt.

Rice

PERSIAN 'BAGHALI POLOW' WITH BORLOTTI BEANS & DILL ... 192

LONG-GRAIN RICE WITH LEMON & TOASTED ALMONDS ... 193

LEBANESE DIRTY RICE ... 194

EGGPLANT PILAF WITH YOGHURT & ZHOUG ... 197

ZUCCHINI BLOSSOM & PRESERVED LEMON RISOTTO WITH RICOTTA & PARMESAN ... 198

Rice originated in the East as many as twelve thousand years ago and we can largely thank Arab traders for delivering it to the rest of the world. It is a grain that arouses fierce loyalty and passionate devotion, and in many cultures it is the axis around which every meal revolves.

Although rice is not indigenous to the Middle East, it has been eagerly embraced by the countries that make up the region; with Turks and Iranians elevating rice-cookery to a culinary art form. (We firmly believe the legendary *tah deeg* – the crunchy, golden base of Persian polows – is an art well worth mastering!) Rice is most often served as a stomach-filling accompaniment to grills or braises, sometimes flavoured with aromatics or drizzled with a buttery saffron liquid. But it can also form the heart of the dish itself, cooked together with other ingredients. This is a technique which is at its zenith in sophisticated Turkish pilafs, Persian polows and Arab biryani-style dishes.

In the main, Middle Easterners use long-grain rice varieties, as these tend to be the least starchy, making them ideal for dishes where the individual grains are intended to remain distinctly dry, fluffy and separate after cooking. Shorter-grain rice is also used, but primarily for stuffings, where it is required to clump together stickily (see pages 105 and 108 for some examples).

Early in his cooking career, Greg spent a whole year making risotto in a restaurant in the north of Italy, and it's a dish he never tires of. So, while it's not a Middle Eastern technique, we are convinced that creamy risottos work very well with Middle Eastern ingredients. We couldn't resist including an example here.

And, finally, as in the West, the shortest grained rice of all is used for puddings. In some Middle Eastern countries entire stores are dedicated to this style of milk-based dessert and we offer a recipe for one of our favourites in the dessert chapter on page 243.

Persian 'baghali polow' with borlotti beans & dill

Our travels around Iran throughout 2009 and 2010 gave us a deep love and respect for Persian cooking – and especially for their impressive repertoire of rice dishes, which ranges from buttery saffron *chelow* to complex layered *polows*, incorporating meat, vegetables, nuts, herbs and all manner of exotic spices. *Baghali polow* is one of our favourites, as it showcases the marvellous affinity between broad beans and dill. Some versions include a final drizzle of melted saffron butter, but this is one rare occasion where we prefer to hold back on the saffron and keep the flavour focus on the vegetables and herbs. The borlotti beans are not strictly traditional, but they add interesting extra texture and flavour.

Persian rice is generally cooked by a parboil-rinse-steam absorption method and it's a technique, once mastered, that results in glorious light, fluffy and fragrant rice. Most important of all is the crunchy golden crust (the *tah deeg*) that this method creates on the bottom of the pot. In the recipe, below, we go into some detail about the way to prepare it and we recommend that you follow it quite carefully. In our experience, it can take a few attempts to really get the hang of the technique, but it's well worth persevering.

SERVES 4

650 g (1 lb 7 oz) broad beans (fava) in the pod or 200 g (7 oz) frozen broad beans

400 g (14 oz) fresh borlotti beans in the pod

200 g (7 oz) basmati rice

1 tablespoon sea salt

50 ml (2 fl oz) vegetable oil

⅓ cup chopped dill sprigs

1 heaped teaspoon dried mint

30 g (1 oz) unsalted butter, melted

1 clove garlic, lightly crushed

1 long strip lemon peel

Greek-style yoghurt, to serve

Bring a saucepan of water to the boil. Pod the broad beans and borlotti beans, then blanch them briefly, separately, in boiling water and peel the broad beans. If using frozen broad beans, slip them out of their skins and set aside.

Wash the rice thoroughly, then leave it to soak in a generous amount of lukewarm water for 30 minutes. Swish it around with your fingers every now and then to loosen the starch. Drain the rice, rinsing it again with warm water.

Bring 1 ½ litres (52 fl oz) of water to the boil in a large saucepan. Add the salt and stir in the drained rice. Return to the boil and cook, uncovered, for 4 minutes. Test the rice by pinching a grain between your fingers or by biting it. It should be soft on the outside, but still hard in the centre. Drain the rice and rinse again with warm water. Toss it several times to drain away as much of the water as you can.

Return the rice saucepan to a medium heat and add the oil and 2 tablespoons of water. As soon as the oil begins to sizzle, spoon in enough rice to cover the base of the saucepan in a thin layer. Gently toss the remaining rice with the beans, dill and mint and spoon it into the pan, building it up into a pyramid. Use the handle of a wooden spoon to poke 5 or 6 holes down through the rice to the base of the pan to help it steam. Mix 2 tablespoons of warm water with the melted butter and drizzle this over the rice. Sit the garlic clove and lemon peel on top of the rice. Wrap the saucepan lid in a clean tea towel and cover the pan as tightly as you can.

Leave the pan over a medium-high heat for 2–3 minutes until the rice is visibly steaming (you'll see puffs of steam escaping from the edges of the pan). Turn the heat down to low and leave the pan completely alone for 40 minutes. Resist the temptation to peek, as this releases the steam and affects the cooking time. The rice can actually sit quite happily over the lowest possible heat for up to a further 20 minutes or so.

When ready to serve, plunge the saucepan into a sink of very cold water; the sudden change of temperature creates a surge of steam that 'shocks' the rice and makes it shrink from the sides and loosens the crusty bottom. All going well, when you invert the pan onto a serving platter, the rice will plop out obligingly in one go, topped with a triumphant crunchy golden crown.

If things don't go to plan, or if the *tah deeg* breaks, it isn't the end of the world. Simply spoon the rice into a warm serving dish and shape it into an appealing mound. Loosen the *tah deeg* from the bottom of the pan and drape it artfully over the top; the only really crucial thing is to distribute it in equal portions. Serve with lots of creamy yoghurt.

Long-grain rice with lemon & toasted almonds

We serve this simple yet elegant rice as an accompaniment to all sorts of braises and other wet dishes.

SERVES 4

300 g (10 ½ oz) basmati rice
30 ml (1 fl oz) vegetable oil
a generous knob of butter
¼ cinnamon stick
5 cardamom pods, crushed
1 star anise
2 bay leaves
strips of peel and juice from ½
    lemon
small strip of orange peel
450 ml (16 fl oz) water
30 g (1 oz) flaked almonds
a few handfuls coriander (cilantro)
    leaves, finely shredded

Rinse the rice several times until the water runs clear. Shake away as much excess water as you can, then set aside for a few minutes.

Heat the oil and butter in a heavy saucepan. Add the rice and stir it around over a medium heat. Stir in the spices, bay leaves and citrus peels, then add the water. Bring to the boil, then turn the heat right down. Cover the pan and cook at a gentle simmer for 15 minutes.

Remove the pan from the heat and, working briskly, fluff up the rice. Cover the pan with a clean tea towel and replace the lid firmly. Leave it for 5–8 minutes to steam; the moisture will be absorbed by the cloth, making the rice fluffier.

Meanwhile, heat a frying pan over a medium heat and toast the almonds for 3–4 minutes, stirring so they colour evenly.

Give the rice a final fluff with the fork and fish out the aromatics, if you wish (we rather like leaving them in). Tip into a serving bowl and scatter on the toasted almonds and coriander.

Lebanese dirty rice

In our view this is THE quintessential rice dish of the Middle East. It is fantastic comfort food: sweet and earthy, with a great tangled topping of caramelized onions. Although we gave a recipe for it in our very first book, *Arabesque*, we just couldn't leave it out from a vegetarian cookbook. Just about every country around the region has a version of this dish because they understand the value of boosting the protein value of rice with lentils. And so the Persians have their *addas polow*, and everywhere there are versions of *mjaddarah* (Lebanon and Syria), *moudjendar* (Cyprus) or *megadarra* (Egypt). Serve it with a sharp, bitter leaf salad.

SERVES 4-6

40 ml (1 ¼ fl oz) olive oil

1 medium onion, diced small

40 g (1 ½ oz) small black (beluga) lentils

1 litre (35 fl oz) water

80 g (2 ¾ oz) long-grain rice, very well washed and drained

½ teaspoon ground cumin

1 teaspoon dried rose petals, to garnish (optional)

Onion topping

2 medium onions, thinly sliced

2 tablespoons cornflour (cornstarch)

½ teaspoon ground cumin

vegetable oil, for deep-frying

For the *mjaddarah*, heat half the olive oil and sauté the diced onion for a few minutes until soft. Add the lentils and half the water, cover and cook for 15 minutes (or until the lentils are just cooked). Add the rice, mix well and continue cooking for a further 15 minutes, stirring every now and then and gradually adding more of the water as it is absorbed.

The dish is ready when the rice grains have swelled and almost burst and the lentils are starting to break down and stain it all a dirty black colour. (Black lentils hold their shape better than the brown lentils that are usual for this dish, so it won't be quite as sludgy.) Add the cumin and stir well.

While the rice and lentils are cooking, soak the onions in enough salted water to cover for 15 minutes. Drain, rinse then pat very dry with kitchen paper. Dust the slices liberally with the cornflour and cumin so they are evenly coated.

Pour vegetable oil into a deep-fryer or saucepan to a depth of around 8 cm (3 ¼ in) and heat to 170°C (325°F).* Fry the onions in batches until crisp and golden, then drain on kitchen paper.

Serve the *mjaddarah* at room temperature topped with the onions and a sprinkling of crushed rose petals.

*Note: We love the crunch of the onion topping and the pretty colour contrast they make with the dirty black rice. However, we acknowledge that this is a rather poshed-up version of *mjaddarah*! If you don't want to soak and deep-fry the onions, then shallow-fry them in a mixture of olive oil and butter until they caramelize a lovely deep brown.

Eggplant pilaf with yoghurt & zhoug

A lovely thick and sticky rice dish, full of satiny chunks of eggplant in a rich tomato base, while the mint adds a refreshing counterpoint. Serve the spicy zhoug on the side with plenty of cold, creamy yoghurt.

SERVES 4

1 large eggplant (aubergine), cut into 1 cm (½ in) dice

salt and freshly ground black pepper

250 g (9 oz) long-grain rice

100 ml (3 ½ fl oz) olive oil

1 onion, finely chopped

1 clove garlic, finely chopped

2 medium vine-ripened tomatoes, chopped

½ teaspoon Turkish black chilli flakes

1 tablespoon roughly chopped mint leaves

1 tablespoon roughly chopped flat-leaf parsley leaves

300 ml (10 ½ fl oz) vegetable stock or water, boiling

a handful of green leaves, to garnish

pita bread and Greek-style yoghurt, to serve

Zhoug

seeds from 4 cardamom pods

1 teaspoon black peppercorns

1 teaspoon caraway seeds

4–6 small red chillies, deseeded

2 cups fresh coriander sprigs

6 garlic cloves

¼ teaspoon salt

1–2 tablespoons olive oil

To make the zhoug, crush the cardamom seeds, peppercorns and caraway seeds in a mortar then sift to remove any large bits. Put the chillies, coriander, garlic, salt and a splash of water into a food processor and whiz to a paste. Mix in the spices then transfer to a jar. Cover the surface with a thin layer of oil and seal.

Layer the eggplant cubes in a colander, sprinkling generously with salt as you go. Sit a plate on top and leave them in the sink for 20 minutes to draw out moisture. After degorging, rinse the eggplants and pat dry with kitchen paper.*

Put the rice in a bowl and wash in several changes of water until it is clear – you want to wash away as much of the excess starch as possible.

Heat 40 ml (1 ¼ fl oz) of the oil in a large heavy-based saucepan over a medium–high heat and sauté half the eggplant until it is lightly coloured. Remove from the pan with a slotted spoon and set aside. Add another 40 ml (1 ¼ fl oz) of oil to the pan, and cook the rest of the eggplant. Remove from the pan and set aside. Lower the heat slightly, add the remaining oil and fry the onion and garlic for about 8 minutes until they soften. Return all the eggplant to the pan and add the tomatoes and chilli flakes. Season with salt and pepper, then throw in the mint and parsley and mix well.

Add the rice to the pan – you don't want to mix it in, but rather layer it on top of the vegetable stew. This stops the eggplant breaking down into the rice. Carefully pour on the boiling stock or water. Return it to the boil without stirring, cover the pan, reduce the heat and simmer for 18–20 minutes.

When the cooking time is up, turn off the heat and remove the lid. Cover the pan with a clean tea towel, replace the lid and leave to stand for 10 minutes to steam. When ready to eat, gently mix the rice and the braised vegetables together, and serve garnished with some green leaves, the zhoug and yoghurt and plenty of pita bread.

*Note: Some people tell you not to bother with salting (degorging) eggplants as nowadays they are cultivated to be less bitter than they were in the past. When you're frying them, however, we think it's important not to omit this step, as it has less to do with the flavour than in drawing out moisture and thereby reducing the amount of oil absorbed. It also helps to fry at a fairly high temperature, as this also reduces the absorption.

Zucchini blossom & preserved lemon risotto with ricotta & parmesan

There's something exquisitely ethereal about zucchini blossoms – not only is their season blink-of-an-eye short, but their fragility means they don't take well to supermarket life. You need to hunt them down at a farmers' market or a good greengrocer, or else grow them yourself (and zucchinis are famously easy for the home gardener).

Their natural long cavity means that zucchini blossoms are frequently stuffed and then deep-fried, but the shredded blossoms also add a glorious colour, wonderful texture and delicate flavour to creamy risottos. Here, they combine with salty-sour preserved lemon and a creamy ricotta topping in one of our new favourite early-summer risottos.

SERVES 4

5 baby zucchinis (courgettes) with
    blossoms attached
30 ml (1 fl oz) olive oil
100 g (3 ½ oz) butter
1 small onion, very roughly
    chopped
1 clove garlic, quartered
300 g (10 ½ oz) Arborio rice
60 ml (2 fl oz) white wine
up to 1 ½ litres (52 fl oz) vegetable
    stock, simmering
¼ preserved lemon, skin only, very
    finely diced
60g (2 ¼ oz) parmesan, grated
80 g (2 ¾ oz) ricotta
1 small handful basil leaves, finely
    shredded
salt and freshly ground black
    pepper

Detach the flowers from the courgettes. Carefully pinch out the stamens and wipe the flowers clean. Slice the zucchinis into tiny discs.

Heat the oil and 2 tablespoons of the butter in a large saucepan and sauté the onion and garlic for 5 minutes to flavour the oil, then scoop out and discard the onion and garlic.

Add another tablespoon of butter to the pan and, when it starts to sizzle, add the zucchini and sauté for 3–4 minutes, or until lightly coloured and tender. Remove with a slotted spoon and set aside.

Add the rice to the pan and stir for a few minutes to coat each grain of rice with the buttery oil. Add the wine and let it bubble away until evaporated. Next, ladle in enough simmering stock to cover the rice by a finger's width. Cook over a medium heat, stirring with a wooden spoon from time to time, until most of the stock has been absorbed.

Add the same quantity of stock and cook as before, until most of the stock has been absorbed. Meanwhile, shred the zucchini blossoms.

Add a third of the amount of stock (reserve around 100 ml / 3 ½ fl oz for the final stage) and when half of the liquid has been absorbed, add the preserved lemon, zucchinis and blossoms and stir gently until the stock is all absorbed.

Stir in the reserved stock, the remaining butter and 40 g (1 ¼ oz) of the parmesan. Cover the pan and allow to rest away from the heat for a few minutes.

While the risotto is resting, blend the rest of the parmesan with the ricotta and basil leaves.

Season the risotto, to taste, then spoon into serving bowls and top with small blobs of the cheese mixture. Serve straight away.

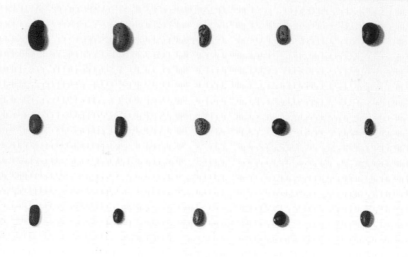

Legumes

BAKED BEANS WITH TURKISH SPICES & CRUNCHY CRUMBS ... 202

SPICED PUY LENTILS WITH PORCINI & HERBS ... 203

LENTILS WITH SWEET CARROTS, DATES & GOLDEN CREAM ... 204

LEBANESE SPICED CHICKPEAS & EGGPLANT WITH PITA ... 206

ROASTED TOMATO & CHICKPEA CURRY WITH COCONUT & CORIANDER ... 209

Pulses, beans and peas – often called legumes – are some of the very earliest cultivated crops – and are still some of the easiest, cheapest and most reliable to grow. They have played a vital role in our diet through the ages, especially in poor and rural communities, and for this alone we should pay them the respect they are due. Unassuming in appearance they may be, but they are nutritional superstars, crammed full of protein, vitamins and minerals – essential in any predominantly vegetable-based diet. When combined with cereal grains, they provide a meal that contains virtually all our protein requirements, and is more than a match for a diet based on animal proteins.

While they are often grouped together under one heading, legumes, in fact, come in a huge range of shapes, sizes and textures, each suited to its own method of preparation. Brown and green lentils, for instance, break down relatively easily, which makes them ideal for soups (page 95), while tiny Puy and 'beluga' (black) lentils retain their shape well, making them better suited for salads. And, as any Middle Easterner understands only too well, one of the main joys of pulses is their ability to take on other flavours. We love to use smooth starchy white beans in bakes and casseroles, while chickpeas form the base for an almost unfathomable range of snacks, soups, stews, stuffings and dips – think of those deliciously salty roasted chickpeas, the darling of street vendors, or a rich and creamy hummus (page 71), crunchy fried falafel (page 114), chickpea dumplings, fritters and breads.

Baked beans with Turkish spices & crunchy crumbs

Dried beans often seem a little austere or even, dare we say it, dull. But this way of baking them slowly in the oven, with plenty of aromatics and a touch of chilli heat, really transforms them into something special.

Serve the beans as is, with warm bread and lots of Crème Fraîche Butter (page 52) or jazz them up with this crunchy sourdough crumb topping. Either way, use the tastiest tomatoes you can find. In the winter, we suggest vine-ripened cocktail tomatoes, which are fairly readily available and have an acceptable flavour, albeit less intense than summer tomatoes. As with many braises, the flavours of this dish develop over time, so you can happily serve them a day (or even two) after making.

SERVES 4

250 g (9 oz) dried cannellini beans, soaked overnight

300 g (10 ½ oz) vine-ripened tomatoes

3 shallots, quartered

6 cloves garlic, lightly crushed

4–5 thyme sprigs

2 bay leaves

40 ml (1 ¼ fl oz) extra-virgin olive oil

40 ml (1 ¼ fl oz) Turkish red pepper paste* or tomato purée

1 tablespoon good-quality harissa*

1 tablespoon pomegranate molasses

450 ml (16 fl oz) vegetable stock

½ teaspoon freshly ground black pepper

big squeeze lemon juice

1 teaspoon sea salt

Crunchy crumbs

150 g (5 ½ oz) stale sourdough bread

1 clove garlic, grated

zest of 1 orange, grated

1 tablespoon chopped thyme leaves

¼ teaspoon salt

40 ml (1 ¼ fl oz) olive oil

Preheat the oven to 160°C (320°F).

Drain the soaked beans and rinse them well. Tip into a medium-sized roasting tin and scatter on the tomatoes, shallots, garlic and herbs. Mix the oil with the pepper paste, harissa and molasses then add it to the stock. Pour over the beans and season with pepper. Don't add any salt at this stage. Cover with a sheet of greaseproof paper, followed by a sheet of foil. Bake for 1 hour, then add the lemon juice and salt and return to the oven, uncovered, for a further 45 minutes, or until the beans are very tender and most of the liquid has evaporated. Set aside for up to 4 hours until ready to serve, or proceed with the crumb topping, below.

To make the crumb topping, break the sourdough bread into pieces and whiz in a food processor to coarse crumbs. Add the garlic, orange zest and thyme leaves and continue whizzing to fine crumbs. Stir the salt and oil into the crumbs and scatter it on top of the beans in an even layer. Return to the oven for a further 15 minutes, or until the crumb topping is crisp and golden.

*Note: Both Turkish red pepper paste and harissa are available from Middle Eastern grocers, specialist food stores, and even some supermarkets. Alternatively, make your own, using the recipes on pages 69 and 56.

Spiced Puy lentils with porcini & herbs

We're almost embarrassed by how often we make this salad – or some version of it. Generally, tiny Puy lentils make an ideal basis for salads. They cook quickly, hold their shape well and their earthy sweetness is a great foil for all kinds of vibrant, herby dressings. Use this as a basic recipe and play around with it until you find your preferred combinations (and see some of our favourite ideas below). The porcini mushrooms here are optional, but they do underscore the earthiness of the lentils and add a lovely, slightly chewy texture.

SERVES 4

25 g (1 oz) porcini mushrooms
    (optional)
250 g (9 oz) Puy lentils
1 bay leaf
1 sprig thyme
40 ml (1 ¼ fl oz) extra-virgin
    olive oil
juice of 1 lemon
salt and freshly ground black
    pepper
3 spring onions (scallions),
    shredded
1 loosely packed cup coriander
    (cilantro) leaves, shredded
¼ loosely packed cup mint leaves,
    roughly shredded
⅓ loosely packed cup flat-leaf
    parsley leaves, roughly
    shredded
Labneh, strained for 12 hours
    (page 73) or soft goat's cheese,
    to serve

Dressing

2 small cloves garlic, crushed with
    ½ teaspoon sea salt
juice of 1 lemon
50 ml (2 fl oz) extra-virgin
    olive oil
1 teaspoon Dijon mustard
salt and freshly ground black pepper

If using, cover the porcini mushrooms with warm water and leave to soak for 15 minutes.

Place the lentils in a pan of cold water with the bay leaf and thyme and bring to the boil. Do not salt the water as it toughens their skins. Lower the heat and simmer for 20–25 minutes, or until the lentils are tender. Drain well then tip into a mixing bowl. While the lentils are still warm, stir in the oil and lemon juice and season generously with salt and pepper. Stir in the spring onion and herbs.

Fish the porcini mushrooms out of their soaking liquid and pat them dry. Chop them roughly and stir them into the lentils.

Combine the dressing ingredients in a small jar with a lid and shake vigorously. Pour onto the lentils and mix in thoroughly. Dot with blobs of labneh or goat's cheese and serve straight away.

Variations

- Turn the salad into a heartier meal with soft-boiled eggs

- Replace the herbs with dill and flat-leaf parsley and add a diced ripe pear

- Instead of labneh, crumble on 50 g (1 ¾ oz) Home-made Shankleesh (page 72)

- Omit the mushrooms and add avocado and ruby grapefruit segments

- Top the salad with long shreds of Sweet Peppers and Shallots in Lemon Oil (page 83)

- Try a combination of flat-leaf parsley, pomegranate and feta. Or rocket (arugula) leaves and pieces of charred lemon. Or small cubes of roasted pumpkin (squash) or sweet potato

Lentils with sweet carrots, dates & golden cream

The essential earthy quality of lentils means they make a great foil to robust flavours. Dark green leaves, caramelized onions, chill and garlic are all excellent, as are sweet dates and carrots, which we use to great effect here with a lightly curried cream dressing. Nutty little Puy lentils or black (beluga) lentils are best as they maintain their shape well.

SERVES 4

100 g (3 ½ oz) Puy lentils

½ small onion, halved

1 clove garlic

1 sprig thyme

1 bay leaf

small piece cinnamon stick

good pinch sea salt

40 ml (1 ¼ fl oz) extra-virgin olive oil

½ medium carrot, finely shredded

3 Medjool dates, pitted and finely
    diced

1 cup shredded flat-leaf parsley
    leaves

⅓ cup roughly chopped tarragon
    leaves

a small handful of watercress, rocket
    (arugula) or snowpea tendrils,
    to garnish (optional)

Golden cream

1 tablespoon olive oil

1 shallot, finely diced

½ teaspoon ground ginger

½ teaspoon ground coriander

½ teaspoon ground cumin

¼ teaspoon turmeric

150 ml (5 fl oz) pure (double or
    heavy) cream

2 tablespoons lemon juice

115 g (4 oz) Greek-style yoghurt

salt

Rinse the lentils well then combine them with the aromatics in a small pan and cover with plenty of water. Simmer for 15 minutes, or until tender. Don't add salt as this will make the lentils tough!

Drain well and, while still warm, toss with the salt and 1 tablespoon of the olive oil.

To make the golden cream, heat the oil in a small saucepan and add the shallot and spices. Sweat the shallot for 5 minutes, or until soft. Add the cream and lemon juice and bring to the boil. Simmer for 5 minutes then stir in the yoghurt. Season, to taste, and set aside.

Add the carrot and dates to the lentils, together with two-thirds of the golden cream. Stir well and chill until ready to serve. (It will keep well for around 8 hours.)

Just before serving, mix in the herbs, then mound the lentils onto a serving plate. Make a well in the top and fill with the remaining golden cream. Drizzle with the remaining oil and serve at room temperature. Top with green leaves, if using, or serve with a salad on the side.

Lebanese spiced chickpeas & eggplant with pita

This is our take on a traditional and very popular dish called *fatteh*. There are endless versions of this all around Lebanon (and other parts of the Levant) but all include stale, fried or toasted pita as a base, which is then topped with yoghurt and chickpeas – and then anything else that takes your fancy!

Some versions of *fatteh* use spiced lamb or chicken, but we favour eggplant – and for this recipe, the long, Japanese variety, with its rich flavour and silky texture. It's a brilliant way of using up bits of leftover bread, but the complex layering of spices and the contrasting textures make it much, much more than the sum of its parts.

SERVES 4–6

500 g (1 lb 2 oz) vine-ripened
  tomatoes
extra-virgin olive oil
2 medium onions, thinly sliced
2 long green chillies, seeds
  removed, finely shredded
½ teaspoon ground ginger
½ teaspoon ground cinnamon
½ teaspoon ground allspice
½ teaspoon freshly ground black
  pepper
250 ml (9 fl oz) vegetable stock
sea salt
640 g (1 lb 7 oz) eggplant
  (aubergine), peeled and cut
  into fat wedges
250 g (9 oz) cooked chickpeas
  (good-quality tinned will do,
  at a pinch)
1 pita
250 g (9 oz) Greek-style yoghurt

Preheat the oven to 200°C (400°F). Arrange the tomatoes in a roasting tin and drizzle with a generous tablespoon of oil. Roast for 10 minutes, or until the skins are slightly coloured and splitting away from the flesh. Set aside until cool enough to handle, then peel away the skins.

Heat another few tablespoons of oil in a heavy-based flame-proof casserole or saucepan and add the onions, chillies and spices. Sauté very gently for 10 minutes, or until very soft and translucent.

Add the vegetable stock to the pan and bring to the boil. Add ½ teaspoon of salt and reduce to a simmer. Tip in the tomatoes with their roasting juices and simmer for 15–20 minutes, or until the liquid has reduced by around a quarter.

Meanwhile, arrange the eggplant in a large roasting tin and toss with 100 ml (3 ½ fl oz) extra-virgin olive oil and a sprinkling of salt. Roast for 15–20 minutes, or until tender. Shake the pan from time to time to ensure they colour evenly.

Add the chickpeas to the tomato mixture and continue cooking for a further 5 minutes. Finally, add the cooked eggplant (keep the roasting tin to one side and the oven on) and stir in very gently.

Roll up the pita into a tight roll and shred into ½ cm (¼ in) strips. Scatter into the eggplant roasting tin and drizzle with a little more oil. Cook for 5–7 minutes, shaking from time to time, until the bread crisps and browns evenly.

Spoon the *fatteh* into a deep serving bowl. Dollop the yoghurt around the edge of the bowl and then scatter the toasted bread over the top. Serve straight away.

Roasted tomato & chickpea curry with coconut & coriander

There is a large Indian population in the Arabian Peninsula and we've become increasingly interested in vegetarian Indian food. This light and fragrant curry is one of our favourites recipes, as it is very simple, relying on just two primary ingredients. Don't be off put by the long list of ingredients in the spice blend: you can find them all at the supermarket and it really doesn't take long to bring them all together. As curries go, this one is pretty straightforward. Serve it with Naan Breads (page 36), Long-grain Rice with Lemon & Toasted Almonds (page 193) or even – very non-traditionally – couscous.

SERVES 4

1 kg (2 lb 4 oz) medium-sized vine-ripened tomatoes, stalks attached if possible

80 ml (2 ½ fl oz) olive oil

salt

6 cardamom pods, crushed for seeds, then crush the seeds

½ teaspoon fennel seeds

¼ teaspoon black mustard seeds

6 cloves

2 star anise

1 small dried red chilli

1 teaspoon ground cumin

1 teaspoon ground coriander

½ teaspoon turmeric

½ teaspoon freshly ground black pepper

1 medium onion, grated

3 cloves garlic, grated

1 tablespoon grated fresh ginger

250 ml (9 fl oz) coconut milk

400 g (14 oz) tin chickpeas, well rinsed and drained

chopped coriander (cilantro), rice, naan bread and Greek-style yoghurt, to serve

Preheat the oven to 180°C (350°F).

Arrange the vine-ripened tomatoes in a roasting tin. Drizzle on half the oil and sprinkle with a little salt. Roast for 10 minutes, or until the skins are just starting to split. Set aside 12 of the nicest tomatoes then peel and chop the rest. (Save the skins for making stock, page 88.)

Heat a frying pan over a medium heat. Add the cardamom seeds, fennel and mustard seeds, the cloves and the star anise and fry for around 2 minutes, stirring frequently, until golden and aromatic (but not burnt!). Tip into a mortar, add the dried red chilli, and grind everything to as fine a powder as you can manage. Sieve to remove any larger bits and combine with the cumin, coriander, turmeric and black pepper.

Heat the remaining oil in a casserole or heavy-based saucepan. Add the grated onion, garlic and ginger and sauté for around 10 minutes until soft and translucent. Add the spices and fry for 2–3 minutes, stirring them around in the oily onion mixture. Add the chopped tomatoes to the pan, together with the coconut milk and season to taste. Heat to just below boiling point, then lower the heat and simmer gently for around 15 minutes.

Add the chickpeas to the pan, together with the 12 reserved tomatoes. Simmer gently for 8–10 minutes, just until the tomatoes have warmed through. You want them to retain their shape.

Sprinkle on plenty of chopped coriander and serve with rice, naan bread and plenty of yoghurt.

Pasta & couscous

FREGOLA WITH ZUCCHINI, CITRUS & BASIL ... 212

GOAT'S CHEESE DUMPLINGS WITH FRESH & DRIED MINT ... 214

BUTTERED EGG NOODLES WITH ARTICHOKES, CÈPES & SAFFRON ... 216

MIXED SPRING GREENS WITH GOLDEN RAISINS & COUSCOUS ... 217

WEDDING COUSCOUS WITH HERBS & FLOWERS ... 219

Depending on our ethnic origin, we tend to think of pasta as belonging to Italy or to China or Japan. But pasta dishes also have an important role to play in Middle Eastern cooking. Stuffed pasta dumplings, known as *shish barack* in Lebanon or *manti* in Turkey, are popular all across the Middle East and noodles, which the Iranians call *rishteh* and are called *rishta* in Lebanon and Syria – a word that translates to 'thread' – are used in a huge variety of dishes. They are added to soups, baked with vegetables in a tomato sauce, and cooked with rice or lentils to provide an interesting texture contrast. We also like to use short pasta, such as Greek orzo or Sardinian fregola, as a base for salads. And let's not forget that couscous, the national dish of the Maghreb is, in effect, a kind of pasta, being made from finely rolled grains of semolina, a by-product of flour manufacture.

Couscous is of Berber origin, synonymous with the North African countries of Morocco, Algeria and Tunisia where it is eaten every day. Traditionally, the miniscule 'grains' are steamed slowly over a bubbling stew of meat or vegetables and they swell and soften in the fragrant steam to an ethereal light fluffiness. The couscous is poured into a large round tray, shaped into a mound and served with the broth and stew, often accompanied by a harissa-spiced sauce. There are also larger types of couscous, with grains up to the size of a pea, and these varieties are generally cooked in the broth, rather than being steamed atop a stew.

Today, couscous has taken over the world and with it has gone the lovingly and slowly prepared dish of the Maghreb. In its place, is a time-saving impostor 'cooked' with boiling water from the kettle. While we regret the loss of romance, we fully accept that few people these days have the time or inclination to cook couscous in the ancient manner. We remain huge fans of this clever, versatile ingredient that lends itself so well to so many different recipes and we enjoy it in all its guises, both traditional and contemporary, savoury and sweet. At its plainest, couscous can be eaten for breakfast with milk and fruit (see page 21), or buttered and served alongside an exotically spiced Moroccan tagine; we also like to throw handfuls of couscous into soups, combine it with gently braised vegetables for hearty meals or toss with herbs, nuts and dried fruits in summery salads.

Fregola with zucchini, citrus & basil

Fregola is one of our new favourite things! It's a toasted semolina pasta from Sardinia and utterly gorgeous to look at, as the individual grains are variegated shades of cream through to dark chestnut brown, depending on the level of toasting. It has a nutty flavour, which goes really well with sharp citrus fruit. We especially love the bitter-sour tang of ruby grapefruit, but clementines, tangelos or blood oranges (when in season) are also lovely. If you're making your own citrus oil, you'll need to start a day ahead of time.

SERVES 4

1 litre (35 fl oz) vegetable stock
    or water
150 g (5 ½ oz) fregola
salt and freshly ground black pepper
Citrus Oil (see below), or buy a good-
    quality mandarin oil
50 g (1 ¾ oz) blanched hazelnuts
1 ruby grapefruit
1 orange
2 baby zucchini (courgettes), cut
    into tiny dice
2 spring onions (scallions), thinly
    sliced into rounds
¼ cup shredded basil leaves
¼ cup shredded mint leaves
¼ cup snow pea tendrils

Citrus oil

125 ml (4 fl oz) grape seed oil
125 ml (4 fl oz) good-quality olive oil
zest of 2 oranges
1 bay leaf
¼ teaspoon coriander seeds

For the citrus oil, combine the oils in a small saucepan. Use a microplane grater to zest the oranges over the oil, to capture any oils that are released as you grate. Heat gently, just to blood temperature, then remove the pan from the heat. Leave to infuse for 24–48 hours, then strain and decant into a sterilized bottle or jar.

Bring the vegetable stock to the boil and cook the fregola for 10 minutes at a healthy simmer. When cooked it should be tender, but still have a slight bite. Tip into a sieve to drain for a few minutes, then tip into a shallow tray. Season with salt and pepper and drizzle on a tablespoon of citrus oil. Toss and leave to cool.

Heat a dry frying pan over a medium heat and toast the hazelnuts for 3–4 minutes, stirring frequently, until they are golden brown. Chop roughly and set aside.

To prepare the grapefruit and orange, use a very sharp knife to peel them, taking care to remove all the bitter pith. Holding the fruit over a large mixing bowl to catch the juice, carefully slice each segment out of its skin casing and into the bowl.

To assemble the salad, add the zucchini, spring onions, herbs and chopped hazelnuts to the fregola. Add a few tablespoons of citrus oil and toss gently to mix everything together well. Serve straight away.

*Note: You can buy various citrus oils from good delicatessens, but it's easy enough to make them yourself and they are a joy to have on hand for all your salads. Our favourite is mandarin oil, although this is tricky to make successfully at home. We tend to use orange zest and the quantities here make 200 ml (7 fl oz), as it's not really worth making in smaller amounts. The oil will keep in the fridge in a sealed sterilized jar for up to 1 month – and we guarantee you will use it! Use a mild-flavoured olive oil, not extra-virgin, which will overpower the citrus flavour.

Goat's cheese dumplings with fresh & dried mint

One doesn't usually associate pasta with Middle Eastern cuisine, but noodles and dumplings, in particular, are popular in several countries around the region. Stuffed pasta dumplings, called *manti*, are a key feature of Turkish cooking, and it's thought that they date back to the eighth century, when they were introduced to Anatolia from Northern China by the Uyghurs. The very best *manti* are teeny-tiny, and require a great deal of patience and skill to make. (See our earlier book, *Turquoise*, if you are interested in learning how to make them.) In this larger form they are much more forgiving, and just as delicious. *Manti* are usually stuffed with minced lamb and served under a blanket of creamy yoghurt. Our vegetarian version are stuffed with herb-spiked fresh goat's cheese and dressed in a light and tangy pomegranate vinaigrette.

SERVES 4

Pasta dough

2–3 large eggs

1–2 tablespoons olive oil

250 g (9 oz) pasta flour (superfine '00' grade), sifted, plus extra for dusting

1 teaspoon salt

Goat's cheese filling

1 teaspoon butter

1 shallot, very finely chopped

1 small clove garlic, very finely chopped

250 g (9 oz) fresh goat's cheese

¼ teaspoon salt

freshly ground white pepper

finely grated zest of ½ lemon

½ teaspoon dried mint

1 teaspoon shredded mint leaves

egg wash, made from 1 egg white beaten with 1 tablespoon water

Tomato-pomegranate dressing

2 medium vine-ripened tomatoes, finely diced

1 shallot, very finely diced

1 clove garlic, very finely chopped

3 tablespoons pomegranate seeds

juice of 1 lemon

1 tablespoon pomegranate molasses

125 ml (4 fl oz) extra-virgin olive oil

½ teaspoon Turkish black chilli flakes

To make the dressing, combine all the ingredients, except for the chilli flakes, in a bowl and whisk together well. Taste and adjust the balance of sour, sweet and salty, to taste. Pour into a lidded jar and store in the fridge for up to 5 days. Bring to room temperature before serving.

To make the dough, lightly beat 2 of the eggs together with a tablespoon of oil, then add them to the bowl of a stand-mixer with the flour and salt. Use your hands to bring it together to a rough dough. If it seems too stiff, add a little more egg; too wet, a little more flour. Once it has come together, knead with the dough hook on a slow speed for 2–3 minutes until well combined. Turn it out onto your work surface and knead it by hand for a few more minutes until it is very smooth and pliable. After kneading, divide the dough into 2 pieces and wrap them in cling film and leave it to rest and relax at room temperature for at least an hour. It will also keep well in the fridge for up to 2 days.

To make the filling, melt the butter in a pan. Add the shallot and garlic and sauté gently for 8–10 minutes, or until soft and translucent. Remove from the heat and leave to cool completely.

Crumble the goat's cheese into a mixing bowl and add the cold shallot mixture, the salt and pepper, lemon zest and the dried and fresh mint. Mash it all together well with a fork.

When ready to make the dumplings, use a floured rolling pin to flatten out one piece of dough on a floured work surface. Shape into a rough rectangle then roll it through a pasta machine, working your way from the widest setting down to the second-narrowest setting. (We find the narrowest can make the pasta very fragile.)

Lay out the strip of pasta dough flat on your work surface and use a pastry cutter to cut out 6 cm (2 ½ in) discs. Blob a heaped spoonful of filling in the centre of each disc and lightly brush the perimeter with egg wash. To make the traditional *manti* shape, bring up the sides of the dough over the filling and press to seal at the top. Bring the other two sides up, carefully pinching the side 'seams' as you go to seal

them. You are aiming to achieve a four-cornered star-like shape. For an easier option, simply fold the pasta over the filling to form little half-moons and squeeze to seal. Repeat with the remaining dough and filling.

Place the *manti* on a lightly floured tray as you complete them, until all the dough and filling has been used. The *manti* can be kept in the fridge, covered with cling film, for a few hours.

When ready to cook, bring a large saucepan of salted water to the boil. Drop in the *manti* (you'll have to cook them in batches) and simmer for 3–4 minutes, or until tender. Use a slotted spoon to transfer the cooked *manti* to warm serving bowls. Spoon on the tomato-pomegranate dressing, sprinkle with the black chilli flakes and serve straight away.

Buttered egg noodles with artichokes, cèpes & saffron

Noodles are popular in Iran, where they are called *rishteh* (meaning 'thread') and also in Lebanon and Syria (where they are known as *rishta*). They are often served with vegetable sauces or, especially in Iran, in soups. The following recipe uses some of our favourite ingredients: artichokes, cèpe mushrooms (also called porcini) and saffron, flavoured with a popular all-purpose spice mix called *taklia*.

SERVES 4

100 ml (3 ½ fl oz) olive oil

2 shallots, finely sliced

1 tablespoon Taklia (see below)

8–10 saffron threads, lightly toasted
    and crushed

8 good-quality artichokes in oil
    (or see page 158), halved

2 vine-ripened tomatoes, diced

100 g (3 ½ oz) fresh baby peas
    (or use frozen)

½ preserved lemon, skin only,
    finely shredded

60 ml (2 fl oz) vermouth or white
    wine

salt and freshly ground black
    pepper

25 g (1 oz) dried cèpes, soaked in
    100 ml (3 ½ fl oz) cold water for
    10 minutes

400 g (14 oz) fresh egg noodles

a knob of unsalted butter

juice of ½ lemon

a handful of baby herbs to garnish
    (optional)

Taklia

1 tablespoon olive oil

6 cloves garlic, roughly chopped

1 teaspoon sea salt

2 teaspoons ground coriander

vegetable oil, to seal

To make the taklia, heat the oil in a small frying pan and sauté the garlic for 1 minute over a low heat, making sure it doesn't colour. Scrape it into a mortar and pound to a paste with the salt and coriander. Spoon the taklia into a sterilized jar and cover the surface with a thin film of flavourless oil. If you're not eating it straight away, store in the fridge where it will keep for up to 2 months.

Heat the olive oil in a heavy-based pan, then add the shallots and *taklia* and cook over a gentle heat until soft, about 5 minutes. Then add the saffron, artichokes, tomatoes, peas, preserved lemon and vermouth and allow to bubble for a few minutes until it reduces and thickens. Season with salt and pepper.

Remove the cèpes from their soaking water and add them to the pan. Strain the soaking water to remove any bits of grit or dirt and add half of it to the pan.

Cook the egg noodles in boiling water (they only take a few seconds), drain well and tip into a large serving bowl. Stir through the butter. Pour on the braised vegetables, add the lemon juice and mix together well. Scatter over the baby herbs, if using, and serve straight away with warm crusty bread.

Mixed spring greens with golden raisins & couscous

This is a fabulously vibrant couscous dish that makes excellent use of the year's new-season greens: spring greens, pungent mustard greens and wild garlic are all brilliant, and you can usually find them at farmers' markets and farm stores. If you live in a resolutely urban environment and can't get hold of these, then use a mixture of wild rocket or watercress with silverbeet or spinach, and sauté with a clove or two of crushed garlic.

SERVES 4

200 g (7 oz) couscous

70 ml (2 ¼ fl oz) extra-virgin
    olive oil

250 ml (9 fl oz) boiling water

2 shallots, finely sliced into rings

1 head of spring greens, any
    yellowing outer leaves
    removed, finely shredded

2 handfuls mustard greens,
    finely shredded

1 handful wild garlic leaves
    (ramps), finely shredded

40 g (1 ½ oz) golden raisins, roughly
    chopped

Juice of ½ lemon

salt and freshly ground black
    pepper

Greek-style yoghurt, to serve

Put the couscous in a bowl and add a tablespoon of the oil. Use your fingers to rub it into the couscous as evenly as you can. Pour in the boiling water and stir it well. Cover with a tea towel and leave for 10 minutes, stirring with a fork from time to time to prevent the couscous from clumping together. When the couscous is cool, use your fingers to break down any remaining small clumps and to make sure it is all flowing freely. If you're not using the couscous straight away, chill in a sealed container for up to 2 days. To reheat, tip the couscous into a bowl and cover with a tea towel. Microwave on high for 2–3 minutes. This 'mini-steam' should help make the grains even fluffier. If you don't have a microwave oven, warm the couscous through in a saucepan.

Heat the remaining olive oil in a frying pan and sauté the shallots over a gentle heat until they are soft. Increase the heat and add the shredded greens to the pan. Sauté for 2–3 minutes, or until they wilt, then add the chopped raisins and lemon juice and season, to taste, with salt and pepper.

To serve, mound the couscous onto a serving platter and spoon the sautéed greens around. Serve straight away, with plenty of cool, creamy yoghurt.

Wedding couscous with herbs & flowers

Named for the part it played in Lucy's wedding dinner! With its lavish use of herbs, nuts, barberries and pomegranates, and its exotic flower petal garnish, this certainly feels special enough to be part of any celebration menu. But, in reality, like most couscous dishes, it's blissfully easy to put together. It is delicious eaten hot with harissa broth (see below), or at room temperature as a salad. Either way, serve with plenty of yoghurt alongside.

Traditionally, couscous is steamed over a rich broth, which swells the individual grains to flavoursome plumpness. However, most people these days opt for speed and slosh on boiling water instead of the more time-consuming steaming. A word of caution: don't just leave the couscous to sit or it will set into a solid lump. Follow the method described below and you should achieve lovely separate and free-flowing grains.

SERVES 4

200 g (7 oz) couscous

70 ml (2 ¼ fl oz) extra-virgin olive oil

250 ml (9 fl oz) boiling water

1 green chilli, deseeded and finely shredded

finely grated zest of 1 orange

1 teaspoon butter

2 tablespoons barberries (available from Persian stores or some Middle Eastern stores. If you can't find them, use dried cranberries or cherries)

25 g (1 oz) pistachios

2 tablespoons pomegranate seeds

⅓ cup shredded flat-leaf parsley leaves

⅓ cup shredded tarragon leaves

⅓ cup shredded purple basil

a handful of edible flowers, to garnish (choose from violas, nasturtiums, rose petals, borage, cornflower, dandelion, marigold – or indeed any that you can find)

Greek-style yoghurt, to serve

Harissa Broth

1–2 tablespoons Green Harissa (page 56), or to taste

400 ml (14 fl oz) vegetable stock

salt and freshly ground black pepper

Put the couscous in a bowl and add a tablespoon of the oil. Use your fingers to rub it into the couscous as evenly as you can. Pour in the boiling water and stir it well. Cover with a tea towel and leave for 10 minutes, stirring with a fork from time to time to prevent the couscous from clumping together. When the couscous is cool, use your fingers to break down any remaining small clumps and to make sure it is all flowing freely. If you're not using the couscous straight away, chill in a sealed container for up to 2 days. To reheat, tip the couscous into a bowl and cover with a tea towel. Microwave on high for 2–3 minutes. This 'mini-steam' should help make the grains even fluffier. If you don't have a microwave oven, warm the couscous through in a saucepan.

When ready to serve, transfer the couscous to a serving bowl. Add the chilli and orange zest and mix thoroughly.

Stir the green harissa into the vegetable stock and bring to a gentle simmer. Season, to taste, then pour into a serving jug.

Melt the butter in a small frying pan. Add the barberries and pistachios and sauté for a minute, just to warm them through. Add to the couscous, together with the pomegranate seeds and herbs, and toss everything together well. Scatter on the rose petals, if using, and serve with the jug of hot harissa broth and plenty of cold creamy yoghurt on the side so that people can help themselves.

Ices

CRÈME FRAÎCHE ICE CREAM ... 223

BANANA ICE CREAM WITH SALTED DATE CARAMEL ... 225

STRACCIATELLA WITH ORANGE PEEL ... 226

BUTTERMILK SORBET WITH BAY LEAF & LEMON ... 228

PEAR SORBET WITH PROSECCO, CARDAMOM & LIME ... 229

NEGRONI SORBET WITH BLOOD ORANGE & POMEGRANATE ... 231

Given the climate, it's hardly surprising that iced confections are popular in the Middle East. They're the perfect refreshment through the baking-hot summers, and an excursion to the local ice-cream parlour is popular at any time of day – and often long into the warm evenings. In fact, it's thought that early versions of water ices originated in the region: certainly the Persians were familiar with the concept of storing ice and snow from the mountains in ice houses, for use during the summer months.

While the very earliest frozen desserts were little more than fresh fruit juice or wine mixed with snow or ice, nowadays the repertoire in most Middle Eastern countries includes a wide range of amazing fruity granitas and sorbets, as well as creamy dairy ices. A traditional favourite is an ice cream known as *dondurma* in Turkey and its cousin, *booza*, in the Arab world. These dense, 'chewy' ice creams have a wonderful stretchiness and a distinctive flavour which comes from mastic, the resin of a Mediterranean tree. They are traditionally egg-free, thickened instead with salep, from the root of a particular orchid. You'll often see *dondurma* suspended from hooks above the vendor's stall, from where it is hacked down in chunks with a vicious-looking knife. It is usually so dense and hard that you need to eat it with a knife and fork.

In reality, ice creams are rarely made at home in Middle Eastern countries, but they are often bought in from a favourite neighbourhood ice-cream shop and offered as a treat to visiting guests. As in Western countries, the range of flavours is ever increasing; we've included some new and unusual sorbets and ice creams in the pages that follow. None is difficult to make, although the finished result is undeniably better if you have the benefit of an ice-cream machine. Home-made sorbets and ice creams are at their very best when freshly made. After churning, they'll need to firm up in the freezer for an hour or so, but aim to eat them within a day or two of making for maximum flavour and best texture.

Crème fraîche ice cream

This has become our 'go-to' accompanying ice cream as we find it more refreshing than classic vanilla. Crème fraîche has a slight lactic tang and sharpness, which we love and accentuate here with a generous squeeze of lemon.

MAKES AROUND 1 LITRE (35 FL OZ)

250 ml (9 fl oz) milk
170 g (6 oz) caster (superfine) sugar
1 vanilla pod, split and seeds scraped
1 strip of lemon peel, about 5–6 cm
    (2–2 ½ in) long
pinch salt
6 large egg yolks
500 g (1 lb 2 oz) crème fraîche
juice of ½ lemon

Combine the milk, sugar, vanilla pod and seeds, lemon peel and salt in a medium saucepan and heat gently until the sugar dissolves. Bring to a simmer then remove from the heat.

Whisk the egg yolks in a large mixing bowl, then slowly pour on a quarter of the hot milk, whisking continuously. Pour the mixture back into the saucepan and whisk in briskly. Cook over a medium heat for about 10 minutes, stirring continuously with a wooden spoon, until the mixture thickens to a custard consistency. You should be able to draw a distinct line through the custard on the back of a spoon.

Remove the pan from the heat and cool immediately in a sink of iced water. Stir from time to time to help the custard cool down quickly. Transfer to the fridge until chilled.

When ready to churn, strain the custard through a sieve to remove the lemon peel and vanilla pod. Whisk in the crème fraîche, followed by the lemon juice, then pour into an ice-cream machine and churn according to the manufacturer's instructions. Transfer to a plastic container and freeze for at least 2 hours before serving.

Banana ice cream with salted date caramel

Neither of us has ever been drawn to commercial banana ice cream, with its synthetic flavour and bilious yellow hue, but we really wanted to showcase bananas, which are an important crop in Oman, one of our favourite countries on the Gulf. After testing a few recipes, we became worryingly addicted to this version, especially when topped with this irresistible salted date caramel. It's an ode to Arabia!

MAKES AROUND 1 LITRE (35 FL OZ)

400 g (14 oz) ripe bananas (peeled weight), chopped
240 ml (8 fl oz) milk
240 ml (8 fl oz) pure (double or heavy) cream
40 ml (1 ¼ fl oz) Amontillado or medium sherry
6 egg yolks
50 g (1 ¾ oz) caster (superfine) sugar
50 g (1 ¾ oz) liquid glucose
1 teaspoon lemon juice
pinch sea salt

Salted date caramel

100 g (3 ½ oz) unsalted butter
100 g (3 ½ oz) light muscovado sugar
3 bay leaves
100 ml (3 ½ fl oz) pure (double or heavy) cream
⅛ teaspoon salt flakes
80 g (2 ¾ oz) plump Medjool dates

To make the salted date caramel, melt the butter in a saucepan over a low heat. Once melted, stir in the sugar and heat gently until it has dissolved, stirring to help it along. Add the bay leaves to the pan and simmer for a few minutes. Don't worry if it seems to be resolutely un-amalgamated at this stage, it will all come together when you add the cream. Pour it in (watching out for splutters) and stir briskly until it melts magically into a thick, glossy sauce. Add the salt and simmer for a few minutes.

Remove the pan from the heat and tip the caramel into a jar until ready to use. The sauce will keep for up to 2 weeks in the fridge. If you can resist eating spoonfuls directly from the jar, then warm it gently and serve with ice cream.

To make the ice cream, put the chopped bananas in a heavy-based saucepan with the milk and cream. Bring to a bare simmer and cook for 10 minutes. Towards the end of the cooking time, add the sherry. Remove from the heat and set aside for an hour to infuse. Discard half the bananas and transfer the rest, together with the infused cream, to the bowl of a food processor. Whiz to a fine purée then push through a sieve into a clean saucepan. Return to the heat and bring to a simmer.

In a separate bowl, whisk the egg yolks with the sugar and glucose until thick and creamy. Slowly pour on a quarter of the hot banana milk, whisking continuously. Pour the mixture back into the saucepan and whisk in briskly. Cook over a medium heat for about 10 minutes, stirring continuously with a wooden spoon, until the mixture thickens to a custard consistency. You should be able to draw a distinct line through the custard on the back of a spoon. Remove the pan from the heat, stir in the lemon juice and salt, and cool immediately in a sink of iced water. Stir from time to time to help the custard cool down quickly. Chill well in the fridge.

When ready to churn, pour the custard into an ice-cream machine and churn according to the manufacturer's instructions. Transfer to a plastic container and freeze for at least 2 hours before serving.

When ready to serve, tip the caramel into a small pan and warm through gently. Meanwhile, blanch the dates for 1 minute in boiling water. Peel and discard the skins and pits, then dice the dates finely and add them to the caramel. Serve while warm with the ice cream.

Stracciatella with orange peel

Stracciatella – which means '*little shreds*' in Italian – is a universally popular ice cream. The shreds are created by pouring warm chocolate sauce into the ice cream at the end of churning. By some alchemy, the sauce freezes instantly into little crackly flakes. In our recipe, we infuse the custard with orange, which is a lovely counterpoint to the dark bitterness of the chocolate.

MAKES AROUND 1 LITRE (35 FL OZ)

500 ml (16 fl oz) pure (double or
    heavy) cream
250 ml (9 fl oz) milk
1 vanilla pod, split and seeds
    scraped
strips of peel from 1 orange
pinch salt
6 large egg yolks
150 g (5 ½ oz) caster (superfine)
    sugar
70 g (2 ½ oz) good-quality dark
    chocolate (70% cocoa solids)
    chopped

Combine the cream, milk, vanilla pod and seeds, orange peel and salt in a medium saucepan and bring to a simmer. Remove from the heat and leave to infuse for at least an hour.

When ready to make the custard, bring the infused milk to a simmer then remove from the heat and leave to cool briefly. In a large bowl, whisk the egg yolks with the sugar until thick and creamy. Slowly pour on a quarter of the hot infused milk, whisking continuously. Pour the mixture back into the saucepan and whisk in briskly. Cook over a medium heat for about 10 minutes, stirring continuously with a wooden spoon, until the mixture thickens to a custard consistency. You should be able to draw a distinct line through the custard on the back of a spoon.

Remove the pan from the heat and cool immediately in a sink of iced water. Stir from time to time to help the custard cool down quickly. Transfer to the fridge until chilled.

When ready to churn, strain the custard through a sieve to remove the vanilla pod* and orange peel. Pour into an ice cream machine and churn according to the manufacturer's instructions.

While the ice cream is churning, melt the chocolate in a bowl set over a saucepan of simmering water (the bowl shouldn't touch the hot water). When it has completely melted, scrape into a small jug and cool to blood temperature. When the ice cream has all but finished churning, remove the lid and, with the motor still running, pour the chocolate directly into the ice cream, onto the turning blades, in a slow, steady stream. Continue churning for another 20–30 seconds. The chocolate will harden on contact and form little flakes. Transfer to a plastic container and freeze for at least 2 hours before serving.

*Note: Wash and dry the vanilla bean and store with your sugar.

Buttermilk sorbet with bay leaf & lemon

Since creating this recipe as a way to use the buttermilk that is produced when making butter (page 52), we've become addicted to its light tang and subtle sweetness. The bay leaves, coriander and lemon juice add a wonderful citrus-herbal quality and it makes a brilliantly refreshing end to a rich meal. Don't feel obliged to use home-made buttermilk; it's just as delicious with the cultured kind that you can buy from supermarkets.

MAKES AROUND 800 ML (28 FL OZ)

250 ml (9 fl oz) water

210 g (7 oz) caster (superfine) sugar

35 g (1 ¼ oz) liquid glucose

strips of peel from ½ lemon

½ teaspoon coriander seeds,
    lightly crushed

2 large bay leaves

400 ml (14 fl oz) buttermilk

150 g (5 fl oz) Greek-style yoghurt

60 ml (2 fl oz) lemon juice
    (juice of about 2 lemons)

Combine the water, sugar and liquid glucose in a saucepan and heat gently, swirling the pan from time to time, until the sugar dissolves. Add the lemon peel, coriander seeds and bay leaves, increase the heat and bring to a gentle boil. Simmer for 3 minutes, then remove from the heat and leave to cool. Transfer to the fridge until chilled.

Whisk together the buttermilk and yoghurt then chill.

Stir the lemon juice into the cold syrup, then strain this into the chilled buttermilk mixture. Tip into an ice-cream machine and churn according to the manufacturer's instructions. Transfer to a plastic container and freeze for at least 2 hours before serving.

Pear sorbet with Prosecco, cardamom & lime

With their delicate and subtle flavour, we think pears make a lovely fresh-tasting autumnal sorbet, especially when partnered with cardamom, vanilla and cinnamon, as they are here. Choose perfectly ripe pears with a juicy and tart flesh: the French Passe-Crassane are ideal, but if they are hard to find, try Comice or William pears.

This sorbet is best eaten within a few hours of churning as the Prosecco gives it a lovely, almost mousse-like consistency. It will firm up and set harder, the longer you leave it in the freezer. It is still delicious, but not quite as etherial.

MAKES 1.25 LITRES (44 FL OZ)

1.2 kg (2 lb 10 oz) pears, peeled,
    quartered and cores removed

250 g (9 oz) caster (superfine)
    sugar

200 ml (7 fl oz) water

375 ml (13 fl oz) Prosecco

50 g (1 ¾ oz) liquid glucose

1 vanilla pod, split and seeds
    scraped

½ cinnamon stick

14 cardamom pods

60 ml (2 fl oz) lime juice

2 teaspoons rosewater

After preparing the pears, weigh them to achieve 1 kg (2 lb 4 oz) of fruit.

Combine the sugar with the water and 300 ml (10 ½ fl oz) of the Prosecco in a large saucepan. Add the liquid glucose, vanilla pod and cinnamon stick and heat gently, swirling the pan from time to time, until the sugar dissolves.

Meanwhile, toast the cardamom pods gently in a small dry frying pan, then crush them roughly with a heavy knife to release the seeds. Add the seeds to the poaching syrup. Lower the heat and simmer for 5 minutes. Add the pears to the poaching syrup and simmer, uncovered, for around 30 minutes, until the pears are translucent and very tender.

Strain the pears, reserving the poaching syrup. Remove and discard all the aromatics and purée the pears with 200 ml (7 fl oz) of poaching syrup until extremely smooth. The purée should have the consistency of thinnish cream. Whisk in the reserved Prosecco, the lime juice and rosewater then leave to cool. Transfer to an ice-cream machine and churn according to the manufacturer's instructions. Transfer to a plastic container and freeze for at least 2 hours before serving.

Negroni sorbet with blood orange & pomegranate

This palate-cleansing and rather adult sorbet is based on Greg's current favourite cocktail, the Negroni, which combines Campari, vermouth and gin. Its slight herbal bitterness somehow blends seamlessly with pomegranate juice and blood orange. We generally use good-quality fresh juice from a carton, instead of squeezing our own fruit, which means we can enjoy this sorbet at all times of the year.

MAKES AROUND 900 ML (32 FL OZ)

250 g (9 oz) caster (superfine)
    sugar
250 ml (9 fl oz) water
50 g (1 ¾ oz) liquid glucose
250 ml (9 fl oz) pomegranate juice
150 ml (5 fl oz) blood orange juice
20 ml (½ fl oz) Campari, plus a
    splash
2 teaspoons gin
20 ml (½ fl oz) vermouth

Combine the sugar and water in a saucepan and heat gently, swirling the pan from time to time, until the sugar dissolves. Increase the heat and bring to the boil then simmer for 1 minute. Remove from the heat and leave to cool slightly.

Stir the liquid glucose into the syrup. Add the fruit juices, together with the alcohols and transfer to the fridge to cool.

Tip into an ice-cream machine and churn according to the manufacturer's instructions. Towards the end of the churning, add another splash of Campari – a capful should do it – and churn it in. Transfer to a plastic container and freeze for at least 2 hours before serving.

*Note: If you don't have all the components for the Negroni, then just use 50 ml (2 fl oz) of Campari, plus the splash at the end.

Desserts

LEMON POSSET WITH FENNEL SHORTBREAD THINS ... 234

PAVLOVA 'FLOWERS' WITH APPLE JELLY, RASPBERRIES & VANILLA LABNEH ... 236

CHOCOLATE MUHALLABEYA WITH TURKISH COFFEE GRANITA ... 239

MUSCAT CRÈME CARAMEL WITH ORANGE FLOWER CREAM & CANDIED PISTACHIOS ... 240

SAFFRON RICE PUDDING WITH SPICED APRICOTS ... 243

In Middle Eastern countries there is no real tradition of eating desserts, and meals tend to finish with a selection of fresh fruit instead. The exception to this is when guests are visiting, or on special celebratory occasions, when elaborate tarts, gateaux or ice creams will be bought in.

As in most places in the world. sweet treats are very popular although they are usually eaten as snacks during the daytime rather than after a meal. In fact, dairy-based puddings are so well loved that in some countries, such as Turkey, there are shops devoted solely to them and specialist pudding-makers – *muhallebici* – dedicated to the craft. The array of these milk desserts is extraordinary: some are thickened with cornflour, rice or ground nuts; some are flavoured with saffron or flower waters, vanilla or citrus zest; some are enriched with eggs, some with cream. And pudding shops are also the place to find a richly indulgent kind of clotted cream, known as *kaymak* or *ashta* (page 20). This is often rolled into thick logs – firm enough to slice – and used to fill pastries or cakes, as well making a fine accompaniment to poached fruits, or with breakfast bread and jam or honeycomb.

All of this, we feel, gives us a certain freedom when it comes to the dessert course! The recipes in this chapter are, in accordance with our own preference, largely fruit-based. We have drawn upon the ingredients, techniques and flavour combinations that we've encountered on our travels, and reinterpreted them in rather more Western-style desserts than you might find in the Middle East. You'll also find some other lovely dessert ideas in the Ices and Sweet Pastries chapters (pages 220–231 and 244–253).

Lemon posset with fennel shortbread thins

Pure, unadulterated, silky-smooth lemony-ness. The delightfully named posset is an old-fashioned English dish, thought to date back to medieval times, when it was served before bedtime as a warming digestif. Early recipes were little more than milk, curdled with ale, fortified wine or citrus juice. The posset has had something of a resurgence in popularity of late and, although the modern version is undeniably richer, using cream, sugar and lemon juice, it makes a wonderfully refreshing end to a meal. Pretty it up with some Candied Citrus Peel (page 63) and almond flakes if you like, but really, it needs little more than a delicate biscuit – such as the Fennel Shortbread Thins on page 259 – for dunking and scooping.

SERVES 4

grated zest and 120 ml (3 ¾ fl oz) lemon juice (about 2 ½ lemons)

125 g (4 ½ oz) caster (superfine) sugar

450 ml (16 fl oz) pure (double or heavy) cream

½ teaspoon ground ginger (optional)

Candied Citrus Peel (page 63), to serve (optional) or a dab of orange flower or rose petal jam

Fennel Shortbread Thins (page 259), to serve

Combine the lemon zest and juice and the sugar in a small saucepan and heat gently until the sugar dissolves. Bring to the boil, then remove from the heat.

Pour the cream into a different saucepan and add the ground ginger, if using. Heat gently until it comes to the boil. Pour in the hot lemon syrup and return to a simmer, whisking all the time. Simmer for 20 seconds then remove from the heat. Cool slightly then strain through a sieve into a jug. Pour into pretty glasses and chill overnight, or until set.

Top each lemon posset with a small twist of candied peel, if you like, and serve with shortbread biscuits.

Pavlova 'flowers' with apple jelly, raspberries & vanilla labneh

These strikingly pretty meringues are much easier to make than you might think. They are ideal for a dinner party as all the component parts can be made ahead of time. The quantities here are enough to make eight, as we find the recipe doesn't reduce terribly well. However, any uneaten meringues will keep very well for up to 2 weeks in a sealed container.

SERVES 8

Pavlovas

5 large egg whites
200 g (7 oz) caster (superfine) sugar
pinch salt
200 g (7 oz) icing (confectioners') sugar
2 teaspoons cornflour (cornstarch)
300 g (10 ½ oz) raspberries
200 g (7oz) Vanilla Labneh (page 18)
rosewater, to taste

Apple jelly

2 ½ sheets gelatine
250 ml (9 fl oz) apple juice

To make the apple jelly, soak the gelatine leaves in a dish of cold water for a couple of minutes, until soft and slippery then squeeze them to get rid of any excess water. Heat up 50 ml (2 fl oz) of the apple juice and whisk in the gelatine until it dissolves. Mix it back into the rest of the juice then pour into a small shallow container and transfer to the fridge to set.

To make the pavlovas, preheat the oven to 120°C (235°F) and line 2 large baking sheets with baking paper.

Put the egg whites into the scrupulously clean bowl of a stand-mixer. Add 2 tablespoons of the caster sugar and the salt and whisk on a slow speed until the mixture begins to foam. Increase the speed to high and whisk until the foam thickens to form smooth, soft, glossy peaks. Sift on the remaining caster sugar, a little at a time, whisking as you go, to firm peaks. Finally, sift on the icing sugar and cornflour and whisk in briefly until incorporated.

Spoon the meringue into a piping bag fitted with a 1 ½ cm (¾ in) nozzle. On each of the prepared baking trays, pipe 4 pavlova 'flowers', spacing them well apart. Start with a walnut-sized central blob, then surround it with 6 more blobs, to form pretty flower-like meringue nests. Aim to get the peaks of the outer blobs pointing inwards, if you can. Use a knife to flatten the central meringue; this will form a base for the filling. If you feel the flowers are beyond your piping skills, then form the traditional swirled meringue nests.

Bake the pavlovas for 1 ½ hours until they are ivory-coloured and crisp. Leave to cool on the baking sheets for 10 minutes before very carefully lifting the meringue flowers onto wire racks to cool completely.

When ready to serve, cut the jelly into small cubes – they don't have to be precise. Fill the central cavity of each meringue with a generous spoonful of vanilla labneh. Top with fresh raspberries and a scattering of jelly cubes. Add a splash of rosewater and serve straight away.

Chocolate muhallabeya with Turkish coffee granita

Muhallabeya is one of the most popular Lebanese desserts, and it's also one of the easiest you can imagine. When you tell people that it is little more than milk, thickened with cornflour, you can almost feel them shiver with horror. But we say, don't judge until you've tasted it! In Lebanese restaurants, muhallabeya is flavoured with mastic and served with a syrup perfumed with orange flower water – and you do need the syrup as the *muhallabeya* is not, in itself, very sweet. We sometimes serve our chocolate version the same way, drizzled with a coffee syrup, but we like it best of all topped with a refreshing layer of icy-cold Turkish coffee granita.

MAKES 4

Chocolate muhallabeya

60 g (2 ¼ oz) caster (superfine) sugar

30 g (1 oz) cornflour (cornstarch)

500 ml (16 fl oz) milk

40 g (1 ½ oz) best-quality dark chocolate (70% cocoa solids), chopped

125 ml (4 fl oz) water

½ teaspoon instant coffee granules

chocolate-coated coffee beans, to garnish (optional)

Turkish coffee granita

4 teaspoons caster (superfine) sugar

250 ml (9 fl oz) water

3 cardamom pods, roughly crushed

2 ½ teaspoons instant coffee granules

1 gelatine leaf*

Turkish coffee syrup

4 teaspoons caster (superfine) sugar

250 ml (9 fl oz) water

3 cardamom pods, roughly crushed

2 ½ teaspoons instant coffee granules

To make the granita, combine the sugar and water in a saucepan and heat gently, swirling the pan from time to time, until the sugar dissolves. Add the cardamom pods, then increase the heat, bring to the boil and simmer for 1–2 minutes. Remove from the heat and leave to cool for an hour.

Transfer 250 ml (9 fl oz) of the syrup to a small saucepan and bring to a simmer. Stir in the instant coffee and remove from the heat.

Soak the gelatine leaf in a dish of cold water for a minute, until soft and slippery. Squeeze it to get rid of any excess water and add to the hot coffee syrup. Cool for a few minutes, then stir into the remaining syrup. Strain into a rigid plastic container and freeze until firm.

Make the coffee syrup in the same way, but without the gelatine. Leave the syrup to cool.

To make the *muhallabeya*, combine the sugar and cornflour in a small bowl and gradually mix in 125 ml (4 fl oz) of the milk to make a very smooth paste.

Melt the chocolate in a bowl set over a saucepan of simmering water (make sure the bowl doesn't actually touch the hot water).

Combine the rest of the milk and the water in a large saucepan. Add the cornflour paste, melted chocolate and coffee granules, stirring well. Bring to the boil, stirring continuously. Once the mixture boils, remove from the heat and leave to cool slightly before pouring into attractive glasses. Make sure you don't fill the glasses full, but leave space to spoon on a generous layer of the granita or coffee syrup.

When ready to serve, scrape the surface of the granita with a spoon or fork to create crystals and layer on top of the *muhallabeyas*. Alternatively, spoon over some of the coffee syrup. Garnish with a few chocolate-coated coffee beans, if you like, and serve straight away.

*Note: The gelatine might seem like a strange addition to granita, but it keeps the texture nice and firm, instead of it dissolving into a watery layer on top of the *muhallabeya*.

Muscat crème caramel with orange flower cream & candied pistachios

Sometimes it's just impossible to get past the classics – and who doesn't love the seductive wobble of a crème caramel? Over the years, we've made various versions (the mandarin-scented recipe in our earlier book, *Moorish*, is a particular favourite), but we often return to this gorgeous, Muscat-infused silky custard. With its raisin notes and the sugary crunch of candied pistachios, it is the perfect dessert for a golden autumn evening. This recipe will make one large crème caramel or six to eight individual ones, depending on the size of your ramekin dishes.

MAKES 1 LARGE OR 6–8 SMALL CUSTARDS

Custard

200 ml (7 fl oz) Muscat liqueur, Muscatel or Sauternes

50 ml (1 ¾ fl oz) medium-sweet sherry

300 ml (10 ½ fl oz) pouring (single) cream

200 ml (7 fl oz) milk

80 g (2 ¾ oz) caster (superfine) sugar

2 eggs, plus 4 egg yolks

whipped cream, to serve

orange flower water, to serve

Caramel

80 ml (2 ½ fl oz) water

120 g (4 ¼ oz) caster (superfine) sugar

Candied pistachios

100 g (3 ½ oz) caster (superfine) sugar

50 ml (2 fl oz) water

200 g (7 oz) shelled pistachio nuts

To candy the pistachio nuts, combine the sugar and water in a small saucepan over a low heat. Tilt and gently shake the pan from time to time to help the sugar dissolve evenly. Once it has dissolved, increase the heat to medium and simmer for about 5 minutes, or until it reaches the 'thread' stage*, which is 110°C (225°F) on a candy thermometer.

Add the pistachios to the syrup and stir well. Lower the heat and cook, stirring continuously, for around 2 minutes until the sugar crystallizes. Stir until the nuts are evenly covered with sugary crystals, then tip onto a tray lined with baking paper and spread the mixture out roughly. Leave to cool. Break up roughly and, if not using straight away, store in the freezer for up to a month.

To make the caramel, combine the water and sugar in a small saucepan and heat gently until the sugar dissolves. Swirl the pan from time to time to help it along. Once the sugar has dissolved, increase the heat to medium and simmer until it caramelizes to a dark golden brown. Don't stir the caramel once it's simmering. If crystals form on the sides of the pan, use a wet pastry brush to dissolve them. As soon as the caramel is achieved, pour it into a 1.25 litre (44 fl oz) soufflé dish or divide between small, individual ramekins. Swirl to coat the base and sides evenly with caramel, then leave for around 20 minutes to cool and set.

Preheat the oven to 140°C (275°F) and arrange the soufflé dish (or ramekins) in a deep roasting tin.

Combine the Muscat and sherry in a small pan and bring to the boil. Simmer until reduced to 80 ml (2 ½ fl oz), then pour into a bowl and cool completely.

Whisk the cream gently with the milk.

Combine the sugar, eggs, egg yolks and reduced Muscat in a large mixing bowl. Whisk together gently, but be careful not to make it frothy. Gently whisk in the cream mixture then strain into a jug.

Set the prepared mould(s) in a deep roasting tin. Pour in the custard,

then fill the tin with enough hot water to come halfway up the side of the dish. Cover the whole tin loosely with foil and cook in the oven for 1 ½ hours (or 60–70 minutes for smaller ones), or until the custard has just set. It should be soft, glossy and still a little wobbly in the centre – the custard will continue to set out of the oven. Carefully lift out of the water bath and leave to cool. Once cool, cover and chill for up to 2 days before serving.

When ready to serve, run a knife around the edge of the custard and invert onto a serving plate. Garnish with the candied pistachios and serve with plenty of whipped cream and a splash of orange flower water.

*Note: If you don't have a candy thermometer, the thread stage is reached when a drop of the syrup falls from a spoon in a long, unbroken thread.

Saffron rice pudding with spiced apricots

In this ambrosial dessert, tender, sunset-hued apricots make a beautiful sour-sweet counterpoint to the delicate, saffron-tinted rice. Make it when apricots are at their peak in the summer. At other times of the year you can use roasted rhubarb or top with slices of candied blood oranges.

SERVES 4-6

800 ml (28 fl oz) milk

90 g (3 ¼ oz) caster (superfine) sugar

finely grated zest of 1 orange

1 small cinnamon stick

½ vanilla pod, split and seeds scraped

1 tablespoon saffron liquid*

100 g (3 ½ oz) short-grain rice

1 egg yolk

150 ml (5 fl oz) pure (double or heavy) cream

50 g (1 ¾ oz) Pine Nut Praline (page 260), to garnish

edible flowers, to garnish (optional)

Spiced apricots

500 g (1 lb 2 oz) golden caster (superfine) sugar

500 ml (16 fl oz) water

200 ml (7 fl oz) Sauternes or another dessert wine

16 apricots, halved and stones removed

8 cardamom pods, crushed

½ cinnamon stick

finely grated zest and juice of 1 lemon

To make the rice pudding, combine the milk, sugar, zest, cinnamon stick, vanilla pod and seeds and saffron liquid in a large, heavy-based saucepan over a medium heat. Bring to the boil, then stir in the rice and boil briskly for a minute, stirring. Lower the heat and simmer very gently for about an hour, or until the rice is creamy and the milk has been absorbed. If you have a heat-diffuser, this is the time to use it. You don't need to stir constantly – especially for the first 20 minutes or so – but you do need to keep an eye on it to make sure the rice doesn't catch and burn on the bottom of the pan. Remove the pan from the heat and allow to cool for a few minutes.

Meanwhile, whisk the egg yolk with 2–3 tablespoons of the cream, then whisk this into the rice. Leave to cool completely – you can speed this up by scraping it into a bowl set in cold water. Fish out the bits of vanilla pod and cinnamon stick.

Whip the rest of the cream to stiff peaks. Fold it into the cold rice, then cover with cling film and chill for up to 2 hours.

For the spiced apricots, combine the sugar and water in a medium saucepan and heat gently until the sugar has dissolved. Bring to the boil, then lower the heat and simmer for 5 minutes.

Stir in the Sauternes, then add the apricots, together with the cardamom, cinnamon stick, lemon zest and juice. Simmer gently for 10–15 minutes, or until the apricots are tender. Use a slotted spoon to transfer them to a bowl and, when they are cool, carefully slip off their skins. Cook the syrup until reduced by one-third. Strain through a sieve to remove the aromatics, then pour over the apricots and transfer to the fridge for at least an hour, until chilled.

If you want to be fancy, serve individual portions in pretty glasses. Top with the apricots, praline and flowers (if using.) Otherwise, serve at the table in attractive bowls with the apricots on the side. Either way, we sometimes like to warm the apricots, which makes a lovely contrast with the chilled creamy rice.

*Note: To make the saffron liquid, soak 20 threads of saffron in a scant tablespoon of boiling water for 30 minutes.

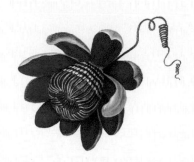

Sweet pastries

BEIGNETS WITH BAY LEAF SUGAR ... 246

PERSIAN SAFFRON TART WITH PASSION FRUIT CURD & MASCARPONE MOUSSE ... 247

SPICED CURRANT SFIHA WITH CINNAMON-GINGER CREAM ... 250

ORANGE BAKLAVA CIGARS ... 252

Is it possible to think of the Middle East and not imagine sticky lozenges of crisp golden baklava? These flaky pastries, stuffed with nuts, drenched in honey or syrup and perfumed with flower water are, perhaps, the food that is most clearly identified with this vast region. They pop up everywhere, from the Arabian Peninsula, through Iran and the Levant, to the Eastern Mediterranean shores of Turkey and Greece, and right across to the far reaches of North Africa.

There are countless regional variations of these honeyed delights but, despite their ubiquity, sweet pastries are considered something of a luxury item, saved for celebrations or religious holidays. But they are also synonymous with the legendary Middle Eastern hospitality, and will be offered to guests with tiny cups of cardamom-scented coffee – and you need this bitter partnering to offset the intense sweetness!

Although translucent filo predominates as the pastry of choice, shredded *kataifi* (a variation on the filo theme) is also popular, as are short- and puff-pastries, pastries made from semolina, and yeast batters for crisp little fritters. The fillings range from ground, cinnamon-spiked nuts (almond, walnut or pistachio) to thick, lactic cream and soft cheese or puréed fruits – dates and apricots are particularly popular.

We've included a few new recipes here, inspired by some traditional favourites from around the region, which can be eaten both Middle Eastern-style as a treat with coffee, or as a more familiar end to a meal.

Beignets with bay leaf sugar

Beignets are a rather sophisticated kind of doughnut – although we prefer to use a choux pastry, instead of the traditional yeast dough, as it makes for a lighter, crisper result. These are elegant enough to serve as dessert – perhaps with ice cream or sorbet (see pages 220–231) on the side.

Fresh bay leaves add a lovely, if surprising, flavour to the dredging sugar, but you could also use a few needles of fresh rosemary or lavender flowers.

MAKES AROUND 24

100 g (3 ½ oz) unsalted butter, diced

1 tablespoon caster (superfine) sugar

300 ml (10 ½ fl oz) water

180 g (6 ¼ oz) plain (all-purpose) flour

3 large eggs (or 4 small–medium eggs)

vegetable oil, for deep-frying

your choice of good-quality fruit curd (or see pages 60 and 247)

Bay leaf sugar

150 g (5 ½ oz) caster (superfine) sugar

2 small–medium fresh bay leaves

To make the bay leaf sugar, pull out and discard the hard central stalks then chop the leaves finely. Put into a mortar with a tablespoon of the sugar and pound as finely as you can to a green, slightly damp, paste. Tip into a larger bowl and mix with the rest of the sugar until evenly distributed. It's easiest to do this with a hand-held blender. Store in a jar until needed.

To make the beignets, combine the butter, sugar and water in a medium saucepan and slowly bring to the boil so that the butter melts completely. As the liquid boils up, quickly add the flour in one go and mix vigorously with a wooden spoon to incorporate it into the liquid. Beat over a lower heat for 3–4 minutes until the mixture is glossy and comes away from the sides of the pan in a smooth ball.

Tip the hot choux paste into the bowl of a stand-mixer. Beat for a minute on medium speed, then increase it to the maximum. Add the eggs, one at a time, then continue beating on maximum for 5 minutes, until the choux has cooled.

Spoon into a piping bag fitted with a 1.5 cm (⅝ in) nozzle and keep in the fridge for at least an hour, or up to 3 hours, until needed.

When ready to cook, pour vegetable oil into a deep-fryer or saucepan to a depth of around 8 cm (3 ¼ in) and heat to 170°C (325°F)*. Prepare a tray lined with kitchen paper and a dish of the bay leaf sugar.

Hold the piping bag over the oil and squeeze out the choux, slowly and steadily. Snip with scissors at 5 cm (2 ½ in) lengths, easing them into the oil gently. Fry in batches for 5 minutes, or until they transform into lovely golden brown puffs. Turn them around in the oil to ensure they colour evenly all over. Drain the beignets on kitchen paper for a few seconds then lift them into the dish of bay leaf sugar and coat them evenly.

Serve while warm with a dish of fruit curd for dipping. Or, make a split in each beignet and spoon in a little curd.

*Note: If you don't have a candy thermometer, the oil will have reached the correct temperature when a cube of bread browns lightly in about 30 seconds. Any faster and it will be too hot.

Persian saffron tart with passion fruit curd & mascarpone mousse

This is a delicious and sophisticated but rather complex dessert, with three distinct parts that each needs to be made separately. The tart must also be chilled for several hours, in two separate stages, before serving. However the component parts can all be made ahead of time and the trade-off for all the effort is a tart that looks sublimely fresh and elegant, with its clean layers, and golden-hued pastry. It is very rich, so will serve up to ten people, easily.

We often double the quantities of the pastry, as it keeps well in the freezer and makes a wonderful all-purpose tart shell for your favourite fillings.

SERVES 10

Saffron pastry

250 g (9 oz) plain (all-purpose) flour, plus extra for dusting

100 g (3 ½ oz) caster (superfine) sugar

finely grated zest of 1 lemon

180 g (6 ¼ oz) unsalted butter, softened, plus extra to grease

¼ teaspoon salt

1 egg yolk

1 tablespoon saffron liquid*, chilled

Mascarpone mousse

150 g (5 ½ oz) caster (superfine) sugar

60 ml (2 ¼ fl oz) water

1 egg, plus 1 egg yolk

1 gelatine leaf

100 ml (3 ½ fl oz) pure (double or heavy) cream

180 g (6 ½ oz) mascarpone cheese

1 teaspoon vanilla extract

splash orange flower water

Passion fruit curd

4 eggs

5 passion fruits, plus 3 to serve

150 g (5 ½ oz) caster (superfine) sugar

1 ½ gelatine leaves

4 teaspoons lemon juice

150 g (5 ½ oz) unsalted butter, cut into small cubes

For the saffron pastry, combine the flour, sugar and lemon zest in the bowl of a food processor and whiz to combine. Add the chopped butter and salt and pulse until it forms sandy crumbs. Add the egg yolk and saffron liquid and pulse until it just begins to come together. Tip onto a lightly floured work surface and knead briefly to bring it together into a ball of pastry. It is fairly stiff and crumbly, but don't overwork it. Shape into a flattish disc, wrap in cling film and rest in the fridge for at least an hour. Alternatively, freeze until ready to use.

To make the mascarpone mousse, combine the sugar and water in a small pan and heat gently until the sugar dissolves. Once completely dissolved, increase the heat and cook, without stirring, for 6–7 minutes, or until it reaches the 'soft ball' stage, which is 120°C (235°F) on a candy thermometer.

At the same time, combine the egg and egg yolk in the bowl of a stand-mixer and whisk vigorously for around 6–8 minutes, until very light and frothy. Turn off the motor.

Measure out 60 ml (2 ¼ fl oz) of the syrup. (Add the pulp from the 3 passion fruits to the remaining syrup and set this aside until ready to serve.) Pour the measured syrup into the whipped eggs carefully, taking care to avoid the sides of the bowl and the whisk attachment. Turn the motor on slowly, then increase the speed gradually to high and whisk until the mixture is cool – around 5 minutes.

Meanwhile, soak the gelatine leaf in a dish of cold water for a minute, until soft and slippery. Squeeze it to get rid of any excess water then mix it with 2 tablespoons of the cream. Zap in the microwave for 5 seconds and stir to dissolve it completely.

Whisk the remaining cream to medium peaks then set aside.

Use a balloon whisk to mix the mascarpone, vanilla extract and gelatine liquid together in a large bowl then pour in a little of the mousse and whisk gently to slacken. Fold in the rest of the mousse and then fold in the whipped cream and orange flower water. Chill in the fridge while you bake and then cool the tart shell.

When ready to bake the tart shell, butter a 33 cm x 10 cm (13 in x 4 in) rectangular tart tin. Place the chilled pastry on a lightly floured work surface and knead it briefly to a workable consistency. Roll the pastry, working fairly quickly so it doesn't warm up too much. Try to keep it in a rectangular shape and roll to a thickness of about 3 mm (⅛ in). Use the rolling pin to lift the pastry carefully onto the prepared tart tin and use your fingers to press it in along the sides and edges, evenly and firmly, so there are no cracks. Don't worry too much if it breaks. Fill any gaps with excess pastry and leave an excess edge all around to allow for shrinkage as the tart bakes. Transfer to the freezer for 30 minutes, or until very firm.

Meanwhile, preheat the oven to 180°C (350°F). Line the chilled tart shell with baking paper and fill with baking beans (or rice). Bake for 18 minutes, then carefully lift out the paper and beans. Return the tart shell to the oven for a further 5–10 minutes, or until the pastry is completely set and golden brown. Remove from the oven and set aside for around an hour to cool completely.

Spread the mascarpone mousse into the base of the cold tart shell, filling it about half full. Chill for 2 hours.

While the mousse is chilling, make the passion fruit curd. Whisk the eggs in a large bowl. Combine the flesh and seeds from the passion fruit and the sugar in a saucepan and heat gently to dissolve the sugar. Once dissolved, bring to the boil, then pour the hot mixture onto the eggs, whisking continuously. Tip the mixture back into the saucepan, and return to the heat, whisking all the time until it thickens. This should only take a few minutes. Remove from the heat.

Soak the gelatine in a dish of cold water for a minute, until soft and slippery. Squeeze it to get rid of any excess water and add to the passion fruit mixture, along with the lemon juice and butter. Whisk until the butter has completely melted. Push the curd through a sieve to remove the passion fruit seeds then set the curd aside for about 45 minutes until it cools to room temperature.

Spoon the cooled passion fruit curd into the tart shell, on top of the chilled mousse and spread the surface evenly. Leave to set for 2–3 hours, so that when you cut it into slices, the neat layers are maintained. Serve drizzled with the passion fruit syrup.

Note: To make the saffron liquid, soak 15 threads of saffron in a scant tablespoon of boiling water for 30 minutes. For this recipe you'll then need to chill it in the freezer for 10 minutes before adding to the pastry; you want it to be very cold when you add it to the pastry, but not frozen, of course!

Spiced currant sfiha with cinnamon-ginger cream

These are a riff on the famous little savoury pies from Baalbeck in Lebanon. Filled with spiced currants and a honeyed curd, they have a wonderfully crunchy sugar coating, and are not overly sweet. Although they are delicious as a teatime treat, we think they are special enough to serve as a dinner party dessert, particularly when paired with this ethereal whipped cinnamon-ginger cream.

MAKES 12

500 g (1 lb 2 oz) butter puff pastry
1 egg white, beaten
granulated sugar, for dusting

Spiced currants

100 g (3 ½ oz) currants
45 g (1 ¾ oz) dark muscovado sugar
45 g (1 ¾ oz) unsalted butter
30 ml (1 fl oz) medium sherry
finely grated zest of ½ orange
½ teaspoon cinnamon
a generous grating of nutmeg

Honeyed curd

80 g (2 ¾ oz) fresh goat's cheese
1 teaspoon honey
splash medium–sweet sherry
finely grated zest of ½ orange

Cinnamon-ginger cream

1 tablespoon honey
¼ teaspoon ground cinnamon
¼ teaspoon ground ginger
150 ml (5 fl oz) whipping cream

Combine the currants with the sugar, butter, sherry, orange zest, cinnamon and nutmeg in a small saucepan. Bring to a boil, then simmer for 1–2 minutes to soften the currants slightly in the buttery syrup. Remove from the heat and set aside to cool.

To make the honeyed curd, beat the goat's cheese with the honey, sherry and orange zest then chill in the fridge for 20 minutes until cold.

To make the cinnamon-ginger cream, warm the honey gently, then stir in the spices. Set aside until completely cold. Stir in the cream, then whip to soft, airy peaks. Chill until ready to use.

When ready to make the pies, preheat the oven to 200°C (400°F) and line two baking sheets with Silpat or baking paper.

Roll out the pastry onto a lightly floured work surface to a rough 45 cm (18 in) square. Cut out twelve 10 cm (4 in) rounds and lift them onto the prepared baking sheets. Place a spoonful of the spiced currant mixture in the centre of each round. Moisten the edges of the pastry with a little water, then pinch the corners together and fold the sides in slightly to form the traditional shape.

Brush them all over with egg white and sprinkle generously with sugar. Bake for 5 minutes then remove from the oven and add a small dollop of honeyed curd into each sfiha.

Return to the oven for a further 5 minutes, or until the sfiha are puffed and golden brown. Transfer to a wire rack and allow to cool briefly. Serve warm or at room temperature. They go very well with a nice cup of tea, otherwise serve them for dessert with the cinnamon-ginger cream or Crème Fraîche Ice Cream (page 223).

Orange baklava cigars

These fruity cigars make a welcome change from the traditional nut-stuffed baklava popular all around the Middle East and Eastern Mediterranean. For good results, try to find the best-quality, thinnest filo pastry that you can. Some of the supermarket filo is fairly thick, which makes for a less refined result.

The traditional method for making pastry cigars suggests folding the long pastry edges in as you roll them up. We find that with this method you not only end up with a high pastry-to-filling ratio but, more importantly, the fragile filo pastry will often split as they bake. After a bit of experimenting with technique, we've found that the best way to extract as much air as possible – and to minimise the splitting – is not to fold the ends in, but to seal them tightly after rolling, leaving a small edge. This is then trimmed neatly after baking. We've described the method in some detail below.

MAKES 8 CIGARS

2 large or 3 medium oranges

1 tablespoon orange marmalade

1 teaspoon vanilla extract, paste or seeds

3 sheets good-quality filo pastry

100 g (3 ½ oz) unsalted butter, clarified (see page 266), plus extra butter to grease

20 g (¾ oz) unsalted pistachio nuts, finely ground

Orange syrup

150 g (5 ½ oz) caster (superfine) sugar

100 ml (3 ½ fl oz) water

6 cardamom pods, roughly crushed

½ cinnamon stick

1 strip of orange peel, about 5–6 cm (2–2 ½ in) long

¼ teaspoon orange flower water or 1 tablespoon Cointreau

To make the orange syrup, combine the sugar, water, cardamom pods, cinnamon and orange peel in a saucepan and heat gently to dissolve the sugar. Bring to the boil, then lower the heat and simmer gently for 5 minutes. Remove from the heat then add the flower water or Cointreau and set aside to cool.

Bring a medium saucepan of water to the boil then carefully drop in the oranges. Cover with a circle of greaseproof paper and weigh down with a small plate to keep the oranges submerged. Lower the heat and simmer for an hour until the oranges are very soft.

Drain the oranges and allow to cool, then slice them thickly and pick out and discard any pips. Transfer the oranges to a food processor and blitz to a very fine purée. Aim to get it as smooth as you possibly can, which will somewhat depend on the sharpness of the blades!

Scrape the orange purée into a clean muslin square (or a tea towel or cheesecloth). Squeeze gently but deliberately to extract as much moisture as you can (it will only be about a tablespoon), then transfer the purée to a bowl and stir in the marmalade and vanilla. Spoon into a piping bag fitted with 1 cm (½ in) nozzle and set aside. It will keep in the fridge for up to 3 days.

Preheat the oven to 150°C (300°F). Butter a small–medium baking sheet or line it with Silpat.

Lay a sheet of filo pastry on your work surface and brush with clarified butter. Top with the remaining filo sheets, brushing each with butter as you go. Use a very sharp knife to cut into 8 rectangles. Pipe a fat line of orange purée along the long edge of each rectangle, leaving at least a centimetre clear at each end so the filling doesn't squish out when you roll up the cigars. Roll them up carefully – a small spatula or knife can help to get things started – keeping the pastry tucked in as tightly around the filling as you can (without squashing) to expel any pockets of air. Seal the long edge with clarified butter then use the flat blade of a spatula or knife to seal the open short ends very firmly.

Transfer to the prepared baking sheet and brush them all over with more butter. Bake for 25 minutes then increase the oven temperature to 160°C (320°F) and bake for a further 10 minutes, or until crisp and golden.

Shortly before the end of the baking, fish out the aromatics from the syrup and bring it to the boil. Pour over the cooked pastries and leave them to cool in the tray. Use a sharp knife to trim the ends neatly, but without exposing the filling. Sprinkle with pistachios and serve as a teatime treat or dessert. They are delicious with Crème Fraîche Ice Cream (page 223), with Ashta (page 20) or with your favourite thick yoghurt or cream.

Cakes & cookies

BITTER CHOCOLATE-HAZELNUT CAKE WITH CANDIED GRAPEFRUIT ... 257

BLACKBERRY-SOUR CREAM CRUMBLE CAKE ... 258

FENNEL SHORTBREAD THINS ... 259

TARBOUCHE – LEBANESE CHOCOLATE MARSHMALLOW CAKES ... 260

While they do a fine and extensive line in pastries and other sweet treats, there isn't a huge selection of cakes and biscuits in the Middle Eastern culinary repertoire. There are a few well-known offerings, such as date- or nut-stuffed *ma'amoul* biscuits, which are regularly turned out in their thousands for religious holidays. *Raybeh* is a kind of Lebanese shortbread, which is also popular, and then there are the famous almond and semolina cakes from Moorish Spain. In the big cities, especially where there's been any kind of French influence, pastry shops will sell versions of French cream-filled gateaux, which appear at special occasions, but generally, the selection is more limited than what we are used to in Western countries.

Rather than provide recipes for these few very traditional dishes – most of which we have covered in our previous books – the following pages include some of the cakes and biscuits that we are currently enjoying making. They each embrace Middle Eastern influence – with plenty of culinary licence thrown in! There's a bitter-chocolate hazelnut cake, which evolved from a delicious Spanish nut cake, a blackberry crumble cake, guaranteed to be a crowd-pleaser, and some very useful fennel-spiced shortbread biscuits that make a great accompaniment to ice creams and other creamy desserts. Then there's a recipe that's just a bit of fun: a recreation of the popular Lenanese teatime treats called 'tarbouche'.

Bitter chocolate-hazelnut cake with candied grapefruit

This cake evolved from one of our favourite Spanish nut cakes, and it demonstrates the natural affinity of hazelnuts with chocolate. It's a simple and rather light sponge cake, rather than the squidgy meringue-style *gianduja tortas* from Italy. In essence, it is all about the nuts! Toasted hazelnuts are ground and folded into the cake batter, but we like to keep some of them a little coarser, which adds a nutty texture to the finished cake.

It's a very versatile cake: instead of the chocolate glaze, orange icing is also delicious. Simpler still, dust it with icing sugar and serve with whipped cream. But best of all, we think, is this easy bitter chocolate glaze and a tangle of candied peel to top it off.

SERVES 8-10

120 g (4 ¼ oz) blanched hazelnuts

120 g (4 ¼ oz) plain (all-purpose) flour

1 teaspoon baking powder

½ teaspoon salt

115 g (4 oz) unsalted butter, at room temperature, plus extra to grease

110 g (3 ¾ oz) golden caster (superfine) sugar

2 eggs, plus 1 egg yolk, lightly beaten

1 teaspoon vanilla extract

¼ teaspoon finely grated orange zest

60 ml (2 fl oz) milk

20 g (¾ oz) best-quality dark chocolate (70% cocoa solids), very finely grated

Candied Citrus Peel (page 63), to garnish

Chocolate glaze

150 g (5 ½ oz) best-quality dark chocolate (70% cocoa solids)

150 g (5 ½ oz) unsalted butter, at room temperature, diced

Preheat the oven to 160°C (325°F). Spread the hazelnuts on a baking sheet and roast them for 10–12 minutes, until golden. Allow to cool.

Increase the oven temperature to 180°C (350°F). Butter and flour the base and side of a 20 cm (8 in) round cake tin and line the base with baking paper.

Place the flour, baking powder, salt and three-quarters of the toasted hazelnuts in the bowl of a food processor. Whiz for a couple of minutes, or until the hazelnuts are finely ground and you can smell their lovely nutty aroma. Pour into a bowl and set aside.

Finely chop the rest of the hazelnuts by hand into coarse, but even crumbs and set aside.

Combine the butter and sugar in the bowl of a stand-mixer. With the paddle attachment, beat at medium speed for around 4–5 minutes, or until light and fluffy. Add the egg mixture, a third at a time, beating well after each addition and scraping down the sides of the bowl as necessary. Mix in the vanilla and orange zest then scrape the bottom and sides of the bowl.

Lower the speed and add the flour mixture in three batches, alternating with the milk. When the batter is just combined, use a rubber spatula to gently fold in the reserved hazelnuts and the grated chocolate. Scrape into the prepared cake tin and smooth the surface.

Bake the cake for around 30 minutes, until a skewer inserted into the cake comes out clean. Leave it to cool, still in its tin, on a wire rack for 10 minutes. Gently run a knife around the edge of the tin and invert the cake onto a plate. Remove the baking paper and leave to cool completely.

To make the glaze, put the chocolate in a heatproof bowl set over a pan of simmering water (it shouldn't touch the water). Stir gently and when it has completely melted, remove from the heat and add the pieces of butter. Beat with a hand-blender, taking care not to incorporate any air. Pour the glaze over the cake evenly and allow to set before topping with candied grapefruit peel.

Blackberry-sour cream crumble cake

One of the joys of this utterly delicious cake is that it is so forgiving! If you don't have blackberries, use raspberries or blueberries. If you don't have sour cream, use yoghurt, or even crème fraîche. The net result is the same: a soft, tender-crumbed cake, with tangy bursts of fruit and a lovely cinnamon-crunch topping. It's as good for pudding as tea time. Keep it in a sealed container in the pantry for up to 4 days, or chill for up to a week.

SERVES 8–10

Cake

180 g (6 ¼ oz) plain (all-purpose) flour

1 ¼ teaspoons baking powder

¼ teaspoon bicarbonate of soda (baking soda)

¼ teaspoon salt

140 g (5 oz) fresh or unthawed frozen blackberries or raspberries

240 ml (8 ¾ fl oz) sour cream

1 ½ teaspoons vanilla extract

140 g (5 oz) unsalted butter, softened, plus extra to grease

200 g (7 oz) golden caster (superfine) sugar

2 large eggs

Crumble topping

120 g (4 ¼ oz) plain (all-purpose) flour

50 g (1 ¾ oz) granulated sugar

80 g (2 ¾ oz) firmly packed muscovado or dark brown sugar

1 teaspoon ground cinnamon

⅛ teaspoon salt

100 g (3 ½ oz) unsalted butter, melted

To make the topping, combine the flour, sugars, cinnamon and salt in a bowl until well blended. Add the melted butter and mix with a fork, stirring until the butter is absorbed and the dry ingredients are uniformly moistened. Set aside.

Preheat the oven to 180°C (350°F). Butter and flour the base and sides of a 23 cm (9 in) square cake tin.

In a medium bowl, whisk together the flour, baking powder and soda and salt until well blended.

Toss the blackberries with 1 tablespoon of the flour mixture until the berries are evenly coated. Set aside. In a small bowl, whisk together the sour cream and vanilla extract. Set aside.

Combine the butter and sugar in the bowl of a stand-mixer. With the paddle attachment, beat at medium speed for around 4–5 minutes, or until light and fluffy. Add the eggs, one at a time, beating well after each addition and scraping down the sides of the bowl as necessary.

Lower the speed and add the flour in three batches, alternating with the sour cream. When the batter is smooth, use a rubber spatula to gently fold in the blackberries. Scrape into the prepared cake tin and smooth the surface.

Sprinkle the crumble topping evenly over the surface, breaking up any large lumps with your fingers. Bake the cake for about 45 minutes, until a skewer inserted into the cake comes out clean. Place on a wire rack and leave to cool completely, still in its tin.

Cut into squares and serve from the tin with tea or coffee or as dessert.

Fennel shortbread thins

Fennel adds an appealing savoury warmth to buttery shortbread. We roll the biscuit dough thinly to make elegant crisp biscuits that are a great accompaniment to ice cream and other creamy desserts, like the Lemon Possets on page 234. They're equally good with a cup of tea or coffee.

MAKES 16–20

120 g (4 ¼ oz) unsalted butter, chilled and diced

50 g (1 ¾ oz) icing (confectioners') sugar

½ teaspoon vanilla extract

140 g (5 oz) plain (all-purpose) flour, plus extra for dusting

⅛ teaspoon salt

finely grated zest of 1 orange

1 ½ teaspoons fennel seeds, roughly crushed

Combine all the ingredients in a food processor and whiz until the mixture just beings to clump together. Do not over-process.

Tip the dough onto a lightly floured work surface and briskly bring it together into a flattish rectangle. Wrap in cling film and chill for at least an hour. Alternatively, freeze until required. It will keep quite happily for a month.

Divide the dough in half and work with one piece at a time; keep the other piece chilled. Roll out between 2 sheets of baking paper to a thickness of 3 mm (⅛ in) – or even slightly thinner, if you dare. Cut the dough into shapes – elegant long triangles, neat rectangles or circles are all good – and carefully lift onto a baking sheet lined with Silpat or baking paper. Refrigerate for another 20 minutes.

When ready to bake, preheat the oven to 160°C (320°F). Bake the shortbreads for 10–12 minutes, or until they colour a very pale gold. Watch carefully in the final few minutes to make sure they don't brown too much.

Remove from the oven and cool on the tray for a few minutes to allow the shortbreads to firm up. Then lift them carefully onto wire racks to cool completely.

Tarbouche – Lebanese chocolate marshmallow cakes

These hugely popular Lebanese teatime treats are a kind of Middle Eastern version of Twinkies or Tunnocks Tea Cakes. They are called 'tarbouche' – which is the Arabic version of a Turkish fez – to reflect their shape.

To make the soft, fluffy marshmallow, you'll need to source Trimolene (a special 'inverted' sugar used for candies, desserts and ice creams) and to follow the recipe very precisely.

MAKES ABOUT 12

Pine nut praline

150 g (5 oz) caster sugar
40 ml (1 ½ fl oz) water
200 g (7 oz) pine nuts

Biscuit base

200 g (7 oz) ginger biscuits
100 g (3 ½ oz) unsalted butter,
   melted

Marshmallow

280 g (10 oz) strawberries, hulled
   and roughly chopped
1 teaspoon rosewater
300 g (10 ½ oz) caster sugar
255 g (9 oz) Trimoline
12 x 1.6 g gold-strength gelatine,
   soaked in 60 ml (2 fl oz) cold
   water for 10 minutes

Chocolate coating

250 g (9 oz) best-quality dark
   chocolate (70% cocoa solids)
50 g (1 ¾ oz) unsalted butter, at
   room temperature, diced
edible flowers to garnish, optional

To make the praline, combine the sugar and water in a small saucepan and heat slowly to dissolve the sugar. Once completely dissolved, increase the heat and simmer for 5 minutes, or until it reaches the 'thread' stage, which is 110°C (225°F) on a candy thermometer*. Add the pine nuts and stir well. The sugar will crystallize as the oils come out of the nuts. Keep stirring until it redissolves to a caramel, which may take 10–15 minutes. Pour onto a baking tray lined with baking paper. Smooth evenly and leave to cool. When cold, pound to coarse crumbs with a rolling pin.

When ready to make the base, preheat the oven to 160°C (315°F). In the bowl of a food processor, whiz the biscuits to fairly fine crumbs (or put them in a sealed plastic bag and bash them with a rolling pin!). Stir in the melted butter evenly. Tip the mixture onto a sheet of greaseproof paper and roll to a thickness of ½ cm (¼ in). Bake for 8 minutes, or until lightly browned, then leave to cool. Cut into 7 cm (2 ¾ in) circles.

For the marshmallow, whiz the strawberries and rosewater in a blender until finely puréed, then pass through a sieve. Combine the sugar with 105 g (3 ½ oz) of the Trimoline and 70 g (2 ½ oz) of the strawberry purée in a saucepan and bring to a boil.

In the bowl of a stand-mixer, combine the remaining 150 g (5 ½ oz) Trimoline with another 70 g (2 ½ oz) of the strawberry purée and the soaked gelatine then whisk on medium speed to combine. With the motor running, slowly pour on the boiling syrup. Continue whisking for 5 minutes or until it cools to room temperature. Spoon into a piping bag fitted with a 1 ½ cm (1 in) nozzle and pipe the marshmallow onto the biscuit bases in a big blob. Smooth the surface evenly with a wet finger. Chill for 2 hours until set.

To make the chocolate coating, combine the chocolate and butter in a heatproof bowl set over a pan of simmering water (it shouldn't touch the water). When they have completely melted, remove from the heat and stir them together well. Weigh out 60 g (2 ¼ oz) of the praline and fold it gently into the chocolate. Spoon over the tarbouche cakes evenly and scatter on the flowers, if using. Leave to set on a wire rack for 20 minutes.

*Note: If you don't have a candy thermometer, the thread stage is reached when a drop of the syrup falls from a spoon in a long, unbroken thread.

Food notes

THE MIDDLE EASTERN PANTRY ... 263

FROM THE FRIDGE ... 266

MEASURING ... 266

OVEN TEMPERATURES ... 267

THE MIDDLE EASTERN PANTRY

While fresh vegetables and fruits are the heroes of this recipe collection, here are some of the ingredients that we usually have in the pantry to help bring out their best. Many are absolute essentials, while others are listed because they are more unusual to a Western cook and so merit some further explanation.

Amardine is dried apricot leather which comes in sheets and is available from Middle Eastern stores and specialty food shops. We use it in recipes – usually cooked down to a paste – as a kind of substitute for apricot purée and also snipped into little pieces for use as a pretty garnish.

Barberries are especially popular in Persian cooking. These tiny red berries have a distinctive tart-sweet flavour and you buy them dried for use in rice dishes, stuffings and omelettes or to make fruit leather. We recommend checking through them for rogue twigs or stones, picking off obvious stems and washing them before use. Barberries can be found in Middle Eastern food stores.

Bulgur wheat, also known as burghul or cracked wheat, comes in numerous grades, from coarse, to medium or fine, and is also available as the whole grain.

Bulgur is a staple widely used in Middle Eastern cooking, often as an alternative to rice.

Couscous has become indispensible in many kitchens nowadays, and there is a wide selection on offer. Just don't choose the pre-flavoured kind, whatever you do.

Dandelions are one of our new favourite bitter salad leaves and we use them, often interchangeably, with other wild salad greens. There are seemingly endless varieties of wild greens around the Eastern Mediterranean and the Middle East – some very region-specific – but dandelions are pleasingly ubiquitous! The younger they are, the milder the flavour and the better they are in salads. As they get older and more bitter, they are better for the cooking pot. Although you can probably find them in your own back garden (wash them very well if you live in a big city) they are increasingly being cultivated commercially. These varieties tend to be longer and finer than the common weed, and range from dark green to pale yellow.

Flour tends to be plain white flour for cakes and pastries and strong white bread flour for baking. We also use pasta flour. Wholemeal flour is not as widely used in the Middle Eastern kitchen.

Flowers have had something of a resurgence of popularity in Western kitchens but they've always been used abundantly in the Middle East, especially in Persian and Ottoman cooking. They are scattered into salads or used to garnish all kinds of polows and stews or they are ground and added to spice mixes or to sweets and desserts. Roses and orange flowers are also used to make jams and sherbets, and are distilled to make essences and flower waters – see below.

Flower waters are distilled from fresh flowers for culinary use and they are an indispensable addition to the the Middle Eastern kitchen. The best known in the West are rosewater and orange flower, which are both used to perfume sugar syrups in which sweet pastries are steeped, and to add fragrance and flavour to cordials, desserts and ice creams. Add flower waters judiciously as some are stronger than others – as with all cooking, taste as you go to achieve the balance that suits you. Flower waters are widely found, but it's worth visiting a Middle Eastern food store to understand the range available.

Freekeh are whole wheat grains, harvested while 'green', or immature. They are fire-roasted, which burns the chaff but leaves the young kernels intact. Freekeh is most often used to make into pilav.

Gelatine products are infuriatingly confusing as there is no standardisation and single leaves from different brands will set different quantities of liquid. Despite this, we still prefer leaf gelatine to powdered, as the flavour is so much better, and we simply follow the instructions on the packet for the quantities required, depending on the brand. If you are vegetarian, then you should substitute the appropriate amount of agar-agar.

Herbs are vital for authentic Middle Eastern flavour and we use flat-leaf parsley, mint and coriander every day. Other favourites are basil, bay, thyme and tarragon.

Koussa are a variety of small, bulbous pale-coloured zucchini which are very popular in the Middle East. They are much easier for hollowing out and stuffing than the traditional darker variety. You can find them in Middle Eastern and Asian food stores and in some specialist greengrocers.

Legumes, such as chickpeas, white beans and various coloured lentils are all important ingredients in our kitchen. We tend to buy them dried, for soaking, but good-quality tinned versions are also good to have on hand.

Nigella seeds (also called 'kolonji') are often mistakenly referred to as black cumin seeds. Nigella seeds will be familiar with anyone who knows Turkish bread, for it is these that are sprinkled over the dough before baking, as they are in Iran too. Nigella seeds are becoming increasingly available through providores, and can be found in Middle Eastern food stores.

Nuts, such as almonds, walnuts, hazelnuts and pine nuts are old favourites, while pecans make a lovely change.

Oils are, in the main, pressed from olives. We like pure olive oil for shallow frying and sautéeing and extra-virgin olive oil for dressing salads. We also use sunflower and rapeseed oil for deep-frying, when you need to heat to high temperatures.

Pepper in our kitchen is usually freshly ground from black peppercorns. For some dishes we prefer to use white pepper – either for the flavour, or where we don't want little black speckles to make a dish (mayonnaise, for instance) look grubby.

Pomegranate molasses is made from boiled and concentrated pomegranate juice. It has an intense sweet-sour flavour, and we often add it to dressings, salads or meat dishes.

Purslane is a sprawling succulent that has a mild, almost cucumber-like flavour and a fresh crunchy texture. It's a popular summer salad leaf in many Middle Eastern countries while both stems and leaves are added to soups, stews and other cooked vegetable dishes. It is prevalent in Europe, North America and Australia but, curiously, is not widely used. We also use winter purslane (sometimes called Miner's Lettuce) which is not the same thing at all. But it is equally succulent in salads and pretty as a picture.

Quinoa is a new favourite of ours, although it's not authentically Middle Eastern. We use it in a similar way to bulgur wheat, in salads and hot pilafs.

Rice is another Middle Eastern staple and we always keep a good-quality long-grain basmati rice in our store for our favourite Persian polows. It's useful to have short-grain rice for puddings and risotto rice as well.

Saffron threads should be lightly warmed before use to release their pungent aroma and flavour. They can be lightly toasted in a dry pan (taking care not to burn them to a crisp) and then ground to a fine powder before using. Alternatively, whole saffron threads can be infused in a small amount of hot water and then both liquid and threads can be added.

Salt comes in two forms in our kitchen. We use a good, fine, free-flowing sea salt for cooking and we use salt flakes for last-minute seasoning. There are endless varieties available, but our favourites are Maldon sea salt from England, Fleur de Sel from France or any of the locally harvested Australian river or lake salt flakes.

Seeds make great additions to salads, as well as baked items. We love sesame, sunflower and pumpkin seeds.

Sour cherries are loved all around the Middle East. They are eaten fresh in the summer months, and turned into sherbets, preserves and fruit pastes all year round. Dried sour cherries have a wonderful, almost vanilla-like quality. If you can resist eating them straight from the packet, they can be added to rice dishes or stews, or poached until soft in a lime-spiked sugar syrup and served with rice desserts or as a topping for ice cream. Ordinary dried cherries (but not glacé cherries) may be substituted, at a pinch.

Spices are the *sine qua non* of the Middle Eastern kitchen. As a minimum, try to stock cumin and coriander seeds, fennel and caraway seeds, cinnamon (ground and in sticks), allspice and paprika. Other more unusual spices are listed separately.

Stock, where called for, is a light vegetable stock and we give a recipe for a straightforward version on on page 88. You could also use a good-quality purchased stock, but we suggest using a liquid (or liquid concentrate) as stock cubes tend to have a rather aggressive dried herb flavour.

Sumac is a dried dark-red berry with a sour, citrus flavour. It may be ground and added to dips or salads and gives a sharp kick to roasts and grills. It is the vital partner to za'atar in the spice paste used to top manoushi pizza breads – indeed, as Greg is fond of saying, 'Za'atar is nothing without sumac'!

Tahini is a thick paste made from ground sesame seeds. It is used to make spreads or dressings and sometimes mixed with molasses to spread on bread.

Turkish chilli flakes (red and black) are a hugely popular seasoning in Turkish cooking. The flavour ranges from mild and sweet to fiercely hot, but we prefer something of medium-heat.

Turkish red pepper paste is a concentrated paste of red peppers which is available from Turkish and Middle Eastern food stores. It comes in mild and hot versions and is used to flavour soups and stews, a little like tomato paste.

Turmeric is a dried, ground rhizome (part ginger family) which has a slightly acrid flavour and adds a vivid yellow hue to savoury dishes. Although it is often considered a sort of poor man's saffron, it should never be used as a substitute, but only in its own right.

Vine leaves are best freshly picked, but these are hard to find unless you grow your own! It's much easier to find jars of vine leaves pickled in brine and you can also find them vacuum packed. Both are quite acceptable.

Vinegars vary in flavour and acidity, and we like to have a selection on hand for salads and to use as a flavour hit in braises or marinades. Our default favourite is apple vinegar, followed by a good-quality white wine or sherry vinegar.

Yeast is nearly always the instant or 'dried active' variety because it is so easy to use. There's no need to cream it to a paste or to activate it with warm water, as you would with fresh yeast. Instead you just chuck it in with the flour (although keep it away from the salt, as this can kill it off before it has a chance to work its magic).

Za'atar is one of the essential herbs of the Middle Eastern kitchen. It is a type of wild thyme with a flavour somewhere between oregano and thyme.

In countries where it grows abundantly, the leaves are used fresh in all kinds of dishes. Elsewhere, you're more likely to find the dried variety of za'atar, which is usually blended with other spices, such as sumac and sesame seeds, and mixed into a paste with olive oil (confusingly, this mixture is also called za'atar!).

FROM THE FRIDGE

Butter is one of our favourite things, especially when home-made (see page 52). We generally use unsalted, or slightly salted butter, although this only really matters in desserts and sweet pastries. It's not going to ruin a dish if you only have the salted kind to hand.

Cheese in the Middle East is mainly the non-melting, fresh, white kind – like feta or the famously 'squeaky' haloumi. We love all kinds of cheese, though, and our recipes also make good use of goat's cheese and European hard cheeses, such as parmesan. These are not suitable for vegetarians, given that they are usually made with animal rennet, but vegetable rennet versions of most of these cheeses are readily available. We also make home-made strained yoghurt cheese (see Labneh, page 73) which has the benefit of being suitable for vegetarians (but not vegans), as it is entirely rennet-free.

Clarified butter is used for making sweets, desserts and pastries, or in dishes where the milk solids in hard butter might burn. You can buy ghee – a commercially produced equivalent – in some supermarkets or in Asian stores. But it is very easy to clarify butter at home: melt butter (preferably unsalted) in a small saucepan until it froths. Strain through a fine, clean cloth (such as muslin or even a Chux) and discard the solids. Keep the clarified butter, covered, in the fridge for up to three months.

Cream is confusing as it comes with varying fat contents, and is called different things in different states and different countries! In our recipes we use pure (double or heavy) cream, by which we mean any cream that has a high butterfat content (roughly anywhere between 40–48%), is thick and unctuous and can be whipped. We sometimes use pouring (single) cream (similar to American half-and-half), which is much runnier and has a butterfat content of around 18%. We also use crème fraîche, which has a butterfat content of between 30–40% and is made by 'souring' cream with a culture. We love it for its slight tang and more nuanced flavour and often prefer it to double cream.

Eggs, and their nomenclature, continue to be fiercely debated in the food industry. The options available to you – whether free-range, cage-free, organic and so on – will depend on where you live. Our own preference is to buy eggs from chickens that have been as humanely reared as possible. We mainly use large eggs, which weigh around 60–65 g (2 ¼ oz), but it's not usually crucial, other than for baking.

Milk in our recipes is full-fat, whole milk, although this is only really important in the ice cream and dessert recipes.

Yoghurt is, perhaps, the single most loved ingredient in our respective kitchens! We use it to accompany just about everything we eat, and it is also an important ingredient in all kinds of soups and braises, as well as making a lovely creamy base for dips and sauces. We tend to use both thick Greek-style yoghurts (which are slightly strained and can have a fat content of 10–13%) and ordinary natural (whole milk) yoghurt, which has a lower fat content (around 4 or 5%) and is runnier. We avoid low-fat yoghurts as they are too watery. We mainly use cow's milk yoghurts as they have a cleaner, fresher flavour than goat's or sheep's milk yoghurts.

MEASURING

When it comes to measuring, we use the metric scale, but acknowledge that there are those who prefer Imperial. We've included both in our recipes, and you should stick to one method or the other and not mix them up. In the main, we weigh things or we measure them by volume. This is because it's the most accurate approach and it's the way professional chefs do it. It's also the most straightforward, given that different countries have different sizes for their 'cups' and tablespoons, which can over-complicate matters when you measure ingredients in this way. (Australian tablespoons are 20 ml, but American and British tablespoons are 15 ml; American cups are 225 ml / 8 fl oz, but Australian and British ones are 250 ml / 8 ¾ fl oz).

The only exception we make is for fresh herbs. Because bunches come in varying sizes and because some amounts are just too light to weigh on most domestic kitchen scales we use measuring cups or tablespoons (American, Australian or British – with herbs, it really doesn't matter).

Our main advice is not to get too hung up about measuring. In the main, a bit extra or less here and there is not going to affect a dish. It's only really important to be accurate with baking and with pastries and desserts.

OVEN TEMPERATURES

Our ovens are fan-assisted, as most seem to be these days, and they heat to a slightly higher temperature than conventional ovens. Reduce the temperature by about 10°C (50°F) if your oven is the conventional kind. Remember, too, that ovens tend to have their own idiosyncrasies and nothing should replace your own understanding of the hot and cool spots within.

INDEX

almonds
Almond-barberry labneh 139
Almond-saffron butter 55
Griddled broccolini with almonds & harissa butter 166
Long-grain rice with lemon & toasted almonds 193
Shredded bitter leaves with roasted grapes, almonds & avocado 135
apples
Apple glaze 24
Apple jelly 236
Apple-walnut butter 57
Glazed apple-raisin fritters 24
Golden bulgur wheat with apple, raisins & yoghurt 182
apricots 263
Apricot-cardamom butter 57
Spiced apricots 243
artichokes
Artichoke & lemon labneh 74
Braised artichokes, preserved lemon & fingerling potatoes with basil crème fraîche 158
Buttered egg noodles with artichokes, cèpes & saffron 216
Farro with slow-roasted tomatoes, artichokes, olives & oregano 187
Ashta 20
Asparagus avgolemono 91
aubergine see eggplant
avocado
Preserved lemon guacamole 71
Shredded bitter leaves with roasted grapes, almonds & avocado 135

Baby carrot tagine with yoghurt & honeyed pine nuts 174
Baby eggplants stuffed with walnuts & chillies 81
Baby leeks in saffron vinaigrette with hazelnut crumbs 148
Baked beans with Turkish spices & crunchy crumbs 202
Baked naans 36
Baked tomatoes with saffron, bulgur & barberries 106
Banana ice cream with salted date caramel 225
barberries 263
Almond-barberry labneh 139
Baked tomatoes with saffron, bulgur & barberries 106
basil
Basil crème fraîche 158
Fregola with zucchini, citrus & basil 212
Shaved zucchini with grana, burrata & basil 142
bay leaves
Bay leaf sugar 246
Buttermilk sorbet with bay leaf & lemon 228
beans, dried
Tomato & bean soup with harissa & honey 95
Hazelnut falafel & tahini-whipped crème fraîche 114
Baked beans with Turkish spices & crunchy crumbs 202
Beignets with bay leaf sugar 246

berries
Blackberry-sour cream crumble cake 258
Breakfast couscous with nuts, seeds & blueberries 21
Pavlova 'flowers' with apple jelly, raspberries & vanilla labneh 236
Rhubarb, raspberry & cardamom fridge jam 58
Summer berry salad with ginger, lime & labneh 18
Bitter chocolate-hazelnut cake with candied grapefruit 257
Blackberry-sour cream crumble cake 258
Blood oranges in spicy caramel sauce with ashta 20
borlotti beans
Fresh borlotti beans with tomato & pomegranate dressing 152
Persian 'baghali polow' with borlotti beans & dill 192
Braised artichokes, preserved lemon & fingerling potatoes with basil crème fraîche 158
breads 32–45
Breakfast couscous with nuts, seeds & blueberries 21
broad beans
Crushed broad beans 66
Egyptian breakfast beans with feta, lemon oil & green chilli relish 30
Persian 'baghali polow' with borlotti beans & dill 192
broccolini
Griddled broccolini with almonds & harissa butter 166
bulgur wheat 263
Baked tomatoes with saffron, bulgur & barberries 106
Bulgur stuffing 106
Golden bulgur wheat with apple, raisins & yoghurt 182
Pumpkin kibbeh stuffed with feta & spinach 118
Spicy Turkish kisir 183
Toasted nuts, seeds & grains with smashed cherries, herbs & goat's curd 185
Winter tabbouleh 145
Buttered egg noodles with artichokes, cèpes & saffron 216
Buttermilk sorbet with bay leaf & lemon 228
butters 50–57
Sizzling mint butter 92

cakes 254–261
Candied citrus peel 63
Candied pistachios 240
caramel 20, 225, 240
cardamom
Apricot-cardamom butter 57
Pear sorbet with Prosecco, cardamom & lime 229
Rhubarb, raspberry & cardamom fridge jam 58
capsicum
Sweet peppers & shallots in lemon oil 83
Tunisian-style vegetables roasted on embers 167
Turkish bread & roasted vegetable salad 150
Turkish red pepper paste 69
carrots

Baby carrot tagine with yoghurt & honeyed pine nuts 174
Honey-roasted carrots with dates, dandelions & Moroccan dressing 160
Lentils with sweet carrots, dates & golden cream 204
Spicy carrot pickle 84
Tunisian-style vegetables roasted on embers 167
Turkish-style carrot labneh 74
cauliflower
Winter tabbouleh 145
Celeriac remoulade with tahini & golden raisins 134
Charred corncobs with almond-saffron butter 168
cheese 266
Home-made shankleesh 72
Parsnip skordalia with garlic, lemon & scarmorza 68
Shaved zucchini with grana, burrata & basil 142
White zucchini omelette with mint & melting gouda 29
Zucchini blossom & preserved lemon risotto with ricotta & parmesan 198
Zucchini blossoms with haloumi in olive-brioche crumbs 102
see also feta, goat's cheese, labneh
Chermoula 153
cherries 265
Middle Eastern granola with pomegranate, sour cherries & pistachios 23
Toasted nuts, seeds & grains with smashed cherries, herbs & goat's curd 185
chickpeas
Egyptian breakfast beans with feta, lemon oil & green chilli relish 30
Hazelnut falafel & tahini-whipped crème fraîche 114
Lebanese spiced chickpeas & eggplant with pita 206
Roasted tomato & chickpea curry with coconut & coriander 209
Spicy red hummus 71
Chilled yoghurt soup with cucumber, currants & walnuts 89
chilli
Baby eggplants stuffed with walnuts & chillies 81
Fennel-Turkish chilli flatbreads 39
Feta cheese straws with Turkish chilli 130
Green chilli relish 30
Green harissa 56
Red harissa 56
Turkish eggs with spinach, chilli & yoghurt cream 26
Turkish red pepper paste 69
Zhoug 197
chocolate
Bitter chocolate-hazelnut cake with candied grapefruit 257
Chocolate muhallabeya with Turkish coffee granita 239
Stracciatella with orange peel 226
Tarbouche - Lebanese chocolate marshmallow cakes 260
cilantro see coriander
Cinnamon-ginger cream 250
citrus
Candied citrus peel 63
Citrus oil 212

Citrus salad with red radicchio & pomegranate dressing 139
Fregola with zucchini, citrus & basil 212
see also specific citrus fruit
Classic labneh in oil 74
coconut
   Coconut-date flatbreads 39
   Roasted tomato & chickpea curry with coconut & coriander 209
cookies
   Fennel shortbread thins 259
coriander
   Roasted tomato & chickpea curry with coconut & coriander 209
   Toasted quinoa with coriander, lime & crunchy pumpkin 180
   Zhoug 197
corn
   Charred corncobs with almond-saffron butter 168
   Fresh corn soup with rice, yoghurt & sizzling mint butter 92
courgette *see* zucchini
couscous 263
   Breakfast couscous with nuts, seeds & blueberries 21
   Mixed spring greens with golden raisins & couscous 217
   Wedding couscous with herbs & flowers 219
Crème fraîche
   Basil crème fraîche 158
   Crème fraîche ice cream 223
   Home-made crème fraîche 52
   Home-made crème fraîche butter 52
   Tahini-whipped crème fraîche 114
Crumble topping 258
Crunchy crumbs 102, 202
Crushed broad beans 66
Crushed hazelnut-rosemary flatbreads 39
cucumber
   Chilled yoghurt soup with cucumber, currants & walnuts 89
   Cucumber, quinoa & tarragon-yoghurt salad 178
currants
   Chilled yoghurt soup with cucumber, currants & walnuts 89
   Rainbow chard with soused currants & pine nuts 155
   Saffron fruit loaf 45
   Spiced currant sfiha with cinnamon-ginger cream 250
   Wild garlic, leek & currant fritters with honey 113

dandelions 263
   Honey-roasted carrots with dates, dandelions & Moroccan dressing 160
   Teta's pie - dandelion, leek & barrel-aged feta 122
dates
   Coconut-date flatbreads 39
   Honey-roasted carrots with dates, dandelions & Moroccan dressing 160
   Lentils with sweet carrots, dates & golden cream 204
   Salted date caramel 225
desserts 232–243
dill
   Persian 'baghali polow' with borlotti beans & dill 192

Summer vine leaves with tomatoes, pine nuts & dill 108
dips and spreads 64–75
dressings 135, 136, 139, 148, 152, 160, 180, 185, 203, 214

eggplant
   Baby eggplants stuffed with walnuts & chillies 81
   Eggplant pilaf with yoghurt & zhoug 197
   Eggplant relish 82
   Lebanese spiced chickpeas & eggplant with pita 206
   North African eggplant pie with pimento sugar 124
   Slow-roasted eggplant with saffron-lemon cream 171
   Tomato & eggplant baked with tarragon-yoghurt custard 173
eggs 266
   Asparagus avgolemono 91
   Pavlova 'flowers' with apple jelly, raspberries & vanilla labneh 236
   Saffron-scrambled eggs 98
   Turkish eggs with spinach, chilli & yoghurt cream 26
   White zucchini omelette with mint & melting gouda 29
Egyptian breakfast beans with feta, lemon oil & green chilli relish 30

Farro with slow-roasted tomatoes, artichokes, olives & oregano 187
Fatima's fingers with goat's cheese, lemon, tarragon & thyme 127
fava beans *see* broad beans
fennel
   Fennel shortbread thins 259
   Fennel-Turkish chilli flatbreads 39
feta
   Egyptian breakfast beans with feta, lemon oil & green chilli relish 30
   Feta cheese straws with Turkish chilli 130
   Green beans with chermoula, shallots & feta 153
   Home-made shankleesh 72
   Pumpkin kibbeh stuffed with feta & spinach 118
   Teta's pie - dandelion, leek & barrel-aged feta 122
figs
   Persian soft herb salad with fresh figs & labneh 136
Freekeh pilaf with spiced roast pumpkin & shallots 188
Fregola with zucchini, citrus & basil 212
Fresh borlotti beans with tomato & pomegranate dressing 152
Fresh corn soup with rice, yoghurt & sizzling mint butter 92
fritters 24, 110–119, 246

garlic
   Green olive aioli 115
   Parsnip skordalia with garlic, lemon & scarmorza 68
   Taklia 216
   Wild garlic, leek & currant fritters with honey 113
ginger
   Cinnamon-ginger cream 250
   Gingered grapefruit curd 60

Haloumi, mint & stuffing 102
Lime-ginger dressing 185
Pear-ginger butter 57
Summer berry salad with ginger, lime & labneh 18
Glazed apple-raisin fritters 24
goat's cheese
   Fatima's fingers with goat's cheese, lemon, tarragon & thyme 127
   Goat's cheese dumplings with fresh & dried mint 214
   Goat's cheese-za'atar flatbreads 39
   Home-made shankleesh 72
   Toasted nuts, seeds & grains with smashed cherries, herbs & goat's curd 185
Golden bulgur wheat with apple, raisins & yoghurt 182
Golden cream 204
grains 176–189
grapefruit
   Candied citrus peel 63
   Gingered grapefruit curd 60
Green beans with chermoula, shallots & feta 153
Green chilli relish 30
Green harissa 56
Green olive aioli 115
greens
   Mixed spring greens with golden raisins & couscous 217
   Rainbow chard with soused currants & pine nuts 155
Griddled broccolini with almonds & harissa butter 166
Griddled flatbreads 36

Haloumi, mint & ginger stuffing 102
Harissa broth 219
Harissa butter 56
Harissa, green and red 56
hazelnuts
   Baby leeks in saffron vinaigrette with hazelnut crumbs 148
   Bitter chocolate-hazelnut cake with candied grapefruit 257
   Crushed hazelnut-rosemary flatbreads 39
   Hazelnut dressing 136
   Hazelnut falafel & tahini-whipped crème fraîche 114
herbs
   Spiced Puy lentils with porcini & herbs 203
   Toasted nuts, seeds & grains with smashed cherries, herbs & goat's curd 185
   Wedding couscous with herbs & flowers 219
   see also specific herbs
Home-made crème fraîche 52
Home-made crème fraîche butter 52
Home-made filo pastry 122
Home-made shankleesh 72
honey
   Honey-roasted carrots with dates, dandelions & Moroccan dressing 160
   Honeyed curd 250
   Honeyed pine nuts 174
   Tomato & bean soup with harissa & honey 95
   Wild garlic, leek & currant fritters with honey 113
Hot yoghurt sauce 105
ices 220–231

jams *see* preserves, sweet
Jerusalem artichoke 'wedges' with green
   olive aioli 115

Labneh 73
   Persian soft herb salad with fresh figs &
      labneh 136
   Vanilla labneh 18, 236
   Labneh, variations 74
   Almond-barberry labneh 139
Lebanese dirty rice 194
Lebanese spiced chickpeas & eggplant with
   pita 206
leeks
   Baby leeks in saffron vinaigrette with
      hazelnut crumbs 148
   Teta's pie – dandelion, leek & barrel-aged
      feta 122
   Wild garlic, leek & currant fritters with
      honey 113
legumes 200–209, 264
lemons
   Artichoke & lemon labneh 74
   Asparagus avgolemono 91
   Buttermilk sorbet with bay leaf & lemon
      228
   Fatima's fingers with goat's cheese, lemon,
      tarragon & thyme 127
   Lemon posset with fennel shortbread
      thins 234
   Lemony lentil soup with saffron-scrambled
      egg 98
   Long-grain rice with lemon & toasted
      almonds 193
   Parsnip skordalia with garlic, lemon &
      scarmorza 68
   Saffron-lemon cream 171
   see also preserved lemons
lentils
   Lebanese dirty rice 194
   Lemony lentil soup with saffron-scrambled
      egg 98
   Lentils with sweet carrots, dates & golden
      cream 204
   Spiced Puy lentils with porcini & herbs
      203
Long-grain rice with lemon & toasted
   almonds 193
lime
   Lime-ginger dressing 185
   Lime-sumac dressing 180
   Pear sorbet with Prosecco, cardamom &
      lime 229
   Summer berry salad with ginger, lime &
      labneh 18

Marshmallow 260
Mascarpone mousse 247
Middle Eastern granola with pomegranate,
   sour cherries & pistachios 23
Middle Eastern pizzas 46
mint
   Fresh corn soup with rice, yoghurt &
      sizzling mint butter 92
   Goat's cheese dumplings with fresh & dried
      mint 214
   Haloumi, mint & ginger stuffing 102
   Sizzling mint butter 92
   White zucchini omelette with mint &
      melting gouda 29
Mixed nut praline 21
Moroccan dressing 180

Mixed spring greens with golden raisins &
   couscous 217
Muscat crème caramel with orange flower
   cream & candied pistachios 240
mushrooms
   Buttered egg noodles with artichokes,
      cèpes & saffron 216
   Mushroom soup with fresh za'atar 97
   Spiced Puy lentils with porcini & herbs
      203
   Tunisian-style vegetables roasted on
      embers 167

Negroni sorbet with blood orange &
   pomegranate 231
North African eggplant pie with pimento
   sugar 124
nuts 264
   Mixed nut praline 21
   Toasted nuts, seeds & grains with smashed
      cherries, herbs & goat's curd 185
   Breakfast couscous with nuts, seeds &
      blueberries 21
   see also specific nuts

oils, infused 83, 212
olives
   Farro with slow-roasted tomatoes,
      artichokes, olives & oregano 187
   Green olive aioli 115
   Olive-brioche crumbs 102
oranges
   Blood oranges in spicy caramel sauce with
      ashta 20
   Citrus salad with red radicchio &
      pomegranate dressing 139
   Negroni sorbet with blood orange &
      pomegranate 231
   Orange baklava cigars 252
   Orange syrup 252
   Stracciatella with orange peel 226

parsley
   Shankleesh salad with parsley &
      pomegranate 140
   Winter tabbouleh 145
Parsnip skordalia with garlic, lemon &
   scarmorza 68
Passion fruit curd 247
pasta 210–216
Pasta dough 214
pastries, savoury 120–131
pastries, sweet 244–253
pastry 122, 128
Pavlova 'flowers' with apple jelly, raspberries
   & vanilla labneh 236
pears
   Pear sorbet with Prosecco, cardamom &
      lime 229
   Pear-ginger butter 57
peas
   Peas with pearl onions & preserved lemon
      cream 165
   Potato salad with peas & Persian spices 157
peppers *see* capsicums
Persian 'baghali polow' with borlotti beans
   & dill 192
Persian sabzi butter 55
Persian saffron tart with passion fruit curd &
   mascarpone mousse 247
Persian soft herb salad with fresh figs &
   labneh 136

pickles 76–85
pine nuts
   Honeyed pine nuts 174
   Rainbow chard with soused currants &
      pine nuts 155
   Summer vine leaves with tomatoes, pine
      nuts & dill 108
pistachios
   Candied pistachios 240
   Middle Eastern granola with pomegranate,
      sour cherries & pistachios 23
pizzas 46–47
pomegranates
   Middle Eastern granola with pomegranate,
      sour cherries & pistachios 23
   Negroni sorbet with blood orange &
      pomegranate 231
   Pomegranate dressing 139
   Shankleesh salad with parsley &
      pomegranate 140
   Slow-roasted tomatoes with pomegranate
      & thyme 79
   Tomato & pomegranate dressing 152, 214
potatoes
   Potato salad with peas & Persian spices
      157
   Braised artichokes, preserved lemon &
      fingerling potatoes with basil crème
      fraîche 158
preserved lemons
   Braised artichokes, preserved lemon &
      fingerling potatoes with basil crème
      fraîche 158
   Preserved lemon butter 55
   Preserved lemon cream 165
   Preserved lemon guacamole 71
   Zucchini blossom & preserved lemon
      risotto with ricotta & parmesan 198
preserves, sweet 58–63
pumpkin
   Freekeh pilaf with spiced roast pumpkin &
      shallots 188
   Pumpkin kibbeh stuffed with feta &
      spinach 118
   Sweet pumpkin sambusek with oregano
      128
   Toasted quinoa with coriander, lime &
      crunchy pumpkin 180
   Tunisian-style vegetables roasted on
      embers 167

quinoa 265
   Cucumber, quinoa & tarragon-yoghurt
      salad 178
   Toasted quinoa with coriander, lime &
      crunchy pumpkin 180

radicchio
   Citrus salad with red radicchio &
      pomegranate dressing 139
Rainbow chard with soused currants & pine
   nuts 155
raisins
   Celeriac remoulade with tahini & golden
      raisins 134
   Glazed apple-raisin fritters 24
   Golden bulgur wheat with apple, raisins &
      yoghurt 182
   Mixed spring greens with golden raisins &
      couscous 217
relishes 35, 82, 197
Red harissa 56

rhubarb
  Rhubarb, raspberry & cardamom fridge
    jam 58
rice 190–199, 264
  Eggplant pilaf with yoghurt & zhoug 197
  Fresh corn soup with rice, yoghurt &
    sizzling mint butter 92
  Lebanese dirty rice 194
  Long-grain rice with lemon & toasted
    almonds 193
  Persian 'baghali polow' with borlotti beans
    & dill 192
  Saffron rice pudding with spiced apricots
    243
  Stuffed zucchini cooked in yoghurt
    105
  Zucchini blossom & preserved lemon
    risotto with ricotta & parmesan 198
Roasted tomato & chickpea curry with
  coconut & coriander 209

saffron 265
  Almond-saffron butter 55
  Baked tomatoes with saffron, bulgur &
    barberries 106
  Buttered egg noodles with artichokes,
    cèpes & saffron 216
  Persian saffron tart with passion fruit curd
    & mascarpone mousse 247
  Saffron fruit loaf 45
  Saffron pastry 247
  Saffron rice pudding with spiced apricots
    243
  Saffron vinaigrette 148
  Saffron yeast batter 116
  Saffron-lemon cream 171
  Saffron-scrambled eggs 98
salads, cooked vegetable 146–161
salads, raw vegetable 132–145
Salted date caramel 225
seeds 265
  Breakfast couscous with nuts, seeds &
    blueberries 21
  Semolina bread with aniseed & sesame 43
  Toasted nuts, seeds & grains with smashed
    cherries, herbs & goat's curd 185
Semolina bread with aniseed & sesame 43
Sesame joujou breads 34
shallots
  Freekeh pilaf with spiced roast pumpkin &
    shallots 188
  Green beans with chermoula, shallots &
    feta 153
  Sweet peppers & shallots in lemon oil 83
  Turkish bread & roasted vegetable salad
    150
Shankleesh salad with parsley &
  pomegranate 140
Shaved zucchini with grana, burrata & basil
  142
Shredded bitter leaves with roasted grapes,
  almonds & avocado 135
Sizzling mint butter 92
Slow-roasted eggplant with saffron-lemon
  cream 171
Slow-roasted tomatoes with pomegranate &
  thyme 79
soups 86–99
Soused currants 155
Spiced apricots 243
Spiced currant sfiha with cinnamon-ginger
  cream 250

Spiced Puy lentils with porcini & herbs 203
Spicy carrot pickle 84
Spicy red hummus 71
Spicy Turkish kisir 183
spinach
  Pumpkin kibbeh stuffed with feta &
    spinach 118
  Turkish eggs with spinach, chilli & yoghurt
    cream 26
Stracciatella with orange peel 226
stuffed vegetables 100–109
Stuffed zucchini cooked in yoghurt 105
Summer berry salad with ginger, lime &
  labneh 18
Summer vine leaves with tomatoes, pine
  nuts & dill 108
Sweet peppers & shallots in lemon oil 83
Sweet pumpkin sambusek with oregano 128
syrups 18, 252

tahini 265
  Celeriac remoulade with tahini & golden
    raisins 134
  Tahini mayonnaise 134
  Tahini-whipped crème fraîche 114
Taklia 216
Tarbouche - Lebanese chocolate
  marshmallow cakes 260
tarragon
  Cucumber, quinoa & tarragon-yoghurt
    salad 178
  Fatima's fingers with goat's cheese, lemon,
    tarragon & thyme 127
  Tomato & eggplant baked with tarragon-
    yoghurt custard 173
Teta's pie – dandelion, leek & barrel-aged
  feta 122
Toasted nuts, seeds & grains with smashed
  cherries, herbs & goat's curd 185
Toasted quinoa with coriander, lime &
  crunchy pumpkin 180
tomatoes
  Baked beans with Turkish spices &
    crunchy crumbs 202
  Baked tomatoes with saffron, bulgur &
    barberries 106
  Farro with slow-roasted tomatoes,
    artichokes, olives & oregano 187
  Lebanese spiced chickpeas & eggplant with
    pita 206
  Roasted tomato & chickpea curry with
    coconut & coriander 209
  Slow-roasted tomatoes with pomegranate
    & thyme 79
  Summer vine leaves with tomatoes, pine
    nuts & dill 108
  Tomato & bean soup with harissa & honey
    95
  Tomato & eggplant baked with tarragon-
    yoghurt custard 173
  Tomato & pomegranate dressing 152, 214
Tunisian marinade 167
Tunisian-style vegetables roasted on embers
  167
Turkish bread & roasted vegetable salad
  150
Turkish coffee granita 239
Turkish coffee syrup 239
Turkish eggs with spinach, chilli & yoghurt
  cream 26
Turkish milk rolls with yoghurt glaze 40
Turkish red pepper paste 69

Turkish-style carrot labneh 74

Vanilla labneh 18
vegetables
  Turkish bread & roasted vegetable salad
    150
  Vegetable 'fritto misto' in saffron-yeast
    batter 116
  Vegetable stock 88
vine leaves 265
  Slow-roasted eggplant with saffron-lemon
    cream 171
  Summer vine leaves with tomatoes, pine
    nuts & dill 108

Walnuts
  Apple-walnut butter 57
  Baby eggplants stuffed with walnuts &
    chillies 81
  Chilled yoghurt soup with cucumber,
    currants & walnuts 89
Wedding couscous with herbs & flowers 219
White zucchini omelette with mint & melting
  gouda 29
Wild garlic, leek & currant fritters with
  honey 113
Winter tabbouleh 145

yoghurt 267
  Baby carrot tagine with yoghurt & honeyed
    pine nuts 174
  Chilled yoghurt soup with cucumber,
    currants & walnuts 89
  Cucumber, quinoa & tarragon-yoghurt
    salad 178
  Eggplant pilaf with yoghurt & zhoug 197
  Fresh corn soup with rice, yoghurt &
    sizzling mint butter 92
  Golden bulgur wheat with apple, raisins &
    yoghurt 182
  Stuffed zucchini cooked in yoghurt 105
  Tomato & eggplant baked with tarragon-
    yoghurt custard 173
  Yoghurt cream 26
  see also labneh

za'atar 266
  Mushroom soup with fresh za'atar 97
  Za'atar biscuits 129
  Za'atar mix 129
Zhoug 197
zucchini
  Fregola with zucchini, citrus & basil 212
  Shaved zucchini with grana, burrata &
    basil 142
  Stuffed zucchini cooked in yoghurt 105
  Tunisian-style vegetables roasted on
    embers 167
  Turkish bread & roasted vegetable salad
    150
  White zucchini omelette with mint &
    melting gouda 29
  Zucchini blossom & preserved lemon
    risotto with ricotta & parmesan 198
  Zucchini blossoms with haloumi in olive-
    brioche crumbs 102

Published in 2014 by Hardie Grant Books

Hardie Grant Books (Australia)
Ground Floor, Building 1
658 Church Street
Richmond, Victoria 3121
www.hardiegrant.com.au

Hardie Grant Books (UK)
5th & 6th Floor
52–54 Southwark Street
London SE1 1RU
www.hardiegrant.co.uk

Chapter illustrations courtesy of the RHS, Lindley Library

A Cataloguing-in-Publication entry is available from the catalogue of the National Library of Australia at www.nla.gov.au
New Feast
ISBN 9781742708423

Publishing Director: Paul McNally
Project Manager and Editor: Laura Herring
Designer: David Eldridge, Two Associates
Photographer: Alan Benson
Stylist: David Morgan
Production Manager: Todd Rechner

Colour reproduction by Splitting Image Colour Studio
Printed and bound in China by 1010 Printing International Limited

Find this book on Cooked
cooked.com.au
cooked.co.uk

ACKNOWLEDGEMENTS

Thank you to all the people who helped bring this book to life, and who made the process so seamless, despite the logistical complexities created by our living in different parts of the world.

First and foremost, thanks to Laura Herring, managing editor extraordinaire, whose calm efficiency and organisational skills were key in bringing it all together on time! She managed it all – and us – with grace and apparent ease. And we'd also like to thank David Eldridge, whose lovely and elegant design makes this book such a pleasure to hold and to look at.

A huge thanks, also, to Alan Benson for his unerring photographer's eye and to the creative styling of David Morgan; their combined artistry brought Greg's food to life on the plate. The photoshoot was fun and inspiring, largely due to these guys, but also thanks to the awesome cooking and management skills of Brooke Payne, Greg's former head chef at MoMo Restaurant in Melbourne. We couldn't have done it without you, Brooke … and it reminded Greg of just how much he misses you!

Thank you to Josue, Sabrina and Franco from Natoora and to Rob Davies of First Choice Produce in Covent Garden. Their dedication to sourcing outstanding fresh produce is yet another reason the food on these pages looks so delicious.

We are, as ever, hugely grateful to Hardie Grant for their ongoing enthusiasm for our ideas. In particular, we'd like to thank Paul McNally, for being the catalyst and for his encouragement and practical support – and for running around London for last-minute ingredients!

And finally, a few personal words: Greg thanks Paul Mitchell and the London Rushbrookes for putting him up (and up with him) on his way through to Kent. We both thank George for partaking of our New Feast so tirelessly and enthusiastically. And Lucy thanks him for everything else.